The View From the Rigging
Memoirs of a Coast Guard Career

Richard Marcott

Captain, USCG (Retired)

Copyright Page

Richard J. Marcott is a retired U.S. Coast Guard Captain. He graduated from the U.S. Coast Guard Academy with a bachelor's degree in General Engineering and he holds a Masters Degree in Personnel Management from George Washington University. He was an Assistant Professor teaching Organizational Behavior at the University of Pittsburgh at Bradford. Chapters of his memoirs have been published in the award winning UPB Literary Journal: Bailey's Beads

Wave Cloud Publications

© 2016 Richard J. Marcott
rjmarcott@atlanticbb.net

The author has recreated events, locales, and conversations from his memories of them. Every effort has been made to make them as accurate as possible. He has retold them in a way to evoke the feeling and meaning of what was said and in all instances, the essence of the dialog is true. The author disclaims any liability for omissions or inaccuracy whether caused by neglect or accident.

First Edition–first Printing, 2016

Print Edition ISBN: 978-1-5356-0395-9

USCG Barque Eagle. Pen & Ink
Drawing by Ray Bryan 1976

Acknowledgements

The cover photo is of a U.S. Coast Guard Academy cadet in the rigging of the USCGC Eagle. All photos are Official Coast Guard photos or private photos belonging to the author.

Dedication

For my daughter
Kimberly Marcott Weinberg

Twenty years from now you will be more disappointed
by the things you didn't do, than by the ones you did do.
So throw off the bowlines, sail away from the safe harbor,
catch the trade winds in your sails,
Explore, Dream, Discourse.
—MARK TWAIN

Contents

Headquarters II

USCG Training Center Petaluma

Preface

You might as well know it right up front. I'm a story teller. My twenty-eight years of active duty in the U.S. Coast Guard has furnished a lot of fodder. My daughter, Kimberly, who suffered through most of my stories throughout her adolescence and into motherhood, has more than once chastised me, "Dad, you really have to start writing those stories down for the grandchildren." The grandchildren, Preston and Maddy, are growing up fast, but no faster than I'm growing old. I finally came to the conclusion that I had better get started.

My stories reference names like: Perry Como, Jacques Cousteau, Ernest Hemingway, and Nikita Khrushchev. There are stories of tragic and triumphant sea rescues, as well as of the brotherhood of Academy classmates. There are stories of command at sea and ashore, and teaching at Officer Candidate School and the National Defense University.

I abandoned an earlier attempt to research my ancestry. Other than discovering family movement from Quebec, Canada, to New York, then Pennsylvania, and finding a few old grave sites, I never discovered them as people. Why did they move? What did they do? What were their lives like? None of the good stuff. It was boring. I was frustrated with my grandparents for never letting us know what their lives were like. Kimberly's pleas took on new meaning. It was time to share my stories.

I have limited my memoirs to stories from my Coast Guard career, from entering the Academy in 1953 to retiring from the Coast Guard Training Center, Petaluma, California, in 1985.

I wanted to tell my tales as plainly as I could, as if I were on the porch on a summer evening sharing a beer with neighbors. Problem—I didn't know how to do that in writing. Enter Dr. Nancy McCabe, Director of the Writing Program at the University of Pittsburgh at Bradford. She was offering a course called "Memoir: Writing From the Self."

I am forever grateful that she allowed me to audit her senior-level course, and I thank her for setting the condition that I participate the same as her regular students. At seventy-five, I gave new meaning to "senior level." The workshop introduced me to the writing style of creative nonfiction (CNF). That is the style I've used in these memoirs.

I define CNF as: writing stories using tools and techniques of fiction writers, such as detailed scenic descriptions, dialogue, and story arcs, to make them readable and enjoyable, all the while staying true to the memoir—the stories must be true.

My stories are as I remember them, without either exaggeration or fabrication. I have recreated dialogue, keeping the character emotions, cadence, tension, and words as accurate to the circumstances as possible. Researched historical and personal events are included as background information to keep the reader grounded in space and time. (I also thought my grandson should know that I paid $2450 for my first car, a brand new 1957 Mercury Monterey.)

My intentions were to make nice three ring notebooks for the kids and family. But my workshop story of the *Minnie V*, a tale of a night rescue in a stormy Chesapeake Bay, caught the imagination and interest of the class. They wanted more. Dr. McCabe asked if I would submit it for consideration to be published in the UPB literary journal, Baily's Beads.

I did. It was selected and published in 2013, and I was hooked.

Now, nearly six years later, Baily's has published four chapters. With over five years of self-study, a sizable reference library of "how to write" books, and other writers' memoirs, I have finally finished mine. I could not have done it without the continued help and encouragement of Dr. Nancy McCabe and her staff of writing professors, and my many friends in the Bradford Writing Group. They have faithfully workshopped my chapters every month for five years. The richness of their forthright candor, always welcome as the only beneficial critique, has kept me on track and encouraged me to keep on. I also thank my classmate Ron McClellan. His cruise journal kept me straight on dates, and scheduled movies, and triggered memories.

The View From the Rigging is structured chronologically by duty assignments from the Academy days to retirement. However, you may enjoy many of the stories as standalone segments. In many ways, my memoirs are like a scrapbook pasted with pieces of life, at times amplified with my musings on events. While I didn't intentionally develop my stories around a theme, I think one evolved. One is rarely in total control of his life. Events intervene that you have no control over and people come and go. The unplanned elements of life lead to either success or failure—depending on how you deal with them.

I hope you enjoy the stories. If you are like me, sometimes that's all I ask for. As Lee Gutkind, often considered the father of CNF, would say, "I hope you see them as good stories, well told."

Introduction

IT WAS AUGUST 1953. I was a new fourth class cadet at the Coast Guard Academy in New London, Connecticut, not three months out of high school in Bradford, Pennsylvania. Still reeling, mentally and physically, from the wild summer of military indoctrination, my class was being transported to board the U.S. Coast Guard Cutter *Eagle* that lay at anchor in New London's outer harbor. She had just returned from the long cruise to Europe with the first and third class cadets who were now headed home on summer leave.

Nobody hid their excitement. We were about to sail a three-masted, square-rigged barque on a two week cruise to Bermuda. My seagoing experience up to this point was limited to a rowboat on Cuba Lake, thirty miles from home.

It was going to be a warm day. When we left the Academy grounds, a faint curtain of heat was already shimmering above the pavement, and the dew no longer dampened the parade ground. The fog had long since burned off.

As the *Eagle* came into view, the silhouette of her tall masts and sleek hull against the background of open ocean and morning sky presented a scene from a Horatio Hornblower novel. As the 40' patrol boats that were transporting us got closer, we could see her white sails, highlighted by the morning sun, furled atop the buff colored yard arms.

The *Eagle*, taken from Germany as part of World War II reparations, was now the school ship for the U.S. Coast Guard Academy. Her masts soared a hundred fifty feet above her three hundred foot hull. She carried five square sails on each the foremast and the mainmast. With a large fore-and-aft spanker on the mizzen mast, and the triangular sails rigged between the masts, the *Eagle* had over twenty-two thousand square feet of canvas, enough to power her to seventeen knots.

Within an hour, we had stored our gear below decks, and were jockeying for a rolled and lashed-up canvas hammock to call our own when an upperclassman entered the compartment.

"Everyone on the main deck, now! Time for up-and-over."

As we scrambled past him to the ladder to the main deck, he cheerfully reminded us that our destination, the main top, was only eighty feet above the deck. To reach it, we had to climb the spider-webbed shrouds to the skimpy triangular iron platform at the center of main yard arm.

We queued up in the well deck to begin the climb. I watched those ahead of me hesitate atop the rail before moving to join the men in the shrouds. Some scampered up like practiced seamen. But most, like me, made it a deliberate, slow, and careful climb, remembering the safety rules: hands on the vertical stays only; keep each foot on a separate horizontal ratline; always have three points of contact—they do break. I watched two classmates freeze for a second, their bodies flattened against the shrouds before regaining their confidence to continue. *Don't look down!*

Nearing the main top, I faced the awkward move of the climb, upside down and backwards, over the edge of the main top platform. Once there, I sat to catch my breath before venturing down the other side. In a self-congratulatory moment, I gazed at the unexpected beauty of the distant horizon and the vastness of the unknown. With my heart slowed to a more normal pace, I allowed myself a momentary dream about what stood over that horizon for me in the years ahead at the Academy, or for that matter, in the Coast Guard.

I looked back at those still in the shrouds behind me. I became conscious of the upperclassmen strategically spread throughout the rigging. Some at the rail helped us get our first step, reminded us of the rules, and left their cheerleader encouragements echoing in our ears. They guided and urged us on, and lent a helping hand if needed. I realized in that moment that we achieved very little by ourselves. People helped, people nudged, and, sometimes...people hindered.

The view from the rigging had lifted my daydream into the future. What lay ahead for me over that Coast Guard horizon would depend, not just on me, but a lot of other people and things that I had no control over: luck, a chain of events, a chance meeting, a set of orders, or unplanned and unexpected external events.

It certainly had been an unexpected chain of events that led me here. Thanks to my high school guidance counselor, I nearly ended up in a career stacking shelves in the A&P. I had competed for several scholarships in addition to applying to the U.S. Coast Guard Academy. When the local Dresser Manufacturing Co. notified her that they were offering me a full scholarship to the University of Cincinnati, she took it upon herself to refuse it on my behalf. Believing I would surely get the Academy appointment, she told them, "Richard will be going to a federal maritime academy." For the last two months of high school, I had no prospects beyond graduation. I envied my friends' excitement while they made plans for college.

By pure chance, when I was randomly assigned to Dressers for a senior-day industry visit only a few weeks before graduation, I learned of their offer. The guidance counselor had never said anything to me. I never spoke to her again.

The officials at Dresser were wonderful. They quickly shifted gears, and before I knew it, I was offered a fully paid five-year co-op engineering program scholarship and the promise of a job upon graduation. At that time I already had a summer job in the drafting department at the Bradford plant, and they had arranged a part-time job in the college library in Cincinnati to help me earn pin money. Then it got complicated.

A week *after* high school graduation, I received a telegram. "Number reached for Coast Guard cadetship." I was to report to the Academy on the 7th of July, less than a month away. After a traumatic week of decision making, including a helpful visit with Mr. George Bell, our high school principal, I phoned Dressers to tell them I wouldn't be to work on Monday. That led to an uncomfortable visit with a panel of Dresser engineers, who had been called in on a Saturday morning to convince me to stay with them.

I had nearly given in to the pressure when one of the young engineers made his point. "Besides, Dressers is an essential war time industry. You'll never be drafted and won't have to go into the military."

That was all I needed. "Sir, I don't know why you would think that someone who has dreamed about West Point and Annapolis since the eighth grade would now be looking for a way to avoid serving in the military. I'm grateful for Dressers' offer, but I've decided to go to the Coast Guard Academy."

I expected to be able to guide my own Coast Guard career by seeking the right education, training, and assignment. But, I also knew that there would be intervening variables that I had no control over. I promised myself that if the unexpected happened (and it did, more than once) I would deal with it and move on.

So my family piled into a borrowed car to deliver their first-born only son—who would also be the only one on either side of the family to go beyond high school—from Bradford, PA to The Coast Guard Academy in New London.

In twenty eight years of active duty assignments, some by design, others by chance, I built a cornucopia of stories that I enjoy sharing. They are all part of my *View From the Rigging*.

U.S. Coast Guard Academy

New London, CT

7 July 1953-1 June 1957

THE UNITED STATES COAST GUARD Academy, the smallest of the five federal service academies, commands the south bank of the Thames River in New London, Connecticut. The overview below reflects the 1953-1957 timeframe. The cadet corps was a single battalion of 600 men, divided into five companies, A-E. There were no congressional appointments. The Academy relied on a single nationwide entrance exam. Graduates incurred a four year active duty obligation in return for a Bachelor of Science degree in general engineering and a commission as an Ensign. The Academy was consistently rated one of the top schools in the country.

During the summers, cadets trained aboard the square-rigged sailing vessel *Eagle*. There were two summer-long cruises to Europe and two short ones, usually to Bermuda. Second class summer (junior year) also provided leadership opportunities while indoctrinating the incoming class.

Cadets lived in a strict military environment. They could not have civilian clothes. They could leave the Academy grounds only on weekends, but not overnight. They could not have cars until a month before graduation. The corps was granted holiday leave during Thanksgiving and Christmas much like a normal college. In addition, everyone had twenty days summer leave before the new academic year began.

Cadets were paid $111 a month, one half of an Ensign's salary, which was placed in their cadet account to pay for books, laundry and dry cleaning, and uniforms. They received a monthly cash allowance ranging from $11 for the fourth classmen to $22 for first classmen.

Attrition was high. The class of 1957 was sworn in with 198 cadets, and graduated 61 Ensigns.

- I -

The Year of the Swab

*TO GRADUATE YOUNG MEN WITH SOUND BODIES, STOUT HEARTS, & ALERT
MINDS. WITH A LIKING FOR THE SEA & ITS LORE & WITH THAT HIGH SENSE OF
HONOR, LOYALTY & OBEDIENCE WHICH GOES WITH TRAINED INITIATIVE &
LEADERSHIP, WELL GROUNDED IN SEAMANSHIP, THE SCIENCES & THE AMENI-
TIES & STRONG IN THE RESOLVE TO BE WORTHY OF THE TRADITIONS OF THE
COMMISSIONED OFFICERS IN THE UNITED STATES COAST GUARD IN SERVICE
OF THEIR COUNTRY AND HUMANITY.*

Mission of the U.S. Coast Guard Academy

IT WAS JULY 7, 1953. After a drive-around tour of the Coast Guard Academy, Dad stopped the car in front of Chase Hall, where I was to check in.
A tall, good looking second-class cadet in a spotless white sailor's uniform
lowered his head to the passenger window and politely explained to my
teary mother, "It would be best to say goodbye now, ma'am. From here on,
your son is going to be very busy... He'll be home for Thanksgiving."

We had arrived in New London, Connecticut, a little later than
expected because of my sister, Pat. At thirteen, she had been fascinated
with the automat. Its marble wall, lined with tiny vaults protecting the pie
behind small windows, reminded her of the post office boxes back home.
She giggled each time she dropped a coin in the slot and a detached hand
delivered a new piece. She loved watching the brass lion's-head spigot,
which stuck straight out of the wall, splashing coffee into the shaking cups
of a constant line of customers.

The family had decided to make a mini vacation out of taking me to the Coast Guard Academy with a New York City stopover. Nobody in the family had been there before. We made it safely into the city with only two trips through the Lincoln Tunnel. My dad, the chauffeur, may have been a good driver, but was not a big city navigator. With no car of our own, we had borrowed Cousin Irene's car. She came with it. So, Dad, Mom, my sister Pat, Irene, and I were ready to see the sights.

After a lot of skyscraper-gawking and a moderately expensive 10 x 12 picture taken on the steps of the St. Patrick's Cathedral with a hundred total strangers, the country bumpkins checked into a Manhattan hotel. Irene, an under five foot tall bundle of loud laughter with a withered face from years of cigarette smoking, kept us in stitches into the middle of the night with animated creeping on the floor and stories about bears in the woods, complete with shotgun sounds.

We all knew the goodbyes were coming, but they felt abrupt. Not much was said. Quick kisses all around, then the family drove away. I turned to follow the second classman through the huge front doors into a world I knew only from books. There was that micro moment of anxiety—hope this is the right thing, first one ever in the family to go beyond high school, the unknown. As Dad drove away, I walked into my new world, fixing on the bold tile in the center of the lobby floor, and told myself, "Yeah, this is where I want to be."

WHO LIVES HERE
REVERES HONOR
HONORS DUTY

I checked in at a long table manned by two commissioned officers. Several second-class cadets stood by in the recreation rooms just off the main lobby. The officers greeted me warmly, checked my name off a list, and handed me a short form.

"When you complete this, Mr. Marcott, please take it to Mr. Ferguson right there in the rec room."

He was easy to find with "J. E. FERGUSON" stenciled in black ink across the jumper of his work whites. I handed him my form. There were other guys scattered around the rec room dressed like me in school slacks, short sleeve shirts, and loafers or plain-toed oxfords that were the uniform of the day. Everyone was trying to look relaxed.

"Good Morning, Mr. Marcott. Welcome to the Academy." His Texas drawl was pleasant, and he flashed an engaging grin. "My name is James Ferguson and I will be your platoon commander. Please follow me," he said, signaling the others to come with us.

He led our small group down a corridor, dorm rooms on both sides. The air was filled with the murmur of get-acquainted chatter. We each were hauling a small suitcase. We were told all civilian clothes would be shipped home. "Two days will be adequate, including underwear."

"OK, gentlemen, stop right here!" Why was Mr. Ferguson shouting? "Set your gear on the deck. This *is* a deck, by the way. You're standing on a deck–not a floor! You're walking in the passageway–not a hall! Now, everyone–backs against the bulkhead. Move! That's the wall, swabs, the wall." He had turned damned mean! We reacted quickly! Some were more bewildered than others and jumped into a police lineup against his precious *bulkhead*.

Mr. Ferguson paced in front of us, clipboard in hand and arms akimbo. "Now, listen up, swabs!" He walked as he talked. "You men are now the Third Platoon, Charlie Company, and we will live in this wing of Chase Hall." He continued, "I'm going to take a moment to see if I can make you civilians stand correctly. Heads up, shoulders back, pull in your chins, heels together against the bulkhead, toes pointed at 45 degrees." He spit out the orders. "Get your eyes in the boat. That's straight ahead, civilians. Pick out a spot on the opposite bulkhead and stare a hole through it! Now brace up!" He stopped in front of one man and put his fist between the middle of his back and the bulkhead. "Pull your back in against the bulkhead. I don't want to be able to get my hand in there, much less my fist. Do you understand me? Arms at your side, fingers together, rig in your thumbs." His pleasant Texas drawl had pitched up to southern overseer. "You low-life swabs know nothing, and can do nothing right until I teach you. You will address me as 'sir' or 'Mr. Ferguson.' You will refer to each other as Mister Gooblatz (universal for 'fill in the name'). When I address you directly, you look at me—and that's the only time you look at me. Understand?"

And so it went for at least another ten minutes. He was not going to let us go until we knew how to stand at attention. A trickle of sweat made its slow, maddening journey down my spine. Finally, backing away toward the middle of the passageway, he read from his clipboard. "I'm going to read names off and assign room numbers. When I say move, you will pick up your gear, go to that room, and take two minutes to get to know your roommate. When I yell 'SWABO,' you *will* be back here, braced up, within fifteen seconds. Now move!"

And so it had begun. Swab indoctrination.

We were destined to be swabs our whole first year, a constant reminder that we were low-life lubbers and fools. Nobody intended the warmer colloquial definition of a colt or calf, one who is awkward with much to learn. No, we were much below that. A similar system exists at all the academies. First year midshipmen at Annapolis were called plebes after the historically lowest Greek social class. The Air Force Academy, which did not exist in 1953, later would call their first year cadets "*doolies*," the Greek word for slaves.

At least I was not surprised by the beastly welcome. I had wanted to attend a service academy since the eighth grade, and had read everything I could get my hands on about West Point and Annapolis as well as the Coast Guard Academy. I knew about the Army beast barracks and the

Navy plebe indoctrination. Many of my classmates did, too. A few, however, appeared unexpectedly lost in a whole new world.

"SWABO!"

"Really? Two minutes already?" With the mad scramble of feet sliding
on the polished deck and Mr. Ferguson yelling, "Move! Move!" the swabs
of Charlie Three made it on time, braced up and eyes in the boat in less
than fifteen seconds.

I never did get my roommate's name. I knew he was from Kentucky,
and that was it. I didn't understand anything else he said...for three days.
And then he left. The 6:00 a.m. reveille, morning exercises, followed by a
run down the hill to the river and back all before breakfast, did him in. He
threw up every morning. One day, he just didn't show up for breakfast and
I never saw him again.

The next few days were a blur of activity. We paraded through dark
basement-issue rooms while disinterested enlisted clerks yelled out sizes
while others stacked your shoes, dungarees, shorts, whites, belts, topsiders,
and a hundred other things on the counter top.

"Keep it moving. Pick your gear up and move on." We blindly stag-
gered back to our rooms with linens and uniforms stacked on our arms up
to our chins.

There was a specified place for everything in our room. Socks, rolled,
front to back in two rows in the second drawer. Shorts folded once, left
side of first drawer. On and on it went. Follow the diagram in the red book,
Cadet Regulations. Furniture placement was not optional. Every room
was exactly the same except for one personal photograph each man was
allowed on the top of his bookcase. Most were of girlfriends. At least some
things changed in the rooms.

While every man was responsible for his personal space, we shared
common household duties through an orderly system. Swabs were assigned as bucket orderlies, window, laundry, mail, and ash tray orderlies.
There were others. We served the needs of the entire wing.

The classroom activities during swab summer included Coast Guard
history, a math refresher to ease us into the engineering-heavy curriculum,

and, of course, *Eagle* seamanship to prepare us to sail the three-masted barque. We had to memorize the name and purpose of more than two hundred lines of running rigging and find their belaying pins in the dark. We learned Morse code, flashing light, and semaphore signaling. Of course, we spent a *lot* of time marching and sweating through physical fitness exercises.

The cadet battalion formed for meals in the quadrangle of Chase Hall and marched to the mess hall and stood in silence behind assigned seats. The cadet Officer-of-the-Day sat at a head table with the battalion staff. He offered a blessing for our food, and then ordered, "Seats!" The mess hall came alive.

The prolonged sound of 600 chairs being moved at the same time lifted in the high-ceilinged hall to meld with a cacophony of calls for, "May I have the potatoes, please, sir." "Please pass the peas, Mr. Gooblatz." Amid the clashing of trays, plates, and silverware, we could make out the yelling of table reporters. "What's the national news today, Mr. Gooblatz?"

Swabs were assigned various reporter jobs. That meant precious time diverted to the library for research. We would prepare an oral report and be ready to answer questions. Reporters covered national, international, and Coast Guard news, sports reports, even Ann Landers and special interests. "What's going on at Slippery Rock College this summer, Mr. Gooblatz?"

The swab "bible" containing all the inane rules we lived by was a white, pocket-size book with an embossed lighthouse beacon on the cover called *The Running Light*. Most of the rules were simple. Swabs must move on the double or march if three or more and stay in the middle of the passageways under the lights. Swabs must sound off before entering an upperclassman's room with their name and home state. "Marcott, sir, Pennsylvania, sir. Permission to come aboard, sir?"

The *Running Light* provided the magic answers to be memorized for routine questions.

"What time is it?"

"Sir, I am greatly embarrassed and deeply humiliated, that due to unforeseen circumstances beyond my control, the inner workings and hidden mechanisms of my chronometer are in such inaccord with the great sidereal movement, that I cannot, with any degree of accuracy, state the exact time, sir. But without fear of being too greatly in error, I will state that it is approximately __ minutes, __ seconds, and __tics, past __ bells, sir."

"How is the cow?"

"Sir, she walks, she talks. The lacteal fluid extracted from the female of the bovine species is highly prolific to the nth degree, sir."

It is hard to find rhyme or reason for much of the stuff of swab year. But I can tell you that step by step we were being molded to fit the Academy mission. By the end of the summer, we looked sharp in uniform, lived in clean quarters, wore clean clothes, we walked tall, marched well, and were stronger. We could field strip our M1 rifles in seconds and keep them clean. We were experts at shining shoes and managing time. We could bounce a quarter off our racks and make tight hospital corners.

Every day we were building loyalty to our classmates and the Academy. We *lived* honor and obedience. We were more resolved. "*Non illegitimus carborundum!* Don't let the bastards grind you down!" We were even more polite.

Swab year was just the initial surge of that sorting out process that would make us "worthy of the traditions of commissioned officers." The developmental cycle continued for four years of the Academy experience with the stakes growing higher each year.

The secret for swab year–recognize the goal and embrace it. Above all, keep a sense of humor. This too would go away. Had we gained "a liking for the sea and its lore?" We were about to find out with a two-week cruise to Bermuda on the U.S. Coast Guard Cutter *Eagle*, America's only square-sailed training ship.

-2-

BERMUDA

"In knocking about aloft on the Royal yards, mind don't let go one rope till you have hold of another, and if you keep in mind this good advice you will never fall from aloft."

Master mariner, Alan Villiers, The Way of a Ship

SOME DAYS BRING YOU ALL the excitement you can stand. The *Eagle* had left Hamilton, Bermuda, our scheduled three-day visit cut to one by an oncoming hurricane. We were headed north, running downwind with as much sail flying as the Captain dared set.

"Mr. Marcott. Come with me." Second Classman Al Breed, our Officer–in-Charge (O-in-C) of the ready boat crew needed a hand. "There's something clanging around on the main royal. We've got to check it out."

"Yes, sir." The royal is the highest sail on the mast, fourteen stories above the ocean, a long climb then a dangerous move onto the footrope. It was dark and raining, and the storm tossed *Eagle* was dancing on the ocean. I felt a little surge of anxiety.

Despite the warm summer air, the rain was cold and irritating as it pelted me with a wind-driven strength I had not felt before. The steel of the crosstrees and yardarm was slippery. We were hard-up on a starboard tack making the dangling footrope a long reach. I was going to have to push off to grab the after jackstay, that one-inch steel safety rod that ran the length of the yard arm. It was the only safety grip when working aloft. We had no safety harnesses in 1953.

The barque was taking heavy rolls. We flailed through a big arc, like the weights on a hundred thirty five foot metronome, first over the deck, then above the black broiling ocean.

"Can you make it OK?" Breed hollered from the shrouds just below me. He cupped his hand by the side of his mouth to overcome the high-pitched wind screaming through the rigging. "Don't take any chances. Be careful."

"Yes, sir. I think I'll be ok."

With that, I timed the pitch of the ship—and pushed off. I grabbed the jackstay with my right hand in a vice grip. I had made it onto the footrope, but my momentum pushed the yardarm further away. It was moving fast, and with the ship dropping beneath us in a steep pitch, I could feel that sickening moment of weightlessness, like cresting at the top of a roller coaster run. The yardarm clanged into the steel stop with a shuddering crash, the lingering vibration numbed my fingers. The braces had not been secured letting the yardarm dangerously free to move as the wind gusts took it. The O-in-C quickly took charge.

"You OK? Hold tight and stay where you are."

"Yes, sir. I'm all right."

"On the main deck!" He called for the ready boat crew.

"Main deck, aye."

"Secure the main royal weather and lee braces. Now!"

"Aye, aye, sir." The answer came from the dark below and the boat crew responded quickly.

Al talked me back onto the shrouds, which were closer and easier to reach now. We stood together for a few moments. "Just take a few deep breaths and, when you're ready, we'll head back down. Good job."

I thought, *I didn't do anything, but hang on.* I was just happy the Academy was not going to have to name an athletic field me after me. (The football stadium, Jones Field, was named for the only cadet to die from a fall out of the rigging.)

Furling the Mainsail

Safely back on deck, it was all over. I rejoined the ready boat crew, huddled under what little protection the pin rail provided, and gave my heart time to stop pounding.

We were clipping along at top speed, bound for New York City. The real purpose of the training cruise was to get us at-sea time to learn the basics of sailing a square rigger and appreciate the power of teamwork. But, it was also was a chance for us to taste the salt air, feel the never-ending ships movement, laugh at porpoises playing in the bow wake, and to marvel at the sunset as it fell off the western rim of the earth. It was a chance for us to test our...*liking for the sea and its lore...* at the moment, I harbored just a hint of doubt.

We had looked forward to getting ashore at Bermuda, but with the hurricane bearing down, it would have been too dangerous to stay. It would have been nice to pick up a wool scarf for my sister, or sneak a pint of British lager. Since we left New London, we had toiled through hours of drills. We set and furled sail, tacked, and wore the ship until we had the maneuvers down pat. All that good *Eagle* seamanship stuff aside, we were sorry to miss the liberty call. The Captain had given us what little chance he could to get ashore. Two duty sections split one day of liberty, and the third section never got off the ship.

The *Eagle* barreled ahead of the storm, spurred on to an average speed of 16 knots, into New York Harbor. Some said we may have set a sailing ship record for the Bermuda to New York run. It was an exciting adventure, but we all looked forward to smoother sailing.

We took on fresh water and minor provisions at the Coast Guard Base on Staten Island. Then we headed for Martha's Vineyard, a triangular shaped island seven miles off the coast of Cape Cod. The Captain hoped to give us at least another day ashore.

We anchored off Edgertown, Massachusetts. Rows of stately federal-style mansions of old whaling captains sat in splendid isolation. It was a touristy, artsy place, with crowds of summer people who strolled the brick sidewalks and stopped in the shade of striped canvas awnings to window-shop the cutesy-stores. It was not a particularly memorable liberty port. I suspect we nearly doubled the population that day. The ice cream was good.

By the time we got back to New London, we were a little saltier, tossing around sea terms like we had just been in a two week Berlitz total-immersion class. We were beyond bulkheads, decks, and passageways. Now we could heave around and take the slack out of lines. We could clew up, sheet home and holystone, and even sing sea shanties. I had come far beyond any Cuba Lake stuff! I cannot compare my first *Eagle* trip to any other experience. Despite my little solo act on the royal yardarm, I was ready for more of ....*the sea and its lore.*

The swab cruise gave us a chance to get to know our classmates, and forced a team effort for success. The second classmen even became a little more human, but never lost control. I thought, *Someday, we may even look forward to serving with them—at least most of them.*

The Academy shifted gears when we entered the academic year in the fall. We became more like any small New England college. The kids were back in town. Our six hundred man corps of cadets may not have had a major impact on New London, but we were conspicuous, in uniform and walking everywhere. We were welcomed in coffee shops, delis, and movie houses.

On Saturday mornings the cadet corps presented a formal military review. Locals as well as tourists lined Mohegan Avenue as we formed on the plush parade ground against the backdrop of Hamilton Hall. The uniform was dress blues, with white hats, leggings, and gloves. The crowd was thrilled by the Coast Guard Band leading the battalion as they passed in review, rifles smartly in line. The National Ensign and the Coast Guard Flag fluttered in full glory. Company commanders each in turn, their bare swords flashing in the morning sun, saluted the visiting dignitary and ordered the marchers, "Eyes...Right!" Strains of *Semper Paratus* filled the air.

Cadets welcomed the fall convening of the Connecticut College for Women, an exclusive women's school, within walking distance of the Academy. The stately gray stone sorority houses and classrooms graced the manicured green acres like English mansions. The freshmen crop of ladies would soon be invited to our Fall Tea Dance, an annual ritual, also known by other not so nice nicknames.

I enjoyed the fall routine: football games, the corps march on, OBJI, our live bear mascot, parents' weekend, and homecoming. But, nothing compared to turning the calendar page to the first day of November.

Thanksgiving would soon be here. I'd finally be going home, the first break since I left my family on the steps of Chase Hall the past July.

Two seasonal maladies invaded the corps each November: channel fever and Dear John letters. Centuries ago, sailors at sea for long periods coined the phrase "channel fever" to describe that overpowering excitement they felt as they got closer to home port. At Thanksgiving, family and friends caught it too. They wrote to cadets more frequently, making plans for the holidays. All letters were welcome, except of course, the *Dear John.*

It was a tradition to share the hated break-up letter. We were still swabs, subject to mess hall harassment. Here's an example of the granddaddy of all, the Dear John.

"Mr. Gooblatz," the first classman at the head of the table said, "I understand you have received a letter that you wish to share with the corps. Please rise on your chair and proceed."

"Aye, aye, sir." The hapless fourth classman then stood, drew his chair back and climbed onto the seat. Standing tall, with the damning letter in hand, he announced, "Attention in the Mess Hall! Attention in the Mess Hall!" The entire corps became quiet, knowing well what was coming, and prepared to execute their duty.

"I am in receipt of a letter from my girlfriend, Margaret, which I would like to share."

Six hundred strong gave a round of appreciative applause, and then quieted.

"Dear John." *A massive cheer arose.*

"It is so hard for me to write this letter. I've been thinking about it for over a week. I care so much for you and want to see you happy." *Cat calls, cheers, and applause.*

"I know that it is going to be too hard for us to continue the wonderful relationship we shared before you left." *Long chorus of boos.* "Please don't hate me. It's something I just must do and I think it is the best for both of us to continue to grow." *Loud cheering and hurrahs.*

"I will always miss you. Please, please, please do come to see me at Thanksgiving so we can talk this over." *Yeas.* "I know I must move on, and of course, you must too." *Boos.* "I hope we will always be good friends; you are one of the best." *Applause, Applause.*

"Sincerely with true affection, Margaret." *A long chorus of hurrahs, boos, applause and cat calls, then, sustained applause.*

The thoroughly humiliated swab would slink back down into his chair, sometimes with visible tears. Most cadets, however, after the fact, felt it had been cathartic.

When the corps cheered and jeered the clichéd phrases, it told them, "It was not all about you." The feelings were universal. The purge of self-pity helped them move beyond, to math, navigation, history, seamanship, classmates, and good thoughts of the future.

I turned the leaf on my desk calendar to Wednesday, November 26, 1953. I thought, *Finally, it's here.* At noon, I joined the mass of uniformed cadets in a dash to the New London train station. I turned from the platform steps into the first car, and joined what seemed like a thousand college students from every school north of New London. The railroad always claimed they put on extra cars, knowing that all college vacations started at noon the day before Thanksgiving. I never believed it.

All I knew was that I made the entire trip standing, suitcase on the deck squeezed between my ankles, fighting the swaying train with one hand on the overhead rack. The air was close and reeked of sweat and stale cigarette breath. The crowd, already worn and hot, had stripped off their coats, hats, and scarves and randomly flung them onto seats, laps, and the deck. The coeds, while still chatty, didn't smile and didn't seem pretty. My flesh never touched fewer than three other people at the same time during the two hour ordeal to New York City.

At Penn Station, the instant the car doors opened, a herd of twenty-somethings, like fire ants scattering from a mound, stampeded into the oblivion of New York City. They were gone in seconds. I waved at a few classmates hurtling to catch the train to Chicago. I boarded a shuttle-bus to Rockefeller Center and the Erie Railroad office where I would begin my lonely overnight trip to Salamanca, New York. Those Chicago bound were there before I was in Salamanca.

-3-

THE FIRST THANKSGIVING

I WELCOMED THE FRESH AIR of Rockefeller Plaza after the stuffy cattle-car ride from New London. My first stop was the Erie Railroad office. A huge banner-like sign screamed "Erie Railroad" above picture windows that let you see the rows of nearly empty wooden bus terminal chairs. Against the back wall was a high ticket counter with a bored agent flipping magazine pages. Movie-size posters scotch taped to bare walls extolled the virtues of Binghamton, Elmira, and, perhaps the only poster-worthy destination, Chicago.

The agent handed me my ticket for the Pacific Express #7 which would depart Jersey City, New Jersey, at 11:00 p.m. Friendly enough, he asked about my uniform. "What does that gold shield on your sleeve mean?"

"That means I am in the Coast Guard. I am a fourth class cadet at the Academy in New London, Connecticut."

Unimpressed, he didn't ask about rank. He knew that without any kind of stripe, I didn't have any. "Going home for Thanksgiving?" he asked.

"Yes, sir."

"You have a good time, and Happy Thanksgiving. Don't miss the bus, which leaves from right in front of the office at 9:30 p.m."

"I won't, and Happy Thanksgiving to you, sir."

I was scheduled to arrive in Salamanca at 5:30 a.m. the following morning. My classmates would be in Chicago long before that. I scouted out a small grill where I could get something to eat later, and headed across to the plaza to kill time watching the ice skaters.

The rink in the sunken plaza was smaller than I expected; it was about one third the size of a football field. The eighteen-foot-high gilded bronze statue of the Greek god Prometheus presided over the rink, posed to bring fire to mankind.

The small skating crowd inched their way around the rink in shuffling mini-glides while holding on to the hand rail. There was a lot of falling down. I guessed that most were tourists checking off their holiday to-do lists: Macy's Thanksgiving Day parade–check; skate at Rockefeller Plaza–check. The center of the rink was willingly abdicated to the few near-pros. A woman in a short white skating outfit with a seasonal happy hat executed smooth jumps and spins. A man in hockey skates impressed the watchers with dramatic chip-spraying stops.

I leaned on the street-level wall, watching the skaters. My mind drifted back to the winters at home in the late 1940s. Recreation Park superintendent, Mr. Applebee, dragged a long water hose to the gravel parking lot behind the high school football field. It ran until the lot was a sheet of ice, then he pronounced it, "Ready for skaters."

A changing and warming hut, made of rough raw pine boards, was tractored out of some remote storage and placed at one end of the rink. There were two narrow benches against the long walls and a pot belly stove glowed between them at one end of the hut. A black chimney-pipe poked through the roof. Smoke curled into the chilly air creating a Norman Rockwell setting. The cozy warmth and strong pine smell of the bare wood was inviting. The hut brimmed with pretty girls who stuffed winter boots under the bench, laced their skates, and doffed their parkas for wool skating sweaters. The room echoed with their high-pitched giggles.

Young tongue-tied men flirted awkwardly while punching their buddies' arms, egging them on to some goofy skating challenge. Of course, everyone followed protocol—white figure skates for girls, brown and black hockey skates for boys. The only exception was Jim Shaw, the high school junior and major heartthrob, who wore black figure skates. He skated so well, nobody dared challenged him.

It had been a long day. I was getting hungry and still faced an overnight train ride. I crossed back to the bar and grill that I had scouted out earlier. As I entered, I noticed a hand- written cardboard sign in the window: *Now---Color TV.* I picked a booth where I could look up at the TV which sat on a small shelf above the bar on the opposite wall. It was a DuMont, one of the big 16" ones. The cathode ray tube poked its bulbous nose through a square frame in a vain attempt to look like a flat screen. As for "color," a cellophane sheet of theatrical lighting gel was scotch-taped to the frame. *Arthur Godfrey and His Friends* cast an eerie orange/yellow glow onto the faces of the bar stool gang. Unimpressed, their jaundiced faces stared blankly at the screen while they sipped beer from pilsner glasses. Nobody talked. Godfrey sang in his nasal twang while strumming his ukulele.

I enjoyed a beer and a burger at the same place every train trip home for four years. I never knew the name of the bar. It was just "My Place in New York." The second year somebody had convinced the owner to take the cellophane off the TV, so I was back to black and white.

I boarded the train in the dark at Jersey City. The cars were all day-cars. The seats were double-wide boards with a nonadjustable partial wicker back. A short distance out of Jersey City, we switched to a steam engine. Finally we were moving west. The rhythmic clicking of the wheels and synchronized rocking of the car nearly put me to sleep. Channel fever kept me awake.

The *Pacific Express* 7 was a milk run. We made nine stops before we got to Salamanca. The conductor passed through the cars balancing himself on the backs of the seats. He announced upcoming stations in muted tones: Port Jarvis, Waverley, Binghamton, Elmira. People stumbled on and off all night. *Who begins their journey at three and four o'clock in the morning?* Corning, Hornell. We were really getting close now.

At one stop, a very pretty girl shuffled into my car and asked if she could sit with me. I had been slumped against the window, half dozing. "Of course," I said. I stood to help her get her bag onto the overhead rack. I was too sleepy for introductions or conversation. She gave it up.

Wellsville, Olean. My stop was next. Roused by the conductor's voice, I was embarrassed to discover that I had slumped, chin on my chest, with my head perched on the precipice of my seat mate's boney shoulder. I was in serious jeopardy of either drooling on her sweater or sliding down onto a softer, more comfortable (more embarrassing), head rest. I roused slowly and apologized with a little fake stretching to hide my guilty comfort moment.

She said, "That's OK, you must be very tired."

I thanked her and explained that I had not slept for twenty four hours. We said very little for the rest of the short ride into Salamanca.

Dad was waiting for me on the platform. I gave him a big hug, "Happy Thanksgiving, Dad."

He broke into his familiar wide smile and said, "Great to have you home, son." He stuck his cigar stub back into the corner of his mouth and we piled into the car for the last eighteen miles to Bradford.

A quick hello to the family, and I was off to bed where I slept until just before dinner. I had forgotten how nice it was to relax on the entire chair, and enjoy family conversation at a leisurely pace. I think the record length of a meal at the Academy, from "Seats" to "Leave at will," was in the neighborhood of twelve minutes.

Mom made sure I didn't have time to lounge around in civvies. I was the uniformed show-and-tell exhibit all afternoon for the relatives, most of whom questioned my status. Was I really a college student or was I in the service?

High school friend Bob Taylor called me Thanksgiving night. He was rounding up friends for a get together on Friday at the pavilion at Cuba Lake, just across the border into New York State where their law granted us a legitimate beer. A typical summer beach place, it was much quieter at Thanksgiving break. Nevertheless, we gathered at a large round table and swapped freshman stories. Bob was going to Allegany College in Meadville, Pennsylvania. There were others from Penn State, and several from the state teachers' colleges: Mansfield, Slippery Rock, and Indiana. It soon became clear that I couldn't compare stories with the wild college frat and sorority bunch. I felt like odd man out.

I don't know how they kept up. Late night parties several times a week, cars, beer, and carousing. When did they study? Nobody talked about that. I was in bed by 10:00 p.m. every night, up a 6:00 a.m. I studied hard, exercised, and struggled to keep up my grades every day. On Saturday or Sunday, maybe a dish of ice cream at the rec hall, or a walk into town for a movie. I lived in a different world.

I liked the nice girl, Janie, who sat next to me. We danced a few times and I enjoyed a little higher level conversation with her than the frat group. Not yet a college girl, she was headed there next fall. It had been so noisy, I had to ask her last name again and where she went to high school.

"I'm Janie, Dick, Janie Upthegrove. I graduated from Okinawa High School."

"Okinawa High? Really? You must be a service brat."

"Yeah, my dad is General Upthegrove. He's head of the U.S. 20th Air Force. He is from Bradford, but I've moved all around the world with my family."

Janie and I hit it off well that night and we agreed to get together over Christmas break. Things were already looking up already.

The trip back to New London was just as gruesome as the one to get home. I arrived at the Academy mid-Sunday afternoon. It had been great to see the family, enjoy a holiday meal, and see old friends. I needed to write to Janie.

Thanksgiving leave was so short, it seemed hardly worth the effort, especially given my travel options. Some cadets did stay at the Academy and ate at the mess hall, and a few were invited into local homes to share their holiday. Others went to a classmate's home who lived nearby. After my first Thanksgiving home alone, I took a buddy with me. My roommate Ron McClellan came home one year and Wayne "Poncho" Arnold another. They made the trip more enjoyable for me too. I remained lifelong friends with both. Ron and I served our first assignment together on the Coast Guard Cutter, *Absecon* in Norfolk, Virginia, and he was best man at my wedding. Poncho left the Academy in our second class year, but we stayed in touch.

The remainder of swab year went well. Hundredth Day came and passed. It marked one hundred days before graduation. To celebrate, the battalion leadership positions were reversed. Swabs were in charge. We enjoyed putting the upperclassmen through the swab indoctrination routines, even for a day. It was always in good sport and taken well by the upperclassmen, but they would remind us, especially while braced against the bulkhead, "Remember, tomorrow will come soon."

We lost a few classmates at the end of the term in January. Some left for academic reasons, others had resigned. The Coast Guard or the Academy experience was not what they had expected or understood it to be. Resignation carried no penalties at this point, and it made sense for both parties to just agree to a no-fault divorce. I never questioned continuing. At the end of the year, I ranked a little below the mid-point academically. I knew I faced hard work ahead. On graduation day, the first class cadets received their commission and loved ones pinned on their new Ensign's shoulder boards. Transformed with their new officer's cap device shining in the sun, they were on their way to their first sea-going assignment—the "Real Guard."

But it was graduation day for swabs, too.

That thin slanted stripe that I now wore may have been the most anticipated in my career. I retired with twenty eight years of active duty and the four broad gold stripes of a captain, but no new stripe felt heavier than the one I put on that day.

Without a break, we moved right on to the next event: a seventy-six day, ten thousand mile summer training cruise to Europe on the *USCGC Eagle*. We were headed to Spain, Netherlands, and Denmark.

— 4 —

THE ATLANTIC CROSSING

ON MAY 30TH, 1954 THE *Eagle* was anchored in the outer harbor of New London, Connecticut. There was a light breeze, calm sea, and a cloudless sky. Everyone felt the excitement. It was our first long cruise. We would be in Santander, Spain, in three weeks.

Our arms were curled beneath the wooden 4 x 4s that extended from the top of the capstan like the spokes of a wagon wheel. The staccato clank of the steel pawl counted off the pace as it dropped onto each link. The preventer kept the chain from running back out. "Keep it movin,' boys. We can't get to Spain unless you get that anchor up."

In the glory days of the great clipper ships, sailors often sang a sea shanty to keep time and set the pace as they did their work. They even had special purpose shanties. One such song, *Oh Shenandoah,* was a "capstan shanty." In later years, after I retired, I sang in a barbershop quartet back home in Bradford. *Oh Shenandoah* was one of my favorites, and every time we sang it I was transported back to that day, to the deck of the *Eagle,* manning the capstan to bring in the anchor on my first long cruise.

A small boat with camera crew from CBS television and *National Geographic Magazine* circled us. They were maneuvering to get pictures and video of the *USCGC Eagle,* the square-rigged barque, under sail, with the world's first nuclear-powered submarine, *USS Nautilus* (SSN 571) in the background. She was outfitting at the Electric Boat Shipyard across the Thames River. The shot would surely compel historical comparisons on tonight's six o'clock news.

The internationally distinguished author, Alan Villiers, one of the world's foremost authorities on the great clipper ships, would be with us for the entire cruise. He was writing an article for *National Geographic* (published in the July 1955 issue. His book, *Sailing Eagle*, covering the same trip, was also published in 1955.)

"Sir, the anchor is up and down." The bosun's status report was relayed from the forecastle to the Captain on the bridge. That meant our bow was directly over the anchor and the shank was vertical. Only the flukes were holding, dug into the soft bottom. Like the built-in hold on a manned rocket launch, everything stopped. We stored the capstan bars and stood by for the next order. Captain Bowman, The *Eagle's* CO, stood on the bridge nearly two hundred feet away, and gave the order.

"All hands to sail stations. Prepare to set sail."

The *Eagle* sprang into organized chaos. Two hundred cadets responded to overlapping commands shouted by the mast captains. Miles of manila line were scrambled all over the deck as cadets, topsiders squeaking on the teak, moved quickly to their stations. Braces, sheets, clew-lines, and halyards, removed from perfect coils, were flaked out for running or were manned by cadets ready to haul away. A mass of eager cadets scrambled up the shrouds, like an advancing wave of humanity, and sounded off as they came to their assigned yard arm. "Coming on starboard! Coming on port!" They pushed off the shrouds to grab the jackstay, then moved to the footropes and loosened the gaskets holding the folded canvas on top of the yard arm.

The *Eagle* rode at anchor with her bow into the wind. Captain Bowman had pre-positioned the yards and staysails on the foremast. He needed the wind to rotate the ship when she was free to move. When he was satisfied the ship was ready, he gave the command, "Break her out."

For the first time, the electric windlass was engaged to power the anchor out of the mud and set the *Eagle* free. The chief of the anchor detail cupped his hands to his mouth and broadcast the report everyone had been waiting for.

"Anchor's away!"

The ship's bow fell off the wind enough to set the fore topsail. Then, as the ship was brought to course, the captain ordered, "Set all sail." One after another, the upper yards dropped their white canvas, then the main and fore courses billowed out in turn, adding their power. We felt the forward movement. We watched the growing wake astern. With the fore and aft sails set, the *Eagle* heeled to port a few degrees. Her bow rose and dipped into the growing Atlantic swells.

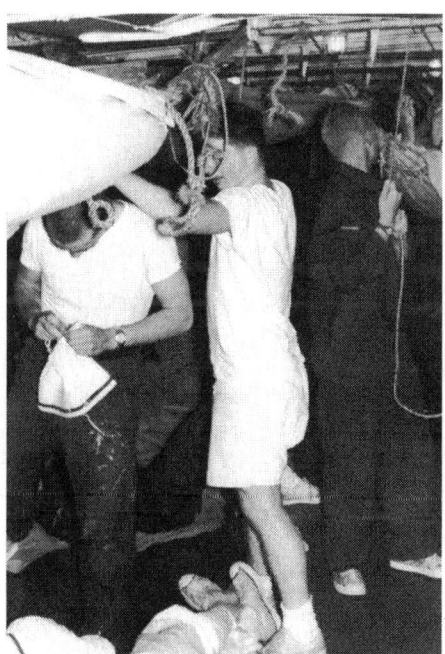

Rigging hammocks in close quarters

By the 31st of May, there was no land in sight and not much ship traffic. We followed the old clipper ship route east, directly toward Spain.

The Coast Guard Cutter *Rockaway* (WAVP 377), an active ocean station vessel, had been assigned to the Cadet Practice Squadron for the summer. She provided an up-to-date platform for the first class cadets learning duties that they would be performing as commissioned officers in the active Coast Guard fleet, often on the same class ship.

On both the *Rockaway* and the *Eagle*, first-classmen stood officer-of-the-deck (OOD), navigator, and engineering watches. Nearly always sailing in company with us, the "*Rock*" was in constant motion practicing convoy station-keeping on the *Eagle* and conducting flashing light, semaphore, and signal-flag drills.

The first-class would swap ships in Amsterdam, our second port. When they were on the *Eagle* they also stood the all-important duties as mast captains, no small task on a square-rigger, with full responsibility for all sail maneuvers.

Our class, on the other hand, rotated through watches similar to those stood by enlisted men on active cutters: quartermaster, helmsman, signalman, lifeboat crew, and messenger. There was a similar split of watches in the engine room. Although we were loathe to run the main propulsion engine, (the original German engine, which had been dubbed, *Elmer*) our engine room provided plenty of experience. The *Eagle* had generators, switchboards, boilers, and auxiliary machinery like evaporators for making fresh water.

The classes of '57 and '55 had sailed together before on the short cruise to Bermuda last year. There is a different atmosphere now, however. As third class cadets, we are on more of a teaching-learning cruise. Within a few days, we settled into routine: work/watch/eat/sleep.

There are three duty sections, each stand eight hours of watch a day. The schedule for a typical day might read:

0600 Reveille.

0630–0745 Breakfast.

0800–1200 Morning watch.

1300-1400 Quarters. Emergency drills.

1400–1600 Ship's work.

1600–1730 Free Time.

1730–1930 Evening meal.

2000–2400 Evening watch.

There was always plenty of ship's work. Anything made of steel was in a constant battle against the sea air, and begged to be chipped and scraped. The Boatswain's precious wooden taffrails needed to be varnished, and his brass always needed to be polished.

If we could find a moment after ship's work, or after chow, some might squeeze in a star sight to feed the voracious appetite of their navigation notebook. With a requirement for one hundred celestial sights, we could not miss an opportunity. Others might jot off a paragraph in a continuous letter home. The evening watch came quickly enough, then, finally to bed at midnight only to do it all over again the next day. Sixteen to eighteen hour days were the norm. Within a week, we had adjusted to sleeping in four-hour chunks supplemented by cat naps when and where we could manage—on a coil of line in the bosun's locker, on a stack of canvas in the sail locker, or on the open deck on a quiet night as part of the ready boat crew.

There were occasional breaks when we rotated into a day-worker job for a few days. Messcooks and laundrymen were not watchstanders. A messcook's day started at 0500, breaking food out of dry stores and reefers for the day's menu, then peeling three hundred pounds of potatoes after lunch. Finally after serving and cleaning up after three meals, the twelve hour shift was over.

Laundrymen, who ran the ship's steam laundry and kept two hundred of us in clean uniforms, socks, and underwear, also had a tough day's work. The real payoff of both day jobs was a full night's sleep.

We received a grade for the cruise that became part of our overall academic record and final class standing. We were graded in deck and engineering performance, navigation (hence the importance of celestial sights), and an all-important "adaptability" grade. It was a highly subjective grade assigned by an upperclassman on everything we did. It was meant to measure our "suitability as a future line officer of the Coast Guard." It comprised 40 percent of our grade. It was possible to flunk the cruise. We had a third classman repeating his long cruise with us because he had received a failing grade the year before. When this happened, it was a last chance effort. Fail again and you went home.

Eagle heeled in heavy weather

We were into the second week of the cruise. It had been rainy and overcast every day, making sun lines and star sights impossible. Until yesterday, the seas had been reasonable, giving us time to gain our sea legs. The storm that had been building all day was forcing another inner ear adjustment. Growing numbers of cadets, and enlisted crew alike, have been drawn to the lee rail. Seasickness is taking its toll. I'm one of the lucky ones—not too affected. I feel a little sleepy for a period, then recover within a day or two.

The chow line was short tonight. The *Eagle* was heeled at a steady fifteen degrees with deeper rolls. Those who were eating either propped one end of their food tray atop their milk glass or held it level with one hand while eating with the other. There was not much conversation, only the occasional sound of crashing metal trays, silverware, and glass bowls, as they slid off the tables onto the tiled deck. It was like living in a house on a hillside, with floors built parallel to the ground—that moved—a never ending carnival ride.

I'm standing the mid-watch tonight with the ready boat crew. There are ten of us huddled on the port side of the open main deck, under the pin-rail in the shelter of coiled lines. The night is dark, heavy inky clouds block out any semblance of light; the sea and sky have merged. We are encapsulated in a black globe. The ceaseless yawing, dipping, twisting, and rolling in heavy seas is wearing thin. The wind whistles through the rigging with surprising force, the pitch changing with each gust. The large mainsail snaps and pops with sound like a cracking whip. Block-and-tackles rattle, and chain-rigged clews clink and clank as they dance to the tune of the sea.

It's not easy staying warm and dry, even with no rain. With every pitch into an oncoming wave, the flared bow of the *Eagle* coughs up a solid sheet of seawater. Now air conditioned by the howling wind, it builds into a man-chilling spray that blows the length of the entire deck. The smell of salt air fills our nostrils. Nobody escapes it.

The bad weather carries good news too. The barque loves it! Fully suited in her twenty-two sails, *Eagle* plows through the ocean with ease, moving us, at fifteen knots, closer to Santander. The weather demands an active watch. We are called to cant yards, secure loose gear, rig safety lines, and trim sails. Time passes quickly. Ding ding...ding ding...ding ding. The high pitched ring of the ship's bell penetrated the howling wind. Six bells, our watch will be over in an hour. Two of us will roust out the relief at 0330.

Entering the berthing compartment is like stepping into deep inner space. A low ambient light from an unknown source creates an eerie scene. Hammocks danced in the dark, swaying together, as if an invisible orchestra was keeping time. I brushed aside the dangling spider webs of hammock lashing cords as I picked my way through the cradled bodies, some strung high, others slung low. I squinted along the red beam from my flashlight looking for the stenciled names of the relief watch. The ship was rolling heavily. Actually, the hammocks were still, suspended in space. It was the ship that was swaying around them.

With no room for hammock spreaders, the sleeping bodies were wrapped in curls of canvas, like caterpillars stretched between tree branches. Sounds and smells, made only by sleeping men, presented when I got close enough to shine my red light onto a face.

I found Arvie Pluntz. I tapped him on the shoulder and flickered my flashlight beam across his eyes a few times. "Good morning, Arvie, time for your watch. It's 0340."

"Yeah, OK, OK." He didn't sound like he meant it.

"Come on, Arv. Don't doze back off," I said, in hushed tones. "Time for your watch."

Arvie's name is Richard V. Pluntz. When we were issued uniforms a year ago, he had set the stencil machine wrong. With no space between his initials— everything he owned read RV Pluntz. Hence, his nickname.

"I'm awake." Arvie grabbed the overhead stay and swung his legs out of his cocoon. When his feet hit the deck, he stumbled, adjusting from the gimbaled comfort of the hammock to the pitch and roll of the deck.

"It's pretty rough out there tonight, Arv."

"OK, thanks. Let me get my pants on and hitch up my can, and I'll be right up."

The "can" Arvie was going to hitch was an empty #2 spinach can that he got from the scullery. He had learned to cope with his constant sea-sickness last year on the short cruise. A couple of punched holes near the top rim, a strand of twine, rigged through his belt loops–he was set to go–his sea bucket always at the ready. I never saw Arvie in bad humor. He stood every watch, did everything required, no complaints, and always with a big smile—but never without his bucket. He was smart and fun to be with. Richard V. Pluntz did not graduate with us. I can't remember the reason he left the Academy, but maybe the thought of spending a major portion of his life with a #2 can tied to his belt had something to do with it.

When we were relieved, we headed below, lifted ourselves into our hammocks and drifted off quickly, our world was finally still. Maybe tomorrow the storm would pass. Even so, there would still be nothing but endless ocean and non-stop movement. Sometimes you just wanted the damned ship beneath your feet to stand still! We enjoyed the extra hour of sleep before the mid-watch was rousted out at 0700.

We ate breakfast, and then mustered on deck for morning quarters. The sun was shining, the ship had stopped lurching, a light breeze was blowing, but the ocean was still there. This was going to be an "air bedding" day. Everyone dragged their hammocks, sheets, and blankets topside, and lashed them to the rail, where they would remain all day. It was not a pretty sight, but the results of fresh bedding were worth it. I think the man who invented Febreze must have been a sailor.

Good weather stayed with us the rest of the way to Santander. Guys huddled during breaks passing around travel brochures and State Department briefing notes on where to go and what to do in the city. (Also what *not* to do and where *not* to go). The world was coming alive again. Ship traffic picked up. Many diverted their course to pass closer than normal, intrigued by the sight of a three-masted square rigged barque on the high seas in this day and time. Someone caught part of the Walcott-Marciano world heavyweight fight on the radio. Radio stations were playing American hit songs in Portuguese. We entered the Bay of Biscay on the 20ᵗʰ of June.

The Pyrenees Mountains that separate Spain and France began to spike on the eastern horizon, rising taller as we closed the distance. I marked the moment as my first (except for Canada) sighting of foreign soil. The western end of the fourteen thousand foot range rises only three to four thousand feet, but they are jagged, in a different league than the rolling hills of Pennsylvania. Everyone is talking about liberty in Santander.

For the last stretch into the more confined bay and harbor, we had to light off the main engine. Elmer's low rumbling vibrations were an unwelcome disturbance after the quiet power of the wind. It was late in the evening when we furled all sail. A large moon, high in the sky, cast a silvery overtone to the picture of a hundred cadets in the rigging. We took the time to ensure a presentable tight harbor furl, no Irish pennants, all canvas tucked out of sight, lashed tightly on the top of the yards.

By morning the city of Santander, was spread before us. Its splendid harbor has been a major port for centuries. Much of the shipping trade with the western nations struck out from here. Low white buildings hugged the waterfront and a few blocks beyond. Four and five story buildings spread to the low hilltops surrounding the city of one hundred fifty thousand people. We docked the *Eagle* on 21 June at 10:30 a.m. A large crowd had gathered on the pier to greet *America's Tall Ship*. We were twenty-one days out of New London, and the deck was finally still.

− 5 −

SANTANDER, AMSTERDAM, AND COPENHAGEN

THE LANGUAGE DIFFERENCE WAS NOT a barrier in Santander. We were like children playing charades with smiling aliens. Mispronounced words dragged from the depths of tenth grade Spanish class triggered fits of laughter. Our hands-across-the-sea moments definitely depended on hands. Communicating was actually fun. The natives were far better with English than we were with Spanish.

The *Eagle* hosted an open house in every liberty port which drew large crowds. In return, cadets were often invited to official receptions and offered a variety of tours. Nightlife in Santander was incredibly late. The city had wonderful open cafes and the food was good, but dinner was not served typically until 10:00 p.m. It was difficult finding anything to eat in the late afternoon or early evening.

We had tour options: an old fishing village, the former royal palace, and tours to the famous Altamira Caves. Ron McClellan, Jerry Minton, Bob Williams, and I took the tour to the caves where the first caveman drawings were discovered. I had seen pictures of the drawings in history books. They looked like bison, and other large animals. Being in the caves themselves put a whole different perspective on the experience and raised unanswerable questions about prehistoric life. Why did they draw the pictures on the walls of caves? Were they intentionally recording history, leaving a message to others, drawing to entertain the clan, or just to decorate the room? Couldn't they have painted them on large, but portable flat rocks so they could show them around, trade, or sell them? It was a fascinating tour.

On the return trip, we stopped at the picturesque fifteenth century village of *Santillana del Mar*, about fifteen miles west of Santander. It had cobblestone streets, and farmers moved their goods in ox carts. We shopped for souvenirs at one of the small store fronts. I bought a goatskin wine pouch that Spanish shepherds wore on shoulder lanyards; their wine was always at the ready. With precise control, they squirted a stream of wine into their mouths from arm's length. We discovered this was not a skill for us to practice while wearing dress khakis. When we came to a street artist, I bought, for a few pesetas, an 8" x 10" colored chalk portrait of me that now lies lost in a box in some deep drawer at home.

Our last stop before returning to the bus was a quaint neighborhood bar, an exemplar of "Cheers," in Boston, where "everybody knows your name." We were welcomed with warm curiosity.

When we departed the bar, we were surprised to hear an American woman's voice behind us. "How nice to see some young American boys again." Startled, we turned to find this smiling gray-haired woman, dressed like a typical American with a white blouse, full skirt, and sensible shoes. She wanted to stroll along with us for a while.

She was the widow of an American watercolor artist who loved painting Spanish landscapes. She had lost her husband a year before. She shared his passion for the area so much that she had remained and lived just outside the village. The big surprise was that she had been born and raised in Chicago and grew up in the neighborhood one block away from Bob Williams.

A large crowd had gathered on the pier to see us depart Santander, on Friday, 25 June . It had been a great liberty port, and most of us wished it could have lasted longer. We enjoyed smooth sailing across The Bay of Biscay. Rumors had it that we would be in Amsterdam by the first of July.

My memories of a quiet Sunday offset any thoughts of past bad days at sea. When off duty, it was a day of relaxation. The forecastle area, from the bow to the stack of balsa life rafts above the forward deck house became the cadet informal lounge and recreation area. Some of us were content to enjoy a good book in the warm sun, shirts off. Others relived the liberty they just had or made plans for the one coming up. A few were flaked out on the deck, catching up on lost sleep, their sextant box next to their head, ready to catch a sun line later.

A fresh breeze carried the *Eagle*, at a slight heel, northward into long friendly swells. The only sound was the whoosh of the dipping bow as it pushed an unending series of wavelets that spilled their energy back to the sea. In the early evening, plankton tumbled in the bow wave, their green phosphorescence light show was as mesmerizing as a campfire's flickering flame.

I stretched out on one of the balsa rafts, content to stare at the open sky in the growing twilight, picking out the early stars. The soft strumming of a ukulele and harmonizing voices rose from the main deck. It was probably Paul Kauffman, our only Hawaiian classmate, with one or two of the thick muscled, big bellied Samoan cooks from the crew. They sang in Hawaiian, a language with only fourteen letters in the alphabet—five of them vowels. How could their singing do anything but enhance the peaceful setting?

I folded my cap into a pillow, entwined my fingers beneath my head, and stared into the deepening blue sky. The music carried me away. *What the hell was I doing in the middle of the Bay of Biscay, on the deck of a square rigged ship?* I thought, *I grew up in Bradford, for God's sake—nobody could have seen this coming.* Whatever force was controlling my journey, I knew I was one lucky guy.

Random thoughts denied me a nap. *Would Janie Upthegrove still be home when I got there? How hard will the fall classes be? Copenhagen sounds great. I hope I stay in Charlie Company in the new set-up. I should write to Janie from Amsterdam; maybe we could have a dinner date at the Ho-sta-ga at the top of the hill going to Olean. I need to find out where Little Civic's band might be playing when I get home.*

Could we be on the same sea that only a few days ago seemed to threaten the continued existence of life? I cringed, recalling the wrenching sounds of the dry-heaves that men suffered when they had nothing left to sacrifice to Poseidon but the three dry crackers they had choked down an hour before. How could it be so bad...yet so good? Only delightful Sundays like this could make men answer the *call of the sea.*

The *Rockaway*, doing station-keeping drills, changed her position to our port beam. Nobody cared. She is just tagging along on her own, like a kid who can't help but skip, leap ahead, and fall behind his mother who is trying to enjoy a Sunday stroll on the Bay of Biscay.

"Keep up now." I finally got off the deck and headed below. "I'm going to catch the movie before I have to go on watch," I announced to nobody in particular. "It's a good one, *Bandwagon* with Fred Astaire and Cyd Charisse."

We entered the English Channel early in the evening of 28 June. The wind was against us forcing us to furl sail and light off "Elmer" if we were going to meet our ETA in Amsterdam. Ship traffic picked up. We were thirty miles south of the Isle of Wight.

In this very spot, ten years ago this month, a mighty armada of 5000 ships of the Allied Expeditionary Force was poised for the bold landing on the beaches of Normandy. Young and scared, American, British, and Canadian soldiers, 150,000 of them, were about to begin their treacherous trip to beachheads called Omaha and Juno. The Normandy invasion, the largest amphibious assault in history, had marked the beginning of the end of WWII.

Although we were nineteen, the decade-old historic event was one we remembered. We shared memories—collecting tin foil and animal fat, and buying saving stamps at school to be changed for war bonds. We had worried about our brothers and uncles. The country had been at war, and *everybody* had played a part.

On the ready boat crew that night, Fred Bruner was holding court in the waist of the *Eagle*. Fred fancied himself a historian, and rightfully so. We marveled at his photographic memory. He could recall the smallest detail of everything he had ever read, and he read prodigiously all things military. He was irritatingly accurate! Though several had tried, often after significant research, to catch him in error, it never happened that I knew of.

Tonight Fred was packing D-Day invasion trivia—it could have been Lord Nelson's defeat of the Spanish Armada. He knew second and third level leaders of each force, their good moves and bad, and the consequences of all of them. We all trusted what Fred told us. We listened respectfully and soaked it up, though we did play with him a little on his delivery. I estimate Fred's comfort zone for conversation at fifteen inches, much inside the personal bubble of most people.

One member of the boat crew, Dave, I believe, made a bet that he could get Fred to move across the deck to the opposite side of the ship without ever touching him or saying anything.

"Hey, Fred, I have a question about the landing at Omaha." Dave moved into the privileged circle.

"Sure." Fred moved closer until he stood directly in front of Dave.

Throughout the Omaha lesson, Dave took small steps backward. Fred closed the gap. He stopped talking only to bookmark a major point when he slowly closed his eyes for three seconds then popped the lids open, as if to ask, "Did you get that?" Fred was not just comfortable at fifteen inches, he *had* to be there. Dave maneuvered the pair on a sinuous backward journey to the other side of the ship. Dave collected his bet. The boat crew enjoyed the moment. Time passed.

The white cliffs of Dover loomed to the north. The 300 foot chalky cliff shone even in the absence of sun. Calis, the closest point on the continent, was a few miles away. Too early for our scheduled arrival, we killed time in the North Sea with more drills.

On the 2 July, we entered the locks of Holland. The narrow canal was busy with ships and barges moving in and out of Amsterdam. It seemed as though we were gliding through flat green fields with outcroppings of Don Quixote windmills. It could have been a picture out of my grade school geography book had only the tulips been in bloom. The paths that paralleled the canal were alive with sightseers on bicycles, peddling along with us, madly waving their arms in welcome.

We were berthed in the confined harbor at the foot of a busy city street. The *Eagle*'s bowsprit extended over the sidewalk and first row of parked cars. For a few days, we were an exciting addition to the cityscape.

I climbed to the foretop for a long-distance view of the wide street that lay in a straight line with the ship. Clusters of cars and hundreds of bicycles paused at the traffic lights, jammed together like marathon runners waiting for the starting gun. When the light changed, the pack moved slowly at first then faster as the next hoard of street vehicles moved into place.

The dock workers who hooked up water and electrical service, and men delivering goods, all wore Dutch wooden shoes as a standard work shoe. I had thought they were relics of the past. They were plain carved wood, work stained, and dinged up from hard use, not painted like those in souvenir shops. Because the arch didn't bend, they created a strange double clop-clopping on the *Eagle*'s teak deck. The sound could not be mistaken as anything else; it was men walking in wooden shoes.

The *Eagle* was a major waterfront attraction on the Fourth of July. All American naval vessels celebrate the occasion by "full dressing" the ship. Every signal flag on the ship was displayed from a line that ran from the blue union jack at the bow, over the trucks of the fore and main mast, 150 feet above the deck, to the flagstaff on the stern. An oversized American flag flew from the tip of the mainmast, above the multicolored string of signal flags. People strolling the pier stopped in their tracks when we held morning colors, precisely at 0800. Every flag had been rolled and lashed to the line with a fine thread. A yank of the halyard broke all flags free at the same instant. They stretched and fluttered proudly in the breeze, as if proclaiming their own independence. The *Eagle* in full dress was an inspiring sight.

Everyone enjoyed liberty in Amsterdam. English was commonly spoken in restaurants, retail stores, and even casual people on the street who frequently stopped us just to say hello to an American.

We were offered many tours. A motor launch trip to small villages like Marken and Volendam, where the locals wore traditional clothing, was popular. Men wore bloused Dutch pantaloons, and women wore winged white hats and aprons. There were tours of cheese factories, diamond cutters, flower markets, and museums with original Rembrandts. I enjoyed a guided tour of the canals of Amsterdam in a glass topped longboat. The Heineken Brewery tour with free beer was a class favorite.

Within a day, cadets were passing the hot word. "Be sure you go to a Rystaffel. It's an experience you don't want to miss."

A Rystaffel (pronounced *rice-taffel*, and means "rice table") is standard fare in many Indonesian restaurants. The influence of the former Dutch colonial empire penetrated deeply into the ethnic restaurant niche. Competition was keen. Living up to the name the "Spice Islands," the famous Rystaffel was served as fifteen to twenty-course meals. The classier fares had even more. I went with a small group to an advertised thirty-six course Rystaffel.

The restaurant served at long narrow tables, guests on each side, with an army of waiters parading luncheon-sized plates of rice and "other things." Each course followed the last with little time between. What we didn't know was how *hot* Indonesian cuisine was. Casual conversation disappeared. Each course was hotter than the one before. That little packet of hot mustard served with Chinese-take-out would rank as half as hot. Other than the rice, nobody knew what the "other things" on the plate were, and we were afraid to ask. Some restaurants served a special Dutch pickle for you to eat between courses to help cool the palate. It was indeed a memorable meal.

We left Amsterdam on 7 July. Good times, good memories.

"Wonderful, Wonderful Copenhagen." Danny Kaye sang those words in the 1952 musical *Hans Christian Anderson*. Our visit to the... "Salty old queen of the sea," began on 14 July. It had been only a week's run from Amsterdam, across the North Sea to this beautiful urban capital of Denmark. A city of over a million people, "the Paris of the North," lies off the eastern coast of Denmark at the southern end of the Kattegat. Sweden is only a few miles across the strait.

Copenhagen's main attraction is the famous Tivoli Gardens. This second oldest amusement park in the world draws an annual seasonal attendance second only to Disneyland of Paris. It is billed as a "Cultural wonderland and historical gem, right at the heart of the city." It is a combination Coney Island and Central Park with acres of meticulously maintained lawns and magnificent flower beds, and amusement rides to please all. In addition, there are historical exhibitions, restaurants to die for, and live theater and movie houses. It was always crowded with thousands of beautiful, happy people.

There was no reason to go anywhere else on liberty, other than Tivoli—unless, of course, you took a tour of the Tuborg Brewery. Not to be outdone by Amsterdam, they generously shared their beer "brewed for Danish kings."

Clusters of cadets in service dress blue uniforms with white cap covers dominated the park scene. We ate in wonderful restaurants, took in shows, visited exhibits, and generally just hung out. Many friendly people were anxious to sit and talk with you. Liberty in Copenhagen was great, but there was so little time.

The iconic small bronze statue of *The Little Mermaid* sits on a rock in the harbor, close to shore. Like the Statue of Liberty that symbolizes the spirit of New York City, or Christ the Redeemer in Rio de Janeiro, the mermaid is the epitome of Danish charm. Myth has it, if you kiss her, you will be drawn back. If I had a chance to return to Europe today... Copenhagen is where I would start.

Our last day in Copenhagen was Sunday, 18 July. Off the coast, near Kronberg Castle, we encountered the Danish sail training ship, *Danmark,* sister ship of the *Eagle.* Both were built in Hitler's Germany and had been given up as war reparations at the end of WWII. A challenge race was on. Two three-masted barques, under full sail, raced northward in the Kattegat Strait. The Danes, with a long history of sail training, sensed an easy victory that was denied by the strategy of Captain Bowman.

Both ships, fast approaching the shoreline, were going to have to tack soon. Tension built. The advantage would go to the ship that could wait the longest for the first move. Captain Bowman engineered a surprise plan that had us make all lines ready, then we crouched to the deck below the bulwark, out of sight of the Danes. We passed commands in a whisper. The three lower braces were married together in our hands, ready for the word. As we drew closer, we could see the crew of the *Danmark* straining through binoculars for signs of life. They had no clue of what was about to happen. We were a silent ghost ship with only two men visible, our captain and the helmsman.

"Helms A Lee!" The Captain thundered his command.

Two hundred cadets leapt into action, and ran away with the braces. There was no hand over hand heaving—we literally "ran away with the braces." Caught totally by surprise, the *Danmark*'s wind was cut off, they never recovered, and the *Eagle* soundly beat her sister ship all the way to the final marker.

A frustrated Danish signalman sent us a flashing light signal. "You are using your engines."

Commander Earle, an Academy officer assigned to the *Eagle*, jumped atop the deck house, personally manned the signal light, and flashed back a message, "No. You are dragging your anchor."

It was a triumph for the upstart sailors from the colonies.

Much like the windjammers of old, the *Eagle* needed the favorable easterly winds of the northern route home. We passed north of Scotland and just south of Iceland. Despite the calendar showing we were in mid-summer, it was cold at sixty-three degrees north latitude, and often overcast. When it was clear, however, we had a lot of time for navigation sights. We had a good horizon and the stars were out from sunset until sunrise—the land of the midnight sun. The navigational chart posted on the bulkhead of the forward mess deck became a center of attention. When the cadet navigator plotted our position on 24 July, we still had twenty-three hundred miles to go.

The days at sea had long since settled into a repetitive routine. We all felt the draw of our fourth, and best, liberty port—home. We did have diversions. Movies again became popular: *Cattle Town, Lili, Gentlemen Prefer Blonds,* and the all hands favorite, *Salome.*

Coast Guard Day is August 4th. It is celebrated at every Coast Guard unit, on land or at sea. We enjoyed a holiday routine. We had goofy pie-eating contests, skits, and a rag-tag cadet band whose uniforms of Bermuda shorts and wool watch sweaters were fitting for an open deck picnic in the north Atlantic. They wore blue uniform cap covers, without the cap frame, tilted to resemble a French beret. A brass piece, a bass drum, a guitar or two, and a leader wielding a toilet plunger baton—The *Horstvessel Furslugeners*—were great fun.

The star attraction of the afternoon was *Papa Santos' Band*. A popular first class petty officer cook, Santos had a practiced string-band of some of his Hawaiian, Samoan, and Filipino cooks and stewards. They were good musicians who played snare drums, ukuleles, and guitars. Papa always stole the show with his home-made bass, an upside down metal garbage can with a tall wooden stick mounted on the side. Two strings ran through the drum and stretched over carved top of the stick. The strings had wood toggles on the end. When Papa manipulated them by twisting and changing the tension, he could strum several notes. He played a mean bass, in his black derby, with a great sense of rhythm and showmanship.

Finally on the 12th of August, New London Ledge Light hove into view. After a pause for a neat harbor furl, we stepped the mast so we could get under the bridge. In a traditional gesture, we gathered our oldest black uniform shoes, the ones worn only in the engine room—steamers, and brought them topside to the rail.

Knowing these battered and scared shoes would never be wearable in uniform again, we threw them at the base of the raised railroad bridge in tribute to the end of a great cruise. Hundreds of shoes filled the air in a black arc that splashed like spattered pebbles at the base of the bridge and sank to the bottom of the Thames River. The growing mound of cadet shoes from years past had formed the strangest fish haven on the east coast.

We had logged 10,339 miles in seventy-six days. Since Copenhagen, we had been at sea for twenty-six. We were ready for home leave.

I don't know when it happened—that brotherhood thing—that un-breakable bond that ties men together for a life time. For over a year we had lived, worked, studied, and played together nearly every day. We had been annealed by the fire of swab indoctrination and shared experiences. We stood tests of self-discipline, physical stamina, commitment to service, and capacity for teamwork. We had been molded into a strong family with

53

Richard Marcott

shared values of honor and duty, and we held a deep respect for the U. S. Coast Guard.

Our entering class of one hundred ninety-eight civilians was now ninety-nine clinging cadet survivors—the brotherhood of 1957. We missed those who were no longer with us, and cheered for all who continued to march. The bonds strengthened after graduation. We worked for the same company. We married sisters, cousins, Conn College coeds, and New London girls. We shared duty stations, and watched each other's families grow. Jack Irwin felt the pull of the brotherhood. He left our class in our swab year. He returned, teary eyed, when he was finally able to make it back to a class reunion—our fiftieth.

After the usual beer and hamburger at "My Place" in Rockefeller Plaza, I boarded the bus to Jersey City for the familiar milk run to Salamanca, New York. The long trip didn't matter this time. I had twenty days leave.

54

—6—

CHRISTMAS TREES AND EE: THE 'TWEEN YEARS

MY BAGGAGE OF BAD STUDY habits in high school caught up with me early in my third class year. High school had been too easy for me. I had graduated twenty-fourth in a class of 244 without really trying. I rarely did homework. I had taken the college prep tract that included the whole math, science, history, and English sequence that prepared one to move on academically. I still had plenty of time for other activities: member of the student council, class president for two years, acted in every class play, partied with friends. I was no party animal—but I had a good time. My slow start at the academy was nobody's fault but mine.

Having said that, however, I believe my high school could have, and should have been, a lot more challenging. In 1953, Bradford was one of the small rust belt communities that pock-marked the hills of western Pennsylvania. We had one public and one Catholic school. Without real comparisons, it was easy think that Bradford High had a strong academic program. After my first peek beyond the Pennsylvania hills, I remember telling my mother, "Mom, we have viewed the world through Bradford-colored glasses."

We were blue collar people. Most of the local grads never left home. They worked the oil fields and refineries, or punched a clock in the factories or clerked at J.C. Penney. Only thirty percent of a graduating class went on to college in the fall. When I stepped through those Chase Hall doors, I found myself in a different league. My academy classmates had stronger high school experiences and a good number had one, even two, years of college.

Calculus was the killer. In the fall term, 1954, the number of cadets in my class failing Calc had reached an unprecedented and intolerable level. Many of us had been serving calculus trees–academic restriction. Trees denied you weekend liberty until we had served a mandatory study hour. (Unsuccessful in my research for the origin of the term "trees," I bowed to the trivia king of the class, Bob Johnson. He reported, "I think it was a carryover from colonial days when the headmaster displayed name-cards of the academically deficient on a mounted board behind his desk. The pegs may have been shaped like tree limbs, hence the term "you were on trees." I'm going with Bob.)

The situation called for drastic measures from the Academy. Thirty of us had half of our holiday leave canceled. We were ordered to return to New London the day after Christmas for remedial instruction–*Christmas trees*. Unfortunately, our math instructors had lost their leave also. It was an intense week between Christmas and New Year's, pumped with five days of calculus, every day, all day. Nobody, especially the Academy, wanted that to happen again.

At the end of the term, there were five of us sitting outside Commander Ralph West's office, nervously awaiting the verdict. The Assistant Commandant of Cadets called us in one at a time. We all expected the, "Sorry-you're-going-home-good-bye-and-good-luck speech." Nobody talked. Too much was at stake. Three classmates had already left West's office, head down, and discouraged. A thumbs-down hand signal hung at the end of their dangling arms... they were going home.

Bob Williams and I, the last two, sat in silence. Our knees bounced in step, anxiety reflex building to a crescendo. The sound of the office door opening triggered instant quiet.

"Mr. Williams." Commander Ralph West stepped to the door and Bob followed him in.

Alone I strangely felt less nervous, and I was resigned to the inevitable. Bob was in the office longer than the others.

Suddenly the door opened, Bob sprung out, huge grin on his face and a double fisted punch into the air over his head as he yelled to me, "Reversion! They're going to let me revert!"

Bob was being set back to the class of 1958. He was going to repeat third class year. There were not many, but he was getting a chance to number himself among the happy five-year-men. I began to feel hope. Maybe the Commander was taking us in order—bad news first, now good news. Maybe I was going to revert too.

"Mr. Marcott."

"Yes, sir." I stood, trying to look confident and stepped into the Commander's office. I came to attention in front of his desk, tucked my hat behind my left elbow, and went to parade rest.

"Mr. Marcott." The commander flipped through my file a bit then looked up. "You have a lot of good things going for you. We think you will make a good officer, but your grades are suffering. We are going to let you continue with your class."

I didn't hear anything for a minute, the sense of relief was overpowering.

"You know," he continued, "our job is not to find ways to lose cadets, but find ways to help them stay. We think you can make it and to help, we're giving you a new roommate, Richard Green, the number one man in your class. Report back to your wing, you'll be changed in the next couple of days. Good luck."

I hoped they had had this same conversation with Rich. He became a great roommate whose focused study habits were an inspiration. I worked hard, and whenever I interrupted him, finger curling his hair in academic reverie, Rich was always there to help.

Bob Williams went on to graduate in 1958 and retired after a successful career as a Coast Guard aviator. Ironically, Commander West was to reap what he had sown. Neither of us knew it then, but the same year I graduated he was given command of the USCGC *Absecon*. He was my first commanding officer.

It was graduation day. The class of 1955, our mentors, and hand-holders for two years, was headed for active duty in the fleet, "the Real Guard." But, it was promotion day for everyone. I snapped on my new shoulder boards, with the second slanted stripe, and smiled to myself, *I hope that Erie RR ticket man in Rockefeller Plaza is still there?* I could give him a better answer on my status now.

I was headed home for twenty days of summer leave a happy man. My Calculus scare was history. I was moving on, and looking forward to the short cruise to Bermuda at the end of the summer as an upper classman. Maybe those who never got ashore two years ago because of the hurricane would make it this year.

Our second class summer was split into segments: indoctrination of the new swab class, weapons training, and aviation indoctrination.

We were flown to Cape May, New Jersey, via CG air, for two weeks of weapons indoctrination in the M1 Garand Rifle and the Colt .45 Cal pistol. The firing range was at the Recruit Training Center at the end of the New Jersey peninsula. The small town of Cape May, one of the oldest vacation resorts in the country, had a year-around population of well under five thousand. In the summer, however, hordes of vacationing families, seeking respite from the brutal big city summers, expanded Cape May to many times that size. It did not offer much as a "liberty town."

Our days were long. We were on the range early every day, and fired and cleaned our weapons into the late afternoon. Reveille was early enough for us to watch the sun erupt from the Atlantic Ocean. It was as though Poseidon had kicked a red beach ball out of its comfortable night's sleep to start every day. The sun ball slowly rose into the sky and changed color, first gold, then yellow, then so white and bright, you couldn't look at it. All the while it grew smaller, but stronger. Soon its strength gave birth to the heat wave that rose from the ground like a curtain that blurred the rifle targets behind its shimmering veil.

On the bus ride to the first shooting position, I tried to picture how far away the five hundred yard line was going to be. In the tight clustered hills where I grew up, I doubt if I had ever seen anything five hundred yards away in a straight line. I had tried to picture myself at the end of the old cinder track at Bradford High School pointing a rifle down the straight-away. If I uncoiled the track until its entire length was strung out before me, and put a target at the end, I would still have sixty yards more to go. That's over a quarter of a mile away. Pressed down into the prone position in the sand, my cheek tight against the hand grip, I was surprised that squinting through that tiny peep-sight I could see three targets. The first task was focus on just one...preferably mine.

It took several days for me to learn how to fight back the sharp kick of the M-1. By the end of the two weeks, I was still nursing a tender cheek-bone where I had been beating myself up with the knuckle of my right thumb. Many of us sported a red welt, the mark of a novice. I did much better the second week. I qualified for the expert rifleman medal.

From Cape May we were flown to Elizabeth City, North Carolina, home of the largest Coast Guard Air Station. We were in for a general orientation on what flying for the Coast guard could be like. I flew in all aircraft types, fixed wing, helicopter, amphibious, sea planes, and even the WWII famous B-17 which the CG used as a long range search plane. Maybe I would like to become a Coast Guard aviator. As a kid I had been intrigued with flying. I spent hours daydreaming in the tall grass on the hill behind my home in Bradford, staring up at the blue sky waiting for small planes from the Emery Airport to wing it over the hill.

I did not make many liberty calls. I wanted to fly as often as I could. We never flew operational missions, but the officers were always glad to take us on check rides and practice flights. I flew a number of orientation flights with one of E. City's better known aviators, Lieutenant Nicholas Ivanosky. I will admit to a tinge of anxiety when I found out his fellow pilots had dubbed him "the mad Russian." I found out why on my first flight with him.

He had this disarming way of explaining the plane maneuvering characteristics while we were flying, then a pause, followed by the crackling intercom. "I'll show you."

"This little OY (a small, single engine Piper Cub type airplane) is great because we can fly it at such low speeds." He continued with, "We use it to hunt out bootlegger stills in the woods. We can slow it right down to about forty miles an hour and skim the tops of the trees. Great view...I'll show you."

He was right. It was a great view. But, I was more focused on the tops of the trees that we were hedgehopping as he reduced then added power to jump the treetops ahead that were, at times, above us, explaining all the while how easy it would be to see a still from here. I took his world for it.

On another flight, in a helicopter, at five thousand feet, he said, "Auto-gyration is a real safety feature of these choppers. You could lose an engine and your controlled free-fall would turn the blades enough to slow your drop rate to the point of safe landing."

I wasn't sure I wanted to hear the next sentence.

"I'll show you."

He cut the engine. A moment of gut-wrenching silence was followed by a long vertical elevator-drop, the whop-whop-whop of the blades increasing speed through the air was the only sound, except for the pounding of my heart. He re-started the engine, our free-fall came to a jerky stop, reversing our descent, and then we regained altitude.

"I didn't want to let it fall more," he explained. "We might have bent a wheel if we had touched down. It would have been safe, but a bit of a hard landing. The engineers don't like that when that happens."

I was with the engineers.

After our short cruise to Bermuda with the new swabs, our second class summer was over. I had loved every minute of it.

Despite the academic bumps in the road, my third and second class years, the *'tween years,* were not all doom and gloom. I didn't mind my restricted military life. I always tried to keep my eye on the goal, an engineering degree and a commission. The comradeship of classmates was priceless. I still had sports, dating, monthly formals, and a mix of and activities like sailing, drill team, church choir, and glee club.

Athletics played an important role at the Academy; it was all part of the *"sound body and stout hearts"* mission thing. Every cadet was expected to be involved in sports. If not at intercollegiate level, then intercompany. Our small six hundred man cadet corps fielded fourteen intercollegiate teams competing with New England colleges like, Wesleyan, MIT, Amherst, Kings Point, Drexel, Worcester, and others. In sailing and rifle and pistol we even challenged West Point and Annapolis.

Soccer was a new sport to me and I had hopes of playing on the newly formed Academy soccer team. We were a club sport for a year before moving up to formal intercollegiate competition. My grades, however, kept me from playing on the varsity team, but through some quirky regulation, I was allowed to remain with the team as manager, which I did through first class year.

A fencing club formed in my third class year, but did not last long. LCDR Short, an instructor at the OCS school (located on Academy grounds) signed on to coach the sport. Nobody had fencing experience. It seemed like a great new sport to learn. I joined the small squad; my weapon was the saber. I soon discovered that it took long hours and intense physical workouts to become a competitive fencer. We had progressed to the inter-squad competition stage, and were about to step up to the club sport level and compete with other schools when our coach had an emergency transfer, and that was the end of that. I took away the indelible memory of the sound and smell of burning steel and sparks as my opponent, who was trying to cut my head off, raked his blade across my steel mesh face mask. Try not to blink. I found it invigorating, competitive, and swashbuckling fun. I was sorry the Academy had to drop the sport.

I enjoyed intercompany sports. I played volleyball and rowed for Charlie Company. When I say rowed, I don't mean like the Georgetown University crew team that, in later years, I would see skimming the Potomac River in a lacy pre-dawn layer of fog. Our "pulling boat" was a two thousand pound double ended surfboat that had been the mainstay of the U.S. Lifesaving Service. Our coxswain was not some little guy crouching over a paddle rudder, but one who stood tall in the stern of the boat and was big enough to handle a twenty foot sweep oar. This boat was designed like the Monomoy Island boats used by settlers off the Massachusetts coast to pound through rough surf and back again with cargos of shipwrecked mariners. (Or illegal whiskey during prohibition.)

Bruce Solomon, the class of 1956, started a precision drill platoon that I was proud to become part of. We practiced for hours to learn the intricate marching maneuvers. We also spun and tossed M-1 rifles, at times, with unsheathed chrome bayonets, end over end over the heads of the squad. We performed exhibitions at Saturday parades and home football games. We were never the caliber of the U.S. Marine Barracks drill team–but we were crowd pleasers.

Cadet social life was a crimped version of what most college students enjoyed; we had no transportation and liberty on weekends only. We did have monthly formals. That usually meant double dating with someone who had a girlfriend with access to a car. My roommate, Ron McClellan, who dated a Conn College girl who had a car, and I often double-dated for formals. In my third class year and into second class year, I was dating a "townie," Sylvia Brickman. Most of our dates were simple: a walk in the park, a movie, or ice cream sodas at the local New London hangout.

When our dates became more frequent, her father, who did not sanction this Irish Catholic cadet dating his Jewish daughter in the first place, telephoned the Assistant Commandant of Cadets. That set me up for another unpleasant visit to CDR. West's office.

"Come in, Mr. Marcott."

"Yes, sir. You wanted to see me?" I had just received a note to report to his office. I had no idea what it was for.

"Mr. Marcott, are you dating a New London Jewish girl by the name of Sylvia Brickman."

"Yes, sir." ...*This is not good.*

"Well, her father does not think it's a good idea. He's pretty adamant. He's called me a couple of times, and he's an angry man. I don't want to keep getting these calls. If I were you...I'd find a new girlfriend."

"Sir?"

"That's my advice, Mr. Marcott. You're dismissed."

"Thank you, sir." I did a perfect about face, and left his office. I was upset that anything like this could happen. I had too much at stake. Sylvia was a nice girl, I liked her, and enjoyed her company. I don't know where the relationship might have gone.

The break-up was not pretty. With hysterical screaming, crying, running on a city street, clearly it was a bad scene, and I felt terrible about it. We both moved on; Sylvia went to nursing school in New York City, and a few years later, I was glad to hear from a classmate who knew her, that she had graduated from nursing school and was doing quite well.

I was surprised to have found a niche in singing. I had never been part of a chorus or choir in high school. My friend, and one time roommate, Wayne "Pancho" Arnold, who had been an altar boy and sang in his church choir for years, convinced me to join the Catholic Choir. I was hooked. I sang second tenor for four years, the highlight of which was a performance at St. Patrick's Cathedral in New York City.

Our choir director was Petty Officer Second Class, Don Janse. Don was a member of the U.S. Coast Guard Band, stationed at the Academy.

He was a talented musician who had composed the music for a Catholic high mass, and had marshaled it through the complex process to gain approval from the Vatican. It was a privilege for our choir to present the inaugural performance of his mass at St. Patrick's. We sang from the high choir loft at the rear of the church looking down upon the gold and white pageantry that enhanced the magnificence of the cathedral itself. It was a memorable experience, made ever more special because...Don was not Catholic.

Barber shop quartet the 574. Arnold, Marcott, Finnegan, Brown

In my third class year, Tom Finnegan, the driving musical force in our class of 1957, wanted to start a barbershop quartet. Tom also sang in the Catholic choir. Poncho and I were quick to sign on, and Tom convinced classmate Jim Brown to join us. We named our quartet the "574." Tom procured the music, taught us what barbershop harmony was all about, and rehearsed us until we were ready for prime time. Poncho sang tenor, Tom was our baritone, I sang lead (2nd tenor melody), and Jim Brown rounded out the harmony as our bass.

Our repertoire was small. We sang old barbershop favorites: *Coney Island Baby, Aura Lee, I Had A Dream,* and *Five Foot Two.* We had great fun singing in the rec hall on weekends for anyone who would listen. I enjoyed singing barbershop. When I retired, I became a charter member, and sang lead with the Bradford barbershop chorus, *The Mountain Laurel Harmonizers,* and sang bass in the quartet, *Northern Knights.* Great times.

I sang with the Academy Glee Club in its first nation-wide telecast in March, 1956. Perry Como, a popular singer of the 1950s, hosted a highly rated weekly variety show. At least one show each season featured a service academy glee club; it was our turn. We were guests along with the Irish tenor, Dennis Day, from the Jack Benny comedy show, and Edie "Rochester" Anderson who was featured as Benny's valet and chauffeur for thirty years. Songstress Jaye P. Morgan was also a guest.

We were bused to New York City, rehearsed all day, took a short dinner break, and presented our program on the *live telecast* from 8:00 p.m. to 9:00 p.m., and then bussed home. It was still the early years of broadcast television. Shows were not taped so they could be fixed later. Como had a weak voice that matched his casual sweater-wearing style. To save his voice, he whisper-sang the words all through rehearsals.

The technical effort it took to produce a TV broadcast was fascinating. We were surrounded by light, sound, camera people, and stage crew all day. They shuffled shelves of equipment, miles of electrical cable, and swinging sound booms around us as if we were not there. They were a friendly bunch that joked and kidded with us. They seemed to like having us there. We got used to the orchestrated chaos, and when our time came, we did justice to *Nothing Like a Dame* from *South Pacific,* and *Semper Paratus.* Of course, the live audience loved us.

The Glee Club appeared the following year at Carnegie Hall. We kicked off a major charity drive for the Children's Asthma Foundation with a fifteen minute spot. There were a number of nationally known performers on the show, most notably, Milton Berle, a well-known stage, movie, and TV comedian. The experience with Berle was not pleasant. When off camera, I found him a foul mouthed former burlesque man who was "always on," cussing his way through a constant stream of sexual innuendoes. It was like he was trying to impress a mob of waterfront sailors. He clearly had no understanding of the Academy. The stage hands and tech crew here were also nothing like those on the Como show the year before, but rather a grouchy, under-worked, group of crabby union guys. "Hey, kid, keep your damned hands off that podium! If that needs movin', I'll move it–you guys can't touch nothin'." The overall atmosphere and the personality of Milton Berle put an unpleasant edge on the grandeur of Carnegie Hall and the sheer excitement of singing there.

My third class Christmas tree experience had helped me get through the gruesome second class year with its heavy engineering curriculum. It included: electrical engineering (EE), thermodynamics, strength of materials, power, fluid mechanics, and physics. I think the only non-engineering course was economics, and that was not a breeze. For the most part, I held my own and pushed my way through all of them—except for EE. I was in extremis again.

The Chase Hall orderly, in dress blues, white cap, web belt, and leggings looked stiff and official standing in the doorway to my room. It was five minutes before "tattoo;" the bugle call that signaled ten minutes until "taps," lights out.

"What are you doing here at this time of night, orderly?" I think I scared him.

"Sir, I am to inform you that you have a phone call on the third deck, booth No. 1."

"They haven't blown tattoo yet. You know the phones are not available until 2200."

"Yes, sir, I know, but the OOD told me you were to take this call right now, sir."

"Very well, thank you, orderly." I'd never had an incoming phone call. I headed for the stairway, my mind racing through all the things that could be wrong at home. This has not been a good day. I went straight to the phone booth, getting evil looks from cadets in line for the phone rush when the bugle blew. I faced them with a hunched shoulder, palms forward gesture, then closed the door, and picked up the dangling receiver. I took a breath, and said, "Hello."

"Marcott?" I did not recognize the voice. At least it wasn't Mom or Dad.

"Yes."

"This is Commander Rivard."

My heart sank. Earlier that afternoon I had been alone in the Commander's Electrical Engineering Lab—the only one in the class taking an EE re-exam. I had already failed the final; this was the *re-exam*. I knew the rules. Pass it and you could remain a cadet at the Academy, but the final exam grade will be used for your GPA. Fail the re-exam and you would be going home.

The commander had watched me through the window in his office door while I was taking the exam. He had come out several times, looked over my shoulder, and mumbled hints, "Damn, Marcott. Don't you remember...?" Twice he had gone to the blackboard and given a micro lecture, something about a squirrel-cage motor. He wasn't giving answers, just trying to focus my thinking. I did not have a good feeling about this. My hand grew moist holding the phone; I held my breath waiting for the news. Finally, the Commander broke the silence.

"I don't know how you did it, Marcott..."

I could feel the smile breaking out on my face and my heart beat faster.

"...but, you failed the re-exam."

My heart skipped a beat. Smile gone. I couldn't speak.

"Now listen to me," he continued in a more grandfatherly tone. "It was very close and you've got a lot of good things going for you, and I believe you're going to make a good officer. So, I'm going to give you a 65.0 (minimum passing score) and you promise me never to apply for any post graduate training that involves EE." Then back to his commander's voice. "You hear me?"

"Yes, sir. Yes, sir. Thank you, sir!"

He hung up.

To this day, I never change a light bulb without thinking of Professor Rivard.

The 'tween years may have been a little harrowing, but they did not detract from my joy of putting on the new stripes of a first class cadet. I had made it! Next stop...my last cadet cruise... to the Caribbean.

—7—

HEMINGWAY AND HAVANA

THE COAST GUARD ACADEMY'S LONG cruise for the summer of 1956, my first class year, was to the Caribbean. The Coast Guard cutters *Campbell* and *Yakutat* would accompany the *Eagle*. Our scheduled ports were San Juan, Puerto; Coco Solo, Panama; and Havana, Cuba. After the excitement of our European cruise two summers earlier, some of my classmates expected San Juan to be nice enough but more like visiting a Florida appendage than a foreign port: rent a car, drive to the rain forest, or hang around the naval base clubs, which would be pretty much it. As for Coco Solo—it was San Juan, with interesting shopping. They were right on both counts.

Shopping in the American Canal Zone was indeed interesting. It was a crossroads market for goods from all over the world. There were native crafts, of course, but you could find Irish linens, Delft china, Italian leather, or German crystal just as easily. Small store fronts jammed the narrow streets.

The shop keepers, who were almost exclusively from India, were pit-bull aggressive. They literally pulled you from the street into their cluttered world, shouting, flailing their arms, and dragging merchandise before your eyes touting their "best value on the street." If you were smart enough to walk out, they would follow you out of their store and into the one just like it next door to lure you back with a cheaper price. Bargaining was as much their national pastime as baseball is to Americans. They seemed slighted, if not dishonored, if you did not argue at least a little. It was their game, and they played it well. I suspect they rarely lost.

I had reason to be more excited about the Panama visit than my classmates were. I was going to visit relatives. Two of my great uncles, Fint and Joe, had ventured to Panama as young men and were part of the construction crew that built the Panama Canal. Uncle Fint remained in the Zone, married a native Panamanian, and raised a family. He had retired as a ship's superintendent, overseeing merchant ships making their way through the canal, but he was now deceased. My cousins Catherine and Margaret still lived in Ancon with Aunt Isabel. I had managed to get an overnight pass to visit them. Nobody in my family had ever dreamed of coming to Panama, although Uncle Fint and his family visited Bradford routinely every other year.

Uncle Joe returned to the states when the canal was completed and remained an adventurer well into old age. A vagabond heater on riveting gangs, he made good money and spent it when he wanted and where he wanted, He built bridges and skyscrapers from Michigan to Louisiana.

Catherine and Margaret picked me up at the pier in Coco Solo and we drove the fifty miles to their home in Ancon, a beautiful place overlooking the Pacific entrance to the canal. Primarily a residential community that housed American civilian and military personnel, Ancon sat on a bald mountain that one approached through rows of banyan trees, and had a 360-degree view across the isthmus. It was easy to see why the Zonians— as the Americans who lived there called themselves—spoke of it as paradise.

We did a little local sightseeing, including a street market where I got a lesson in how to stay in the game with the Indian merchants. Catherine was a close match for the pit-bulls, and I came home with a few nice souvenirs.

The Fourth of July was a big deal in the American territory. The Zonians wore their patriotism on their sleeve and celebrated just like they would if they were back home. Catherine and Margaret took me to a grand dinner-dance at a large hotel in Ancon. It was crowded, with great music, dancing, fireworks, and more. The atmosphere was like New Year's Eve in Time Square.

At one point, I turned toward the long crowded bar and there stood Commander Ralph West, the Assistant Commandant of Cadets. He was one of the Academy officers assigned to the *Eagle* for the summer cruise. But with the ships moored fifty miles away at the other end of the canal, I was surprised to see him. He gave me a knowing smile and turned back toward the bar.

As the evening wore on, he repeatedly swooped in a circle to face us, both arms dramatically outstretched along the bar. He kept glancing at his watch and smiling at us. I thought it best to pay my respects. As I approached, he turned back to the bar and I moved next to him.

"Good evening, Commander," I ventured.

"Good evening, Mr. Marcott," he said, running his finger around the rim of his drink. He lifted his glass, twirled the ice in slow circles, squinted over the rim like he was about to let me in on a secret and said, "Who are those lovely ladies you're with?"

"They are my cousins, sir."

He looked skeptical, tapped his watch with his finger and said, "Pushing it a little aren't you if you're going to make it back to the ship on time?"

Normal liberty was up at midnight. I showed him my overnight pass and said, "Oh, no sir, I have an overnight pass to visit with my Aunt and cousins. They're driving me back in the morning."

"Oh. Well, enjoy your evening, Mr. Marcott." He cut the conversation off and I returned to our table.

A few minutes later, the Commander finished his drink and left. Then it dawned on me. I turned to Margaret, who was in her mid-thirties, very pretty and dressed to the nines for the evening, and asked, "Was he hitting on you, Margaret?"

"Oh yes." She laughed. "Big time. He is pretty good looking."

"I think he had to get back to the ship," I laughed.

We left Panama and made our way across the Caribbean conducting various daily ship exercises. After all this was a cadet training cruise. Finally we could see on the horizon what we had all been waiting for—Havana!

The squadron moored at the coal piers across the estuary from the main city docks where a small crowd was already gathering. The *Eagle*, of course, draws a lot of visitors wherever she goes. Transportation between the central city and the coal pier was via a fleet of small commercial taxi boats. They were doing a brisk business. It was a Sunday, and five hundred visitors had swarmed the *Eagle*, mostly Cubans, but some American vacationers.

We had spent days, pouring over brochures, planning what we wanted to do. Discussion was lively until the crackle of the ship's PA system announced, "Our Ambassador to Cuba, Mr. Arthur Gardner and his wife, have invited cadets to a dance party at their quarters. There is a sign-up sheet on the forward mess deck–it *will* be filled before liberty is granted. Uniform is service dress white. A bus will be on the Pier for transportation."

Someone broke the silent disappointment. "Oh, come on guys, it might be interesting. Remember it is an *official affair*. We'll hang out for an hour or so, do the receiving line bit, and we'll be out of there. We may still have time to get to the city. Besides, this is only the first of our four-day stay. We still have time for other stuff." I followed the lead, and resignedly shuffled my way to the sign-up sheet.

Captain Zittel stood at the front of the bus. With a practiced glance he gave each a quick once-over as we boarded: whites-ok, cap covers-clean, white shoes-polished. He was the SOP (Senior Officer Present), which meant he was in charge, and was giving us the rundown. Clearly he expected a zero-defect visit.

"This is an official visit not expected to be long. A receiving line will be formed for departure when I signal. Conduct yourselves in the same manner as in our Academy receiving lines at any monthly formal. Thank the Ambassador and his wife for their hospitality, shake hands, and keep it moving. The bus will be outside for the return to the ships." Then he paused for effect. "As to drinking—official regulations forbid it—but we will suspend the regulations for the occasion. If the Ambassador should offer, you may accept, and I know you will conduct yourselves as gentlemen."

"Well, at least that's something," an unidentified mumble rose from the back of the bus, followed by a low chorus of stifled snickers. Captain Zittel said nothing.

We arrived at the Ambassador's quarters and were ushered directly to the magnificent patio surrounded by lush gardens and beautifully set tables. We could hear the lively beat of a Cuban band above the crowd's murmur. A number of guests were already there, and our arrival sparked a rise in the background noise. Several adult couples, presumably embassy personnel and Cuban dignitaries, moved to greet us as we entered like a small army. The first surprise of the evening was when a mini-mob of unaccompanied young women, swaying in pretty cocktail dresses to the Latin rhythms, headed our way. Ambassador Gardner's plans for the evening thoughtfully included inviting a number of debutantes. They were described in a photo accompanying an article in the *Havana Post* the following day as "50 Havana beauties." Judging from their smiles as they mingled to introduce themselves, coaxing us directly to the dance floor, they had been looking forward to the party more than we had. But, no question, we were on their side now.

The Ambassador, slightly heavy-set and balding, along with his gracious wife, mingled, making small talk, and generally checking if we were having a good time. "Be sure you take time to meet Ernest Hemingway." he said. "He and his wife, Mary, have been looking forward to meeting you and are really interested in your *Eagle* adventures."

Ernest Hemingway?

It did not take long to find him. His dark businessman's suit and plain tie stood out behind the wall of dress whites that surrounded him like bars in a cage. An occasional pop of a newspaper photographer's flash was a beacon to his entourage. Hemingway sported a neatly-trimmed white beard that framed his already square face into a block. He was a tall, powerfully built man, with deep facial lines from years of outdoor adventures. He seemed to enjoy the animated conversation, drink in hand, asking about our summer on the *Eagle*.

Most of us had read Hemingway's novel *The Old Man and the Sea*, so it was easy to make conversation. We had just entered the Academy the year that it won the Pulitzer Prize for fiction. He and his fourth wife, Mary, now spent a great deal of time in their sprawling home in Havana. He loved deep-sea fishing and often battled swordfish off the nearby coast in the very waters he used as the locale for his simple tale of an old fisherman's victory and defeat.

Cadets chat with Mary Hemingway.
L-R Davis, McClellan, Marcott, Cece

I joined a small group across the room to engage in pleasant conversation with Mary Hemingway. She was an attractive woman with short swept-back hair. She had a narrow face and a small mouth that she pursed into a pretty smile. She was wearing a single pearl choker necklace and carried a small black handbag under her arm. She cradled her drink in white-gloved hands. The *Havana Post* photographer snapped a picture of four of us cadets that appeared in the morning paper.

Some years later, I discovered that in 1954—two years before our visit to Havana—Ernest and Mary had been in two plane crashes within forty-eight hours. They had been on an East African safari when their chartered plane crashed near Murchison Falls. They were rescued by a passing sightseeing boat only to crash again on the takeoff of their rescue plane. The second crash left Hemingway with very serious injuries that included a crushed vertebrae and ruptured kidney. He was still recuperating to some extent when we met him at the Ambassador's Party, but it was not obvious.

The party had been in swing for over an hour when Captain Zittel thought it appropriate that we take our leave. He collared a couple of cadets to start the receiving line. When he approached the ambassador's wife, however, she exclaimed, "Oh Captain, you can't be serious. These young people are just beginning to have fun. Let them stay and dance for a while." The Captain, without much choice, turned to the cadets, hunched his shoulders and ordered, "Well, carry on, men."

And, carry on we did!

The party changed. The music picked up, the dancing became more active, and the women grew more exuberant. I began to think that a debutante's confinement must be more restrictive than ours at the Academy. Champagne was too easy to pluck off the trays of roaming waiters. A few of the girls began swigging their glasses and then tossing them over their shoulders like they were in some decadent 20s movie—some landed in the lawn but others broke on the patio.

Everyone heard the loud splat of a silver serving tray landing in the middle of the blue-green water of the ambassador's pool. Gentleman that he was, the captain of our swimming team declared loudly, "I'll get it." One quick dive into the pool—dress whites and all—and he swam to the side with the tray in hand. Coast Guard to the rescue.

Meanwhile, a small noisy crowd had gathered at the entrance to the formal gardens. A large tombstone-like block of granite with an embedded solid bronze United States seal was the center of attention, along with Ernest Hemingway. He had his jacket off, his right sleeve rolled up, and was about to take a giant swing at the eagle. He had bet classmate Ira "Jake" Jacobson, five dollars that he could "dent the Eagle's beak in one blow."

Handing his half-full rock glass of dark Anejo rum to a cadet, he struck a mighty blow. I don't know why he didn't break all the bones in his hand. He recovered, painfully shaking his hand wildly, coaxing the gentle Caribbean breeze to heal, and fished out a five-dollar bill for Jake. Reportedly, Jake had it signed and framed.

I cannot report, with any degree of accuracy how the party ended. I found myself with a small group of classmates and debs at a Havana amusement park. I was losing my precious twenty-two dollar monthly allowance one dime at a time betting on a rat named "Miguel Raton," who scrambled wildly on a large flat spinning circle to find the cheese. He never once entered the numbered hole that I had bet on. The game of Mickey Mouse was a loser.

Meanwhile, the cadets who had taken the bus back to the ship after the party had found their own game. With enough Anejo still in their veins, a vigorous game of "King of the Royal Mountain" on the huge coal pile at the end of the pier seemed like a good idea. Their dress whites were the big losers here. At least it was the last port on our cruise.

The following day, I joined a group of classmates to see the stage show at the famous Tropicana Cabaret. We were guests of the Cuban Navy. A brochure described it as, "the largest and most beautiful nightclub in the world." Giant fruit trees that had remained standing during construction rose through the roof, some connected with catwalks adorned with show-girls who moved between the trees to the sensuous Latin rhythms. The dancers wore headdresses half again as tall as they were, and costumes that were colorful and enticingly small.

The place was huge. There were two sets of stages with tables to seat 1700. Our Navy hosts had preset our tables with drinks and there were plenty of young women to chat and dance with. The most memorable after-action report was that one classmate, so taken in with it all, proposed to three women on the dance floor in the same night. We like to think it remains a Tropicana record.

1956 may have been the last good year for Havana as well as Heming-way. In November, President Eisenhower recalled Ambassador Gardner who had been exhibiting too much support for the Cuban dictator, Batista. The U.S. was supportive of, what we then thought, were the democratic motives of the rebel, Fidel Castro. In December of that year, the rebels exploded a bomb in the Tropicana, destroying one bar section and maiming one patron. The famous nightclub would never be the same again. Two years later—after Castro ousted Batista—the new communist government took over the Tropicana. The casino was closed, and all the dancers became government employees hired to "exhibit the history of native Cuban dances."

Many critics felt Hemingway was already on his decline in Cuba, de-spite the success of *The Old Man And The Sea*. His body, wracked by too many years of hard living, war, and the physical pain of multiple injuries, had given up. Like others in his family, he also suffered from depression. His story of the old Cuban fisherman was his last significant work. On a morning in early July, 1961, in his cabin in Idaho, Ernest Hemingway took a shotgun from the rack and ended his own life.

The cruise was over. While the squadron was returning to New London—as if we needed another exciting event—we responded to a distress call to search for survivors of the collision between the Italian passenger liner Andria *Doria* and the Swedish merchant ship *Stockholm*. By the time we arrived on scene, air bubbles and flotsam of deck chairs, suitcases, and life rings were bobbing to the surface. The cutters retrieved what they could, sank the empty lifeboats, and took what they had to New York.

Other Coast Guard vessels, on scene earlier, had already removed 1660 passengers. A Coast Guard buoy tender escorted the *Stockholm*, who could proceed slowly on her own power, to New York City. Fifty-two people had been killed in the head on collision.

If our first-class cruise was not the one most looked forward to, it is still the one the class of 1957 talks about the most. Every reunion brings dramatic recall of Hemingway, Havana, late night swims in the Ambassador's pool, coal piles, and the Tropicana. It was a great way to wrap up our cadet sea days.

–8–

GRADUATION

THE MEMORIES OF PANAMA, HAVANA, and Hemingway faded quickly as we disembarked from the squadron ships and prepared to scatter across the country for summer leave. The New London to New York train trip was a breeze compared to Thanksgiving. But, I still faced that gruesome overnight milk run on the Erie RR to get home to Bradford.

I had always enjoyed Bradford summers. In August, the cool morning fog postponed the summer heat and prevented sweltering afternoon temperatures. The lush green hills felt protective, as if they held us in cupped hands. Soft evening breezes carried the smell of newly mown grass, and the sound of peepers announced the arrival of evening. August was great porch weather. Neighbors conversed across quiet streets while youngsters played hide-and-seek before the call to bedtime. Nights invited gatherings around camp fires and barbecue pits. The evenings were made for gathering and sharing of events of the days and times.

My old high school gang, most of them had been home since June, were wrapping up the summer with a round of parties. In a couple of weeks, everyone would scatter back to their colleges for their senior year. An unspoken pall hung over these gatherings; they would be our last until we returned for five year reunions. We were graduating, moving out of the nest to distant cities. Some would marry college sweethearts, build new relationships, and move on to new lives of our own. Everyone felt a nostalgic sense of the inevitable. I know I did. I was going to miss it.

The 1956 fall term at the Academy started like all those before it with one major exception. Now *our* class was in charge of the cadet corps. The battalion positions were posted, and I was pleased to be named Platoon Commander of Charlie Company's third platoon. Especially, since in this presidential year, it meant I would be Platoon Commander for the inaugural parade in Washington.

I enjoyed an easy transition into academics that year. I was still challenged, but I did not spend the year with the sword of Damocles hanging over my head. My first class year was actually fun. I pushed my way through electronics, naval architecture, physics, and maritime law. If you don't count one minor scare in electronics engineering, I was pretty pleased with my grades. In the extracurricular area, I still sang in the Catholic Choir, and Glee Club (including that memorable trip to sing in Carnegie Hall).

At some point during the year, one of the most exclusive Catholic Girls schools in the country, *Duchesne*, sent an invitation for a number of first-class cadets to attend their annual afternoon tea dance in New York City. The *Duchesne Resident School for Girls*, part of the educational system run by the Society of the Sacred Heart, was housed in the magnificent Burden Mansion. The Italian Renaissance-style townhouse was directly across the street on 91st from the Andrew Carnegie Mansion. Clearly we were going to be in an upscale neighborhood. I signed up to go.

A gracious ballroom provided the backdrop. The dance was quite nice, albeit a bit formal. The girls were in sedate dresses and wore white gloves. A raft of nuns patrolled the perimeter of the ballroom—just "keeping order." Most of the girls were daughters of South and Central American diplomats, industrialists, and oil barons, along with a few American girls of the same caliber. The young ladies had plans for an after-the-dance party at the Biltmore Hotel. That was a very different affair. There was no large party room, but, the debs had opened the doors between a series of adjoining rooms on one of the upper floors to accommodate party traffic.

When I arrived at the Biltmore and entered the main lobby, my eye caught the famed "Biltmore Clock." The clock was part of the Palm Court Lounge, a classic landmark mentioned in books by F. Scott Fitzgerald and J.D. Salinger. It was often cited as in, "I'll meet you under the clock at the Biltmore." As I drew closer, I saw a pretty girl standing alone under the clock. She looked strangely familiar. When our eyes met, there was that unexpected moment of mutual recognition.

"Carole? Carole Wolfe, is that really you?"

"Dick Marcott! I can't believe it. What on earth are you doing here?"

I explained the Duchesne dance and that I was now headed to a party in the hotel. "How about you? You look like you're waiting for someone."

"I am. Mary Claire McNerney is meeting me here. She should be here any minute now."

Carole and Mary Claire graduated from Bradford High school a year behind me. They were both popular juniors. Carol explained that they had always been good friends, stayed in touch, and were just meeting to "have a good time in the city." I suggested they join our Coast Guard/ Duchesne group right here in this hotel. When Mary Claire arrived, the three of us engaged in a few moments of small talk, and then headed upstairs for the party together.

The music was loud and different from the tea dance, and what the ladies were serving...was not tea. The party became a little raucous. Carole and Mary Claire were accepted right into the party group and clearly enjoyed themselves. At one moment I saw Mary Claire dashing like a broken field runner from room to room. I could see her coming from three or four doors away. Sprinting amid laughter and giggles, she disappeared for a moment entering each room to jump and spring, as if she were on a trampoline, from bed to bed, then on to the next room closely pursued by a cadet. The unexpected Bradford contingent certainly contributed their bit to make the party a memorable one. Everyone had a great time.

A few days after our return to the Academy, the Superintendent received a "concerned letter" from the Mother Superior who expressed her displeasure and surprise. We got into a little trouble over the party. Informal feedback from the girls at Duchesne, however, was that the "Coast Guard" tea dance had been the best one ever.

When I came home for Christmas in my first-class year, beyond enjoying the holidays with my family and friends, I had a side mission. I had promised Pete Rots, the advertising manager of our yearbook that I would try to get an ad from the Zippo Manufacturing Co. The *Tide Rips*, like most college annuals, was heavily supported by industrial advertisers. In our case, many were huge national companies with a maritime connection: States Marine Lines, Sperry Gyroscope, Babcock and Wilcox, and many others like them.

The world famous Zippo lighter was invented by Bradfordian George Blaisdell and was manufactured only in Bradford, Pennsylvania. I knew the advertising manager. Well, at least I knew his daughter. I had gone to school with Barbara McCutchin from grade school through high school. I thought I might get an ad from her dad.

While sitting in his outer office, I had a sudden bold thought, and decided to give it a try. After the introduction niceties, I said, "Mr. McCutchin, I think we both know that the only people who will bother to look at your ad will be those, like yourself, who might browse through the separate industrial supplement that we send to all the advertisers. Our class would like to make you an offer." I waited for a response. I got a slight smile and a non-committal uh-huh. I moved on.

"If you would present a Zippo lighter to each member of our graduating class, the class of 1957 will take out the same size ad that you would ordinarily buy, giving our thanks for your generosity. When the other advertisers see that, they'll know you cared to go the extra mile." I was on a roll now. "Also, think of how much farther that will get the Zippo product. There may be only 61 of us graduating, but we will carry the pocket lighters all over the country. We are pretty well spread out on both coasts. We'll have the Zippo story to tell from coast to coast."

"I kind of like that, Dick. We'll do it."

When I got back to the Academy, I posted a blank paper in the first class rec room and got every member of our class to sign it. The Zippo lighters arrived with our handwritten personal signatures on one side and the Coast Guard emblem and the "Class of 1957" on the other. Our half page ad in Tide Rips that year read:

The Class of 1957 Thanks You

ZIPPO Manufacturing Company

For the lighters that we shall carry with us

to our every port of call.

I did not know until a few years later that Zippo continued that practice for at least the next two graduating classes, maybe more. Today there is a crazy collector's market for Zippos. I wonder what the entire collection, marking the first year of the event, with personal signatures of every member of the class of 1957 would be worth?

The twenty-third amendment to the U.S. Constitution moved the presidential inauguration day from March 4th to January 20th. It halved the long, contentious, lame-duck period between the November election and the new president moving into office. But, *somebody should have thought about the weather.* The denizens of the District of Colombia tend to think they live in the South. They do not. January weather in Washington, DC can be far from "a nice day for a parade." When the Academy Corps of Cadets disembarked from the train at Union Station for President Eisenhower's second inaugural parade—it was cold.

The pace was lively, and because the band marching behind us was closer, and not in sync with the Coast Guard band ahead of us, it was a miracle the battalion was in step at all.

When it counted, however, as we passed in front of the reviewing stand, and rendered our parade salute to President Eisenhower—we were perfect.

Later that night a number of us had been assigned as ushers at one of the several inaugural balls. There were four locations: The DC National Guard Armory, the Mayflower Hotel, The Sheraton Park Hotel, and the Statler Hotel. I was assigned to the Mayflower.

We received instructions from one of the White House military social aides. "Offer your arm to the lady, and slant a little ahead of her while leading with your elbow extended at shoulder height to 'clear the crowd.' Do not let your lady be jostled."

I dutifully reported in a letter to my mother the names of those that I could recall escorting that evening, and with whom I had exchanged at least a few words. She, in turn, made a list which, years later, I retrieved from a dusty cigar box of assorted souvenirs. I had escorted: Philippine General Romulo, Past President of the United Nations General Assembly; Edward R. Morrow, American broadcast journalist; Prince Romanoff, self-styled Russian Noble; Gene Tierney, American stage and film actress; Senator John F. Kennedy; and Admiral Radford, Chairman of the Joint Chiefs of Staff. She also recorded, at the end of the list, the informal notation that I had also escorted "Mamie's sister, Mrs. Moore."

We returned to New London after the crisp DC weather to face an even colder February in Connecticut. We were warmed, however, knowing that the corps would be celebrating 100th Day at the end of the month; it marked the number of days until graduation. For the swabs, it would be a great day. They would be in charge of the battalion in a total role reversal filled with fun for everyone.

As first classmen, we tolerated, even enjoyed, the short lived antics of the swabs, but we knew the real purpose of this milestone. It marked a shift in our interest and energy toward the real purpose of the spring term—cars and duty assignments.

Everyone got new cars. Denied control of personal movement beyond the gates for four years, we had planned for months. We had poured over brochures and debated power vs. speed. Now we were ready. Every car salesman in the region knew we were guaranteed jobs. We were ripe for picking. There were going to be sixty-one new cars sold in the month of May and all of them wanted a piece of the action. They offered good deals, and the banks gave the best rates. We were low risk, hot-to-trot potential customers with money and a job that would last past three year payments... Uncle Sam would see to that.

I was one of a group of five who opted for a new 1957 Mercury Monterey, a flashy red and white hard top convertible. The deal was sealed by a salesman who arranged to have the cars delivered to us in New York State to avoid the high tax in Connecticut. He picked us up and drove us to Brewster, New York, just across the state line where we signed the papers and drove off in a five-car convoy back to the academy. I paid $2450 for my first car and had a great loan and reasonable insurance through the United Services Automobile Association (USAA) which at the time accepted only military officers as members. They insured hundreds of graduates of all the service academies each year. I knew I would be able to handle car payments of $80 per month even on my Ensign's salary of $222 plus $47.88 for subsistence.

Getting our first duty assignment was a pretty simple process. Our class size made it clear that we were all going to be assigned to a major cutter, either an ocean station vessel, or one of the icebreakers. Headquarters simply sent a list of billets that had to be filled by our class. At least two of us would be assigned to each ship. Everyone was equally qualified and eligible for any of the assignments, so we just signed the list next to the ship we wanted. The first go-around would determine if there were any conflicts.

Some preferred to be near family—at least on the same coast. Others looked forward to spreading their wings a little or sought the adventures promised by serving on a polar icebreaker. Some just wanted to be together with a buddy on any ship no matter where it was.

Ron McClellan and I had pretty much felt that way. We got along really well as roommates and had built a strong friendship. We thought it would be neat to be assigned together. With Ron from Kansas City, Missouri, and me from western Pennsylvania, the East Coast seemed logical. We both wanted to give a shot at a little southern weather, rather than New England. The USCGC *Absecon*, a 311' ocean station vessel in Norfolk, Virginia, fit the bill for both of us. It was open. We got it. As I recall there were few, if any, conflicts. There may have been a friendly swap, or maybe a rock, paper, scissors shake out. If there had been a real conflict, we *were* a military organization after all—the senior man got what he wanted—simple as that.

Ring Dance

Finally it was May—graduation week. My whole family had come. Mom, Dad, Nana, my sister, Pat, and the twins, Bonnie and Connie, were in New London for a few days. I had fixed Pat up with a date for the graduation dance with a cadet from the class of '59, Joe Vorbach.

I was surprised, and really pleased, that an old family friend, Air Force Chief Master Sergeant LeRoy "Skip" Martin had also made it for my graduation. Skip and his brother, Jack, had boarded with Nana, in days before my time. They had both joined the service a year before World War II. Skip joined the Army Air Corps, and Jack the Navy. They were my military heroes while I was growing up, and the few times they both managed to get leave at the same time, there was great banter of Army vs. Navy as they vied to get me in line for their service. When I was in high school, it was West Point vs. Annapolis.

Jack, who had been at Pearl Harbor when it was bombed in December 1941, got out a few years after the end of the war and returned to raise his family in Olean, New York. We saw him often. Skip, who made the Air Force his career, had served in Europe and the Pacific as a flight engineer in a squadron of A-26 medium range bombers.

I knew my sister, Pat, was going to be glad to see Skip also. She was four years younger than me, and was the apple of Skip's eye. As plane captain for one of the A-26's, he had the traditional privilege of naming his aircraft. While assigned in the European campaign, he named his plane, *My Princess Pat,* after my sister. Skip was serving on active duty in his last assignment before retirement, at an aviation repair and supply center in Mechanicsburg, Pennsylvania. Dad told me skip would be in uniform today. Great. That meant I could fit him right into my plans.

It was a long standing tradition in all the services that newly commissioned officers give a dollar to the enlisted man who rendered him his first salute. As I left the graduation ceremonies, I had my silver "Liberty Dollar" at the ready. I was determined it was going to Skip. I spotted him coming toward me, his Air Force summer tan service dress uniform with the Air force blue combination cap stood out in the sea of dress whites.

He wore a big smile as he stopped directly in front of me, braced at attention, and snapped off a smart salute. "Congratulations, Ensign Marcott."

I returned the salute, and flipped the silver dollar in the air.

When we moved to a damp-eyed acceptable manly hug, Skip said into my ear, "I can't wait to call Jack and tell him what he has missed."

"I know. Thanks, Skip. You made my day."

It was over. I had made it. Our final ceremony was indoors. It didn't matter. Following our proud march-in to the strains of the *Triumphal March of Aida*, our class listened as Assistant Secretary of the Treasury, David W. Kendall, gave the graduation address. The Superintendent presented our diplomas and the Commandant of the Coast Guard handed us our commissions. We choked our way through our last singing of the Alma Mater then stepped off smartly to the recessional, *Semper Paratus*. To a man, we were now...

"...Strong in the resolve to be worthy of the traditions of the commissioned officers in the United States Coast Guard in the service of our country and humanity," Sir!

*R. J. Marcott First
class yearbook photo*

Goodbyes to graduating classmates were not the same as in high school. We knew we would see each other again. After all, we worked for the same company, at least for the next four years, and many of us beyond that. Over a career, our paths would cross many times. That proved to be one of the greatest aspects of a Coast Guard career.

I drove back to Bradford in company with the family. We relived the wonders of May week for a few days. I got together with high school friends, dated a few times, and all in all enjoyed a great leave. Even so, I was anxious to move on to my first duty assignment. Although, my orders were to the *Absecon*, before I could join Ron in Norfolk, I had to return to the Academy for temporary duty for the summer. I packed up my new car, and hit the road to return to New London.

That was only the second year for the new program of using a small cadre of graduating ensigns, rather than second class cadets, to oversee the indoctrination of the incoming fourth class. I had sought assignment to the *Absecon*, but the interim temporary duty was a surprise. It would not be the only time a chance set of orders would change my world—but this one was a biggie—that was the summer I met my wife, Carol.

USCGC *Absecon*
WAVP 374

Norfolk, VA

Gunnery Officer & Deck Watch Officer
September 1957-February 1959

The U.S. Coast Guard Cutter *Absecon* WAVP 374 was one of the major cutters assigned to International Weather Patrol. The 311 foot class vessel was built for the Navy as a seaplane tender and was later transferred along with others of the same class to the Coast Guard after World War II. For weather patrol duty the Coast Guard also used 327 foot *Secretary* Class cutters, which were built for the Coast Guard in 1936, and a number of 255 foot *Owasco* class cutters, also built specifically for the Coast Guard.

The Weather Patrol program, shared by several European nations, called for the ships to maintain station in a two hundred ten mile square area in the open ocean. Ships rotated through 21 day patrols. Their primary duty was to collect and provide weather information through regularly reported surface and upper air wind observations. Their air search radar and radio beacon served as navigational aids. They also provided search and rescue assistance when needed. From the beginning of the program in 1939, stations operated around the clock, in both the Atlantic and Pacific Oceans, every day of the year, including during World War II.

In 1957, the United States manned Ocean stations, Bravo, Charlie, Delta, and Echo. Bravo was in the reaches of the North Atlantic west of Greenland. Station Charlie was south of the tip of Greenland along the main airline routes, Delta was on the northern shipping routes, and Echo was in the mid-Atlantic between Bermuda and the Azores Islands.

The Absecon, like all the major cutters, maintained wartime readiness through participation in the U.S. Navy's refresher training program at Guantanamo Bay, Cuba. East coast vessels also provided platforms for the CG Academy cadet summer training cruises. All new academy graduates were assigned to sea duty on either one a weather cutters or a large Coast Guard icebreaker.

—9—

CAROL

I AM SURE ALL THREE of us heard the alarm clock, but Don reacted first, flailing his arm in an arc to smack the doze switch. De and I, who were sharing the double bed this week, barely moved. Just let Don do his thing. He swung his feet to the floor, and switched off the oversized fan on the sideboard. The single bedroom in our rented apartment was wall to wall bed. It had one double and one single with standing room only in between. We took turns rotating to the single.

Don lightly tickled his belly, hands moving in large overlapping circles. Then, with a single cobweb-clearing head shake, he stood up. He was wearing standard issue one-size-fits-all baggy boxer shorts, with the cloth tie-to-fit bows on the hips. With no elastic, his three snap front waist band drooped like a white smiley face holding up his belly. Don had been a full-back on the Academy soccer team. Still built like a tank, he was fighting his weight a little. He shuffled out the bedroom in his bare feet, scratching his hair awake with one hand while still ministering to his belly with the other, and headed for his routine morning chore—brew a pot of coffee.

Suddenly, I heard the hollow sounds of slapping bare feet running back to bed.

"Guys! Get up!" Don was almost gasping, "There's a woman on our couch! Didn't you hear me? Get up! For Christ's sake, some woman is sleeping on our couch! Get up!"

I raised my head, then leaned up on one elbow and said. "Oh, yeah. That's ok, Don, that's just Carol." I let my head drop back to the pillow. De never moved.

A training cadre of our graduating class had been assigned to temporary duty at the Academy to indoctrinate the incoming fourth class. We were scattered in rental houses throughout the city. Don Morrison, De Combs, and I shared an apartment in a stately old Victorian house on Montauk Avenue. It had a huge wraparound porch with an awning. Magnificent maples and oaks lined both sides of the street. Their nearly touching tops formed a comfortable green street tunnel. The neighborhood reminded me what it must have been like in the whaling days when lonely wives of bearded sea captains paced the "widow's walk" high on the roof tops, pining for a glimpse of their husband's ship returning from a year or two at sea.

Our apartment was small with basic furniture in a postage-stamp living room that opened to a dining/kitchen area. We had only a minimum of kitchen utensils, and we needed to increase the inventory. Borrowing was the only answer. Bradford was too far, and Don's family lived in Seattle, so De was elected to procure what he could from his mom on Long Island. He invited me to go with him and stay overnight. "We might even get a date, if you're up to it."

"Sure, why not."

"I've had a few dates with my sister Helen's physical therapist. She has a sister I can probably fix you up with."

"Sounds good to me."

We got an early start on Friday to beat the heavy traffic. Every move on Long Island is planned around the traffic. We arrived at his mom's house by mid-afternoon. In short order, we had a cardboard box of dishes, pots and pans, and silverware loaded into De's car. After a pleasant dinner with his family, we headed out for our date with the Berlinghoff girls, Eleaner and Carol.

As we pulled into the driveway, we could see them through the bay window. Good, they were ready. Their mom greeted us at the door. Quick, but pleasant introductions followed, and then we turned to face the tall sisters. I could see where this was going. The younger one was very pretty, so I figured she was probably De's date.

But, when El stepped forward to greet De with a platonic hug, I couldn't believe it—Carol was my date! She flashed her sparkling eyes and pretty smile as she reached to shake hands. "Hi, Dick, I'm Carol. Nice to meet you."

I have no idea what I said.

As we headed out to De's car, we babbled our way to a safe first-date decision; we would go to the movies. *Island in the Sun*, starring the new sensation Harry Bellefonte, was the unanimous choice. Carol and I both enjoyed the night of easy conversation and lots of laughs. At the right moment in the movie, I had even made the lame my-little-finger-accidentally-touch-her-little-finger-move, and was rewarded when she took my hand in hers.

De and I walked the girls to the door when we took them home.

Carol held my hand and said, "Thanks, Dick. I really had a good time."

My second reward was her light kiss on my cheek, like a longtime friend saying thank you. She was pretty neat.

The following morning before we left, El phoned De. She said, "De, both Carol and I had a good time last night. The Academy sounds really interesting and we'd both like to see it. Is it OK if we drive up some weekend?"

"You bet."

Two weeks later, El and Carol arrived in New London in El's new blue '57 Ford Fairlane convertible. With the top down, hair blowing, and wearing sun glasses, they were sassy college girls cruising for Ivy Leaguers, or at least a couple of Coast Guard Ensigns.

De and I had reserved one of the Academy's twenty six foot *Knockabouts*, an easy sailing, fixed-keel sloop. We made one stop at the deli to pick up bagged lunches and drinks, and then we were off to a great afternoon sail on the Thames River. After a whirlwind tour of the Academy, the girls drove home the same day. I knew I wanted to see Carol again.

Two weeks later, I drove south to pick her up and bring her back to New London for an overnight visit. I had reservations for her at the Mohegan Hotel. The plan was for her to take the train home.

I arrived in Roosevelt on Saturday around 10:00 a.m. She came running out the door to greet me as I pulled into the driveway.

With a welcoming smile, she yelled, "Hi! You made it. Any trouble?"

She looked pretty in a light summer dress, with a scoop neckline and a whirl of pleated skirt that layers of crinolines expanded into a puffy circle. She bounced happiness.

"Come on in." She gave me a quick hello kiss and I followed her into the house.

Her mother rose from her secretary, where she had been pretending busy work, and greeted me, "Hi, Dick. Hope you had an easy trip."

We skipped through the mundane niceties: the weather, my car, Bob's not in from his route yet, and Carol has looked forward to the visit.

Carol spoke up. "We should get going. Can you get my suitcase, Rich, please?" Nobody had ever called me Rich. I kind of liked it.

There was a Saturday night party at one of the cadre's houses. It was typical wall-to-wall people, with their furniture moved to clear a small space for dancers. Saucers and cereal bowls adorned all available flat surfaces, proffering a bounty of chips and dips. There was beer, of course, but nobody went crazy. We were a pretty conservative bunch, actually.

Carol enjoyed meeting my classmates and had a good time. But, when I took her to the Mohegan, she said, "I'm not sure I feel well, I need to get some sleep. I'll see you in the morning."

I drove home to Mauntauk Avenue.

I hadn't been home ten minutes when the phone rang. Somehow, I knew it would be Carol. "Rich, I feel terrible. I want to get out of here, can you come get me...please. I don't want to be alone."

"I'm on the way."

It was a quick trip. Carol was ready to go. She looked miserable, sitting on the edge of the bed, suitcase on the floor beside her. She whimpered, "Let's go."

We checked out of the hotel under the skeptical glare from the night desk clerk, and drove straight to the house.

We sat together at our small kitchen table for a few moments, quietly whispering. I spoke through her cupped hands that were propping up her head. "It's really getting late. You better get some sleep. You can sleep here on the couch if you want. You'll feel better in the morning."

Before I could crunch some pillows together, she had mysteriously removed her crinolines that now stood like a white miniature teepee on the floor at the end of the couch. She smoothed her dress, laid down, said good night, and she was off to dreamland.

"Rich?" Carol's whining broke through my fog.

I sat up in bed, remembering I had left her on the couch. "Carol! Are you OK?" I hollered.

De was stirring now, while Don sat wide-eyed at the foot of his bed trying to look serious in his skivvies. Impossible. I had to chuckle, "I'm sorry, guys. I'll explain later." Then Carol answered that she was fine and I said, "I'll be right out."

Within a few minutes, we were all at the breakfast table, laughing, kidding Don and Carol as to who was more surprised.

De just shook his head and said, "Man, I wish I had seen that."

I took Carol to the train station, and as she waved from the train steps, I called out, "See you in a couple of weeks."

It was mid-August. I was anxious to see Carol before I had to report to the *Absecon*, in Norfolk. I wanted to get to know her better. I asked De for suggestions for a good place to go for a date.

"Try Guy Lombardo's East Point House."

"Really? You mean *the* Guy Lombardo?"

"Yea, really." De said, "You know, Royal Canadians, New Year's Eve, Roosevelt Grille, Auld Ayng Syne and all that? He lives in Freeport. There's always a band playing his music, sometimes he is even directing. Where the hell is Bradford, anyhow?" He paused and smiled, "You gotta get out more, boy."

Oh, I knew Guy Lombardo and his "sweetest music this side of heaven." As a kid, I listened to him on the radio every New Year's Eve. Mom and Dad went out with friends. At the stroke of midnight, Nana, who had stayed home, gave my sister and I old pots and pans and wooden spoons. After our ritual, Auld Ayng Syne sing-a-long with the radio we would run into the yard, bang the pots, and yell Happy New Year until the cold January night chased us back into the house. Oh yeah, I knew Guy Lombardo. Going to East Point house would be a big deal for me. I phoned Carol, set the date. She sounded excited, and said she would make reservations.

Driving up to the nightclub, I was disappointed. It looked like a long flat barge or boxy river cruiser with a line of narrow picture windows facing the sound. There was a small deck under the overhang surrounding the building. A few early diners were strolling the deck checking out Guy Lombardo's famous racing boat, *Tempo VI*. He was a Gold Cup champion, almost as well-known as a cigarette-boat racer as he was a musician.

Carol followed our waiter, weaving a path between the tables that were dispersed around the dance floor like white islands. She looked great in a lavender cowl-necked dress with a full circle skirt.

The waiter held her chair, then mine, smoothed the white linen table cloth, snapped the napkins open, and flared them onto our laps. "Do you care for drinks first, sir?"

We ordered.

Waiters moved among the tables, lighting the single candles; the frosted chimneys forced a soft flicker of light over the linen. I looked at Carol and said, "You know, this is our first date on our own. I like this." She smiled in return.

Halfway through dinner, the orchestra began setting up. Tables were filling while murmurs of conversation joined the background of clinking silverware. The flat globed ceiling lights were dimmed, making our candle-lit table seem more private. We were far enough away from the band to enjoy conversation along with the music. Carol had a simple, honest style that made her easy to talk to.

She had grown up in Roosevelt, went to Hempstead High School, played in the band, had a small circle of friends, dated a few boys, but for the last two years, only Warren. He was two years older but she had known him all through grade school and Sunday school. She mostly double dated with her best friend, Joyce. When she followed her sister to college at Courtland State, she and Warren drifted apart, like most high school romances.

The band was playing *Harbor Lights*, one of my favorites. "Want to dance?" We moved slowly with the music. Neither of us would be mistaken for a good dancer, but it was nice holding her close and smelling her faint perfume. The vocalist crooned, "...but you were on the ship... and I was on the shore." That was not a good thing to think about, if this relationship was going to grow.

When the set was over, we returned to our table. I told her more of my background and how I ended up going to the Academy. Then, I asked her why she did not stay in college.

"I was never much of a student, even in high school. I was always overshadowed by El who had skipped a grade and started college at sixteen. When I wrestled with French and geometry, all I heard was, 'I don't know why you can't get this? Your sister was so smart.'"

She paused, hunched her shoulders, and turned her hands up. "So I tried for three semesters, and this last Christmas, I told my parents I didn't want to go back." She continued, "They were very supportive. Actually, I doubt if they were surprised. So, I went back after break, cleared out my stuff and joined them in Florida for the last part of their vacation."

The band broke into another favorite, *Red Roses for a Blue Lady*. "Let's dance." I said, and she gave me her hand and we moved to the edge of the now crowded dance floor. Moving in tight circles, cheek to cheek, I asked softly, "So what happened to Warren?"

"We just never got back together." She arched her back, turned toward me with a sheepish grin and surprised me, "I should tell you. I was engaged for a short time to another guy, George."

"Really? You've been engaged?" I blinked to clear my head for this story.

"Yes. I met George at *Abraham & Strauss*, where I worked part-time during the summer and school breaks. He was my supervisor in the gardening department. He was a little older than me, a Korean War vet. I discovered he had a lot of family baggage and personal problems and he was sort of a whiner. So I called it off just before this last Christmas. When I got home from Florida, I got a job at Met Life, where I am now." She smiled. "That pretty much brings you up to date."

I didn't say anything, just pulled her closer and finished the *Red Roses* set. As we headed back to the table, I said, "Do you think you could get away from Met Life a few days? I'd love for you to come home to Bradford with me before I have to leave for Norfolk?" She squeezed my hand. I took that as a maybe.

The trip to Bradford went smoothly. We drove west on Rt. 17, (now I-86), slowly working our way through the same New York towns I used to creep through on the Erie RR. They were mostly single industry towns, now threatened with becoming part of the rust belt as they lost their manufacturing base.

We turned south toward Bradford at Seneca Junction. Ten miles to go. Carol, wrinkled her nose toward the slightly open passenger window and said, "What's that smell?"

"That's oil. We'll be passing the Kendall Refinery in a few minutes." I could smell it, too. Funny, I had never smelled it when I lived here, but, I did now.

This was unfamiliar territory for Carol. Bradford was a city of mixed industrial, small business, and neighborhood districts, spread like outstretched fingers into shallow valleys of protective green hills. It was a far cry from the flat miles of suburban houses where she grew up.

We had a great visit. My family welcomed her with open arms.

Mom was a little reserved, as usual, until she had her properly categorized. "She's probably from money, being from New York."

"Mom! Her dad's a village milkman! Honestly, I wish you'd stop that stuff."

"Well, we'll see," she retorted, tipping her chin up and away, eyes cast on the ceiling as she noisily ppfftted a cloud of cigarette smoke skyward. She would never change.

We made the obligatory rounds to the relatives. The Whalens and the Brophys (aunts and cousins) lived next to us, but Grandma and Grandpa Boyd and three of mom's sisters and their families lived on Center Street. If Carol was going to experience culture shock, it would be there.

It was a poor blue collar neighborhood. The houses were small, owned by the same landlord, who ignored most needed repairs or paint. The men worked long hours on oil leases in the hills, or in factories. They came home expecting dinner on the table, and coffee already saucered and blown. Then they would have a couple of beers, watch some wrasslin' on the new TV, and head off to bed early. Carol was wonderful; she charmed them all.

We went for dinner and dancing at the Brook Club, the closest thing to a night club in town. The Little Civics Quartet was playing. We loved his easy dance music in the Lombardo-Glenn Miller style, and he became our favorite band. Even after we were married, we sought him out every time we came home.

We left Bradford, both feeling good about the trip. Turning on to RT 17, we chatted softly, re-living the good moments. Carol slid over close to me, squeezed my right arm with both hands, and snuggled her head into my shoulder. We glanced at each other. I smiled and said, "You know, it could be like this all the time."

"I know. I think I'd like that." She smiled and squeezed my arm again.

That was it!

Whatever we read into that... we were detailing wedding plans before we had traveled fifty miles. Religion loomed, as Carol said, "You, know, my dad is going to have problems with the Catholic thing. He's had Catholic issues before and is still a little bitter about his sister marrying into the church."

I admitted to questioning a few things in my own mind lately, and told her, "I won't let that be a problem. I am willing to get married in your church, and there will be no question of raising the children Catholic." Then I added, "I want to ask your dad formally, though."

"Let me talk to him first."

We got to Roosevelt on Thursday and I left for Norfolk on Sunday. In between, we confirmed that it would be a military wedding, in her church, with her minister. I had checked the Atlantic Area Commander's deployment schedule for Ocean Station duty, and knew the *Half Moon,* out of Staten Island, along with the *Absecon* and the *Ingham,* in Norfolk, would all be in port next March. So, I could get classmates as ushers, and hoped Ron and I could get leave at the same time so he could be best man. I also sent my miniature ring to Herf-Jones to mount an engagement setting. I couldn't believe how much I changed my life in the last two months. I had spent more time deciding what car to buy.

—10—

THE PAMIR

EARLY ON THE MORNING OF August 10, 1957, Captain Johannes Diebitsch of the German Merchant Marine paced the deck of the *Pamir*, a four hundred-foot barque. She had just cleared the harbor of Buenos Aires, Argentina, her subsidizing cargo of barley stowed below. With all her square sails set, the *Pamir* was beginning her 7000 mile journey home to Hamburg, Germany.

The permanent crew of thirty-five professional merchant mariners and the fifty-one young teenage cadets, ages fourteen to seventeen, had not been home since July. Everyone was anxious. Eighty-six souls on board—only six would ever see home again.

The *Pamir* was the last commercial sailing ship to carry cargo around Cape Horn. That was in 1949. Outmoded by modern bulk carriers, the *Pamir* was a financial burden to her shipping company who, while still using her to carry cargo, leased her out as a training ship for German Merchant Marine Cadets. Although, Captain Diebitsch was experienced in commanding square-rigged training ships, he had never been Master of a cargo ship. Pressured for time by the home office and obstructed by a dock strike, Captain Diebitsch opted for the dangerous alternative of loading the barley in loose bulk form. He planned on using his ship's crew, despite their inexperience, to install baffling, after they got underway, to prevent the free surface effect of shifting cargo that could jeopardize the ships stability.

On September 2, a strong squall line that had formed in West Africa moved off shore into the Atlantic Basin. The storm, churned by the warm waters in the five degree northern latitudes near the Cape Verde Islands, became cyclonic. The storm grew in strength on its westward journey toward the United States. The U.S. Weather Bureau ordained it Tropical Storm *Carrie*. It was the third storm of the 1957 season, the first year they were officially given names.

On September 9th, after the long drive from Carol's house in Roosevelt, NY. I reported for duty on the *Absecon* as a deck watch officer. I was quickly pulled into the hectic activity of preparing for Ocean Station Patrol. The ship was assigned to station Echo, in the mid-Atlantic, halfway between Bermuda and the Azores.

It was great to see Ron again. We exchanged quick updates of our summers; Ron enthusiastically accepted the best man job. He then helped me get my gear aboard and into the quarters we would share on the second deck. We were assigned to what had been temporary aviators' quarters when the Navy operated the *Absecon* as a seaplane tender. It had all the atmosphere of an open ward with 8 bunks, separated by black pull curtains. A small gray metal desk with a fold down top and a few drawers was crammed alongside a metal bunk. It was fine for the fly-boys who were only aboard for a short time, but we were bachelors trying to make the unwelcoming space into our seagoing home.

With no portholes, the only light came from our desk lamps. We were bombarded by the constant hum of the circulating air vents, and subjected to dank smells emanating from the Chief's head across the passageway. We both looked forward to moving to the main deck officer's staterooms next year. For now, as the most junior officers aboard, the "Ensign Locker," as the rest of the ship called it, would have to do.

All week long, the main deck was a series of all-hands evolutions. The chief petty officers kept long lines of crewmen moving boxes, and nondescript containers hand over hand from trucks on the pier, up the gangway, through narrow passageways, down tiny hatches to storage compartments, and reefer lockers in the bowels of the ship. The engineers, clustered on the fantail, knelt like children on Christmas morning, hovering over their prized shiny metal pieces. Each part was lovingly separated from the straw and grease packing, and checked against invoiced lists of machinery parts. The strange tools for weather observations were all brought aboard and properly stowed: huge white balloons, electronic radiosonde boxes that would dangle beneath them to transmit wind speed back to the ship, and large tanks of helium.

On Friday, at the end of my first week, the *Absecon* slipped cleanly from her berth to begin her five day journey. As we cleared Cape Henry, the Captain ordered a course change to due east to take the ship just north of Bermuda and on to Station ECHO.

On the way to the gunnery office, I passed through the wardroom where our navigator, LT Jim Fleishell, was huddled in conference with the weathermen at the end of the table. There were four assigned by the National Weather Bureau to all ocean station patrols. Before satellites, their observations on these patrols were the primary source of weather forecasting for the U.S. This business was all pretty routine for them. They had reported aboard just a few hours before sailing. They would berth in the Ensign locker with Ron and I.

As I grabbed a cup of coffee, one departing weatherman drained his, started to leave, and turned back to LT Fleishell. "As of the eighth, that tropical storm is now Hurricane *Carrie*, a Category IV, packing winds of 155 MPH. She's headed just south of Bermuda. Looks like a tough trip." As he turned and headed below, I watched the wardroom steward scamper back to the mess deck. I knew that in a matter of minutes even the engineer on watch in No. 2 engine room would have the scuttlebutt—the *Absecon* was headed directly into a hurricane!

Fortunately, we had a few days to gain our sea legs and get the ship buttoned down before the onslaught of *Carrie*. By Tuesday afternoon, we could read the telltale signs. Wind streaks danced like pinstripes on a gray ocean, keeping time with the 30-40 mph gusts. White caps formed, only to be blown flat, like truncated pyramids, spitting their frothy spray downwind to hang above the trough. The eerie music of the wind in the rigging got louder and changed tone with the wind's speed. Ocean swells mounted larger and longer. Agonizing human forms, ignoring the pelting rain and wind, bent over the lee rail praying for relief or death—a few not caring which.

As sixty foot waves towered and moved swiftly beneath us, the ship rose like an express elevator, then balanced on the crest, bow and stern sagging under their own weight, as though she were waiting for an unseen force to break her back like a giant snapping a twig over his knee. Screws thumped loudly as they flailed in the free air, the rudder, with no water, was useless. Then the wave slid quickly beneath us leaving the 2600 ton flat bottomed ship to plummet, released by the hand of God, to crash with a shuddering thud into the bottom of the next trough. The ship shuddered in a vibrating fit that seemed to last forever, only to have the merciful moment of stillness interrupted in seconds with the following crest collapsing tons of angry green water, hammering the foredeck, nearly back to the bridge. The ship buried her nose into the next wave, courageously climbed the steep wall at an eerie angle, only to repeat the action over and over again. *Carrie* was my first hurricane—ooh, that she would be the last.

On Monday, the 16th of September, *Carrie* made an unusual move. The cooler ocean temperature and an upper level shear turned her northeast. Bermuda and the U.S. east coast would be spared. Reduced in intensity, but still a Category I with winds just below a hundred miles an hour, *Carrie* now took aim directly at the Azores. Happy with the havoc she had played in the mid-Atlantic, she now turned into the path of the northerly bound *Pamir*.

The German Training Ship Pamir

"MAYDAY, MAYDAY, MAYDAY. Four-masted barque Pamir in severe hurricane--Position 35 degrees, 57 minutes North and 40 degrees, 20 minutes West–All sails lost– 45 degree list–ship is taking water–danger of sinking."

At 12:57 on the afternoon of Saturday, September 21, that ominous message sparked all the ships at sea into action. Response is universal and quick, for all sailors know that "...there but for the grace of God..." By Sunday morning, all ships within two hundred miles were advised to proceed to aid in the search for survivors. The *Absecon,* immediately started the three hundred mile dash, engines straining to reach full speed. Search and Rescue (SAR) was now our first priority. The *Pamir* was sinking!

The Sunday *New York Times* alerted the world to the tragedy, with a featured article with file photos of the *Pamir,* and an inset map showing her position in the Mid-Atlantic. The world was now eager to follow the fate of fifty-one young men, who on Friday were giddy in the romance of sailing a square-rigged Cape Horner. On Saturday, they were scared, cold, and alone in the storm-tossed sea, clinging to life itself, desperately wanting only to get home. The *Pamir,* had missed the wrath of the Category IV *Carrie's* westward passage. She had sailed on northward, only to encounter the still dangerous storm on its reversed eastward journey toward the Azores. The last garbled radio transmission from the *Pamir* was received shortly after one o'clock.

The *Pamir* sank 680 miles west-south west of the Azores. Merchant ships were reporting their on scene ETA's and offering whatever assistance they could provide. The U.S. Air Force 57th Air Rescue Squadron out of Lages Air Force Base in the Azores, was anxious to provide search assistance, but was unable to launch their aircraft, hampered by the hurricane winds as *Carrie* bore down on the islands.

Hans Georg Wirth, one of *Pamir's* permanent crew, gave his account of that horrible Saturday in a *Readers Digest* article in June 1958.

*"When the ship capsized, nobody had been lowered into boats.
Nobody even jumped overboard. All eighty-six men just slipped
into the cold Atlantic with the overturned ship."*

The official German investigative authority confirmed most of the facts as reported by the survivors. Unable to hold her head into the wind, the *Pamir* slid into the trough, could not recover, and capsized. The shifting cargo of barley, with nearly the free surface effect of water, was deemed a major contributing factor. The once proud hull of the last Cape Horner took men and boys with her, and released others to fend for themselves.

The *Pamir* floated keel up for a half hour before being quietly consumed by the unforgiving sea. She descended to the Atlantic graveyard, 12,000 feet below the still churning surface, confirming her place in history as one of the greatest sea tragedies of all time.

For most of the overnight run to the *Pamir's* position, Ron and I were huddled in the wardroom pouring over the chart of Atlantic Ocean Currents and the National SAR manual.

In the wardroom, the green felt table cloth had long since been replaced by a green rubber mat. The twelve chairs remained tethered to the table, with their double snap hooks preventing them from becoming flying missile hazards. Our ship bounced, rolled, dipped, and sprung itself through the swells at full speed. A half full coffee pot had been secured with an ingenious Rube Goldberg rig of wire coat hangers of the steward's personal design. He was not going to let his officers go without coffee.

That night, when we finally tried to get some sleep, the sounds of the ship pounding into the swells and the boiling swirls of bow spray along the weather deck were different when you lived below decks. We were keenly aware of the thin layer of very old steel between us and the ocean we were trying to defy. We did not get much sleep with the roar and vibration of all four engines straining. Then, there were the thoughts. I couldn't clear my mind thinking of fifty-one young men being forced to fight for their lives long before they should have to.

The messenger of the watch, shaking my shoulder, shining a small flashlight in my eyes, half whispered, "Sir, it's almost sunrise. Are you awake, sir?"

In a balancing act, Ron and I lurched out of the wardroom in a wide stance, timing the roll of the ship, steaming mug of coffee in one hand, the other reaching for the ladder. Then, the ship reduced speed. The engines lost their sound of urgency, the pitching dampened, and the bow settled, as the *Absecon* snuggled into the full support of the sea.

As we came onto the bridge, LT Fleishell greeted us with a cheery good morning. It was still dark! "Let me show you guys where things are," he said, pointing us toward the chart room. The Captain had taken Ron and I off watch rotation to work directly with the expected fleet of merchant vessels from all over the world. The dull red glow of the chart room night light reflected an eerie magenta shade onto Jim's face. The bridge, set for nighttime steaming, was still totally dark. The dimmest hint of pre-dawn light crept onto the horizon trying to displace the thin line of gray clouds that clung to the edge of the earth.

I quickly went over the night communication log. The HMCS *Crusader* had arrived this morning to join the search along with the merchant ship *President Taylor*, that had arrived on scene late last night. Upon our arrival, we were designated On-Scene-Commander (OSC). That meant we were responsible for search planning and execution; we directed all ships and aircraft movement in carrying out the plan.

"Captain's on the bridge!" The quartermaster made the standard announcement.

A chorus greeted him with smart salutes, "Good morning, Captain."

Saying nothing, CDR West casually brushed at his cap brim with his right hand, which we all took as a returned salute, and lifted himself into the leather upholstered Captain's chair that was mounted on a high pedestal. The chair could be moved to the open starboard wing in good weather. The Quartermaster of the watch buzzed the Captain's steward on the sound powered phone, "Bring the Captain's morning coffee to the bridge."

Ron and I emerged from the chart room and reported to the Captain that we were ready to start the search. The morning sky was gradually working its way to blue with a thin overcast layer of clouds. We recommended a slow speed, and close sweep width to take the best advantage of the early effort. The Captain set a sweep width of five hundred yards and a speed of ten knots.

I stepped out to port wing to grab that first deep breath of the sea air. Sipping my coffee, I watched flying fish, darting in a ragged formation, flying a few feet above the contour of the swells, for as much as a hundred yards. Then, darting back under for a few seconds to regain their power, they leapt into the air again, staying just clear of their predators seeking breakfast.

I moved back into the chart room, and we began the first leg of the search.

Hans Wirth, the *Pamir* crewman, reported in his *Reader's Digest* article that by Tuesday morning his lifeboat had only five survivors. The effects of ingesting salt water were destroying their brains. Crazy with hallucinations, one went over the side, yelling, "I have to find the Captain. He needs to know." Others saw land, even city buildings, and began swimming for them. One man, just trying to get exercise, went for a swim around the boat and was never seen again. Earlier, during the night, one crewman had slumped into the boat bottom, water up to his armpits, dead. With a prayer for his soul, they lowered his body over the side.

Having seen search planes fly overhead, even ships pass nearby, with no recognition, they knew they had to increase their visibility. They managed to make a small mast by tearing out wooden seats and flying a torn T-shirt as a make shift flag. Everyone was losing faith.

Late that afternoon, U.S. merchant vessel *Saxon* appeared on their horizon. She was lowering her boats! The five survivors were near the end of their ordeal.

The growing number of search vessels had reached armada size, led by the *Absecon*. We started each day's search with planes from Loges AFB.

They crisscrossed the line, staying just ahead of the flanking movement and extended the range to each side.

Captain West strolled confidently onto the bridge each morning. He moved to the port and starboard wings, checked the sea conditions, and the lineup of ships in place for the day. He checked the radar, looked at the chart, and got a short briefing from the Officer-of-the-deck (OOD). Ready to begin, he lifted his handsome frame into his bridge chair. (Captain West bore a remarkable resemblance to the movie star, Clark Gable...and knew it). He propped his non-regulation half wellingtons on the foot-bar, loosened his top shirt button, revealing his *definitely* non-reg red and white horizontal striped T-shirt, like he was a French sailor underneath it all, and ordered us to commence the search, "OK, move 'em out." Captain West may have had a flamboyant style, always on stage, but nobody questioned his professional seagoing ability.

The spirit of the crew waned as the day went on with no contact. Buoyed by the *Saxon*'s find, we knew we were in the right area. The once-promising day dragged on. The lookouts were rotated through meals. One or two searching merchant ships requested, and were granted, release to keep from jeopardizing their own cargo. New arriving ships replaced them. Nobody saw anything, search planes reported, "No joy, no joy."

Just as the day was drawing to a close, sunset only an hour away, the voice tube that runs from the flying bridge lookout to the overhead of the bridge, came alive. "Bridge—Lookout. Target two points off starboard bow, estimate 300 yards." It was the excited voice of Chief Watson, doing extra lookout duty. All binoculars turned in that direction, the OOD changed the *Absecon* course to close the target. Soon everyone could see him! A lone survivor slumped on the after thwart, arm weakly strung along the gunwale. The boat was badly broken, barely floating with seawater lapping over the gunwales.

He was a pitiful sight. He was alone, face and lips swollen, sloshing in water up to his armpits. He'd had neither water nor food for over three days and was exhausted from the sheer effort of staying alive. We launched a small boat, and the crew moved him carefully into a rescue basket, wrapped him with blankets, and returned to the ship. As the deck force eased the stretcher out of the boat and headed to sick bay, everyone within ear shot could taste his first words. "May I have a Pepsi, please?"

Günther Hassalbach was a twenty-two-year-old *Pamir* crew member. He said he was one of twenty-five men who started in this boat. Then, suf-

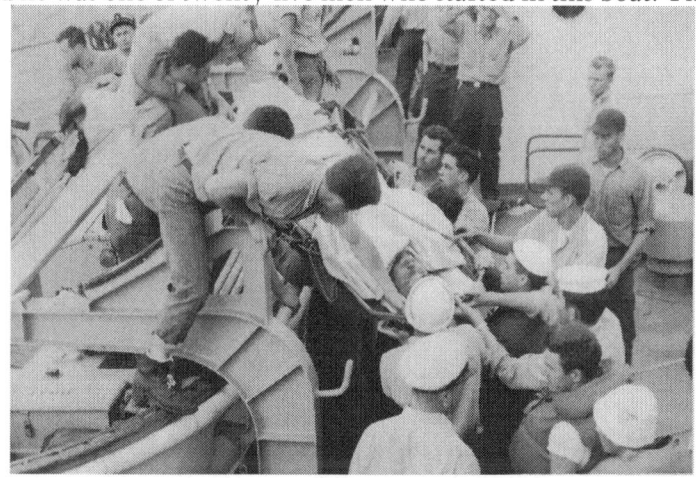

Loan survivor is brought aboard Absecon

fering the same fate as those in Hans Wirth's boat, they gradually lost men to the sea. There had been eight survivors in Günter's boat that morning. By sunset, when we picked him up, he was alone...the last survivor of the *Pamir*.

The next day, we rendezvoused with the French Ocean Liner *Antilles,* in her transatlantic crossing, and transferred Günter to her so he could get hospital care from her doctor and we returned to the search. The *Antilles* took Gunter to Puerto Rico, where he was treated and flown home. All search activity ended after nine days. With seventy ships and twenty aircraft from fifteen different nations, it was touted, at the time, as the largest sea search in history.

Richard Marcott

The following year, the German government presented the U.S. Coast Guard with a large oil painting of the *Pamir* and the *Absecon* received a bronze plaque that was mounted on the ship for all to see.

The plaque read:

To the officers and men of the U.S. Coast Guard Cutter ABSECON in appreciation for their outstanding performance of duty in the intensive search operations for the crew of the lost German Training Ship "PAMIR" between 21 and 29 September 1957. Assisted by U.S. aircraft and by more than 68 vessels of many nations. The Absecon directed the search which resulted in the rescue of six seamen 558 miles southwest of the Azores. These operations are in keeping with the Coast Guard's biggest traditions of seamanship and valor.

Presented by the Government of
The Federal Republic of Germany

—*11*—

WE'LL MEET AGAIN

THERE WERE SACKS OF MAIL stacked on the pier when the *Absecon* returned from Ocean Station patrol. I was so glad I had several letters from
Carol. I whipped through the highlights, then went back, not to the first
one, but the last one. I reread it several times: "Well, the mailman came
today–so I guess we're officially engaged now."

I hadn't seen her in more than two months. I wasn't looking forward
to the long trip to Long Island, New York, but that's where Carol was and
that was where I was going for the weekend. I left the ship before lunch
trying to beat the sailors. That didn't happen. Not on a Friday. It seemed
like half the U.S. Navy was getting out of Norfolk.

I eased my '57 Mercury onto the end of the car line. The loadmaster
bellowed directions and waved furiously, moving us into position to load
onto the next Little Creek–Kiptopeke ferry. The *Del MarVa* had pulled
out just as I arrived. The terminal agent changed the huge red arrow on
the clock-sign on the overhead archway: *Next Ferry at 2:00 p.m.* I had to
wait an hour.

I rolled down the window and tamped a fresh bowl full of London
Dock pipe tobacco into my favorite straight-stemmed briar. I sucked at the
Zippo flame, staring down my nose at the growing circle of embers. The
rising cloud of smoke encircled my head, spreading its soothing aroma of
freshly lit tobacco. With my pipe clinched in my teeth, I surrendered my
body to the plush white leather seat, leaned my head back, and thought
about Carol's letter.

She had written that she had rushed home from work every day, and rifled through the mail until she found the orange postal notice for an insured box.

"Mom," she whooped, "the package came. I'm going right back out to the post office. See you in a bit."

There was nothing in the box. Her mailman was "still out on the route."

She said she drove back home, then backtracked what she knew was George's route. She had known her mailman for years, babysat for his children. Swinging up and down the side streets, she spotted him, bag over his shoulder, on Henry Street. She tooted the horn and slid her old Dodge coupe alongside the curb. She popped out, waving, "Hey, George. Do you have my package?"

"Just this little box from Herf-Jones," George said, giving her the prize with a smile.

Carol ran home, tore into the box, and yelled, "Mom, it's here! It's here! My engagement ring!"

We had missed the traditional moment when many cadets got engaged—the ring dance. Amid the strains of *Cherry Pink and Apple Blossom White* and *Unchained Melody*, beautiful women in colorful gowns, and handsome cadets in dress whites, swirled by, whispering quietly to each other. Flickering lights, reflected from a rotating crystal ball followed the dancers like flitting moths.

Whenever an engaged couple strolled up the ramp to stand beneath the crown of a giant plaster replica or our class ring, nearby dancers paused to share the moment. The cadet presented his miniature, a traditional engagement ring for all service academy graduates, and kissed his fiancée while they both accepted the smiles and quiet applause from the dance floor.

For Carol, the moment had to be by proxy, from the mailman, while I was at sea. I had sent the ring to Herf-Jones to change the setting. Given the ship's schedule, it made sense to have it sent directly to her house. At least we took pleasure knowing her ring would be unique. It was an exact replica of my class ring (which limited it to sixty-one). Reset with her tourmaline birth stone and a small diamond arrangement, there were none like it in the world, nor would there ever be.

The sounds of revving engines, parents herding their kids back into cars, and the staccato thumps of car doors, jolted me back to reality. Finally, *The Princess Anne* was maneuvering into the dock, ping-ponging her way between the narrowing pilings, as if forcing her way into a funnel. No need for precise ship handling here. The docking team secured the ship in a noisy, but precise ballet of deck hands, shouting over the din of running chains and clanking ramps. From the ferry, the hollow roar of several hundred cars and trucks starting their engines at the same time echoed off the high cave-like bulkheads.

I opened my driver's door, banged out my ashes on the rocker panel, and closed the door and the window to ward off the impending fog of exhaust fumes. The cars offloaded, in rhythmic double bumps over the steel ramp. The hulking blue and white ferry, nearly four hundred feet long, could move as many as a hundred and twenty cars and twelve hundred passengers across the eighteen mile entrance to the Chesapeake Bay. With seven ferries in the system, Route 13 had become the shortest and most popular way south from New York and New England.

In a practiced routine, big trucks were first, stacked inboard to outboard on either side of the centerline engine room cowling. The cars were loaded the same way, all according to a weight and balance plan orchestrated by the loadmaster.

The Princess Anne, pulled out, and headed north toward the Kiptopeke terminal on Cape Charles. The ferry's double-ended pilot house made it easy for cars to drive straight on, then straight off on the other side. I knew the crossing would take an hour and a half, so I squeezed out of my

Mercury and made my way topside for a ham sandwich and some fresh air.

The sea was calm. The bright blue sky sported a narrow band of wispy clouds on the horizon. People had migrated to the open topside deck to enjoy the pleasant afternoon on this beautiful October day. A few couples strolled hand in hand, watching others snuggled on the rows of benches. A handful of obnoxious kids circled the perimeter in imaginary chase. A growing flock of seagulls swooped and squawked at each other, fighting for the best position over the wake to snatch bread crumbs tossed into the air by giggling teenagers. Sailors were clustered in random groups, noisily sharing their plans for their liberty weekend. A few remained aloof, retreating to remote benches, their necks crunched deep into upturned peacoat collars like turtles, deep in private thoughts.

As we crossed Thimble Shoal Channel, I leaned on the starboard rail, took the last bite of my sandwich, and re-stoked my pipe. The sun cast a bright streak on the rippling wavelets. Like a beam, it guided my thoughts over the horizon. It was hard not to think of our last patrol, when the German training ship, *Pamir,* sank. The tragic loss of young lives was a reminder of the power of the sea, and Hurricane *Carrie.* That had been less than a month ago. I wondered how long it would take me to let it go.

We pulled into Kiptopeke on time, 3:30 p.m. Reversing the disciplined order of boarding, the loadmaster emptied the cars over the noisy ramp.

A wolf-pack formation of cars headed north on U.S. 13. One by one, drivers broke off while the big-rigs blew by us like we were out for a Sunday drive. Seven hours to go. With one short stop for a snack, I could probably make it to Roosevelt, New York, before midnight.

My drive was accompanied by the steady hum of tires and my low pitched radio that changed from static, to music, to sports, as I dialed in whatever station was in range. I had plenty of time for mind-drift. Random scenes danced in and out of my head: my high school prom, saying goodbye to dad and mom on the steps at Chase Hall, Thanksgiving visits, graduation, meeting Carol. I chuckled to myself, "Poor Carol. After my nebulous, when-the-hell-did-it happen, what-did-I-say proposal, now she had to get her engagement ring in the mail."

A welcome sign alerted me that the Delaware Memorial Bridge was ahead. I had been on the road for four hours. I crossed the bridge, and within a short time merged into heavier traffic on the New Jersey Turnpike.

Hunger pulled me into the first Howard Johnson's Plaza. There were no other choices. They had an exclusive contract. If you were going to eat on the Jersey Turnpike, it was going to be at Howard Johnson's. I skipped the all-you-can-eat fish special, and wolfed down a platter of their famed macaroni and cheese. Lots of ketchup. Good stuff. With not enough time to choose from twenty-eight flavors, I grabbed a small plain vanilla cone for the road. As I exited the plaza, the famed Ho-Jo's orange roof with their trademark "Simple Simon and the Pie Man" weather vane, faded away in my rear view mirror. I was on the road again.

At some point, I became aware of a faint odor that triggered thoughts of home. I cracked the window. Oil! Through the latticed power-line towers, I could see the distant silhouette of tanks: flat, short, tall, thin, and onion domed. They formed a dark base that sprouted tall chimneys. Clouds of billowing smoke rose from some while others stood as silent sentries with red blinking aircraft warning lights. A few flashed burning flames.

In the darkening twilight, thousands of white lights built their Etch a Sketch profile of tangled pipes, and cracking towers. These huge refineries stood unaware that they owed their birth to the oldest refinery in the world, the Kendall Refinery, back home in Bradford, Pennsylvania. I felt a little smug.

My exit to Staten Island was coming up. I crossed the Island to the 69th Street Ferry, then checked the cheat-sheet I had taped to the dashboard, *Follow the Belt Parkway to Southern State, then Exit 21 to Nassau*

Rd. I pulled into the Berlinghoff driveway at 65 West Roosevelt Avenue a few minutes after 11:00 p.m.

It had been a long day, but I perked up when I saw Carol running to the door to greet me. Her mom, in her bathrobe, stood behind her. Her dad had been long since in bed (way too late for an early-rising milkman). Her mom chatted with us amicably.

"How was the trip? Are you enjoying the ship? I'm excited for Carol. I'll see you at breakfast." Then, in a polite move, she said goodnight and went off to bed. I was so tired that within a few minutes I was headed to the small bed in the attic, and Carol to her bedroom. It wasn't even midnight.

Oh yeah—she was wearing her ring. So, I had missed the bended-knee-slip-it-on-her-finger moment too. But, although the seahorse tails and eagle wings of her miniature have rounded to smooth gold over fifty-five years, the magic of the ring still works for us.

I managed a few trips to Roosevelt between ocean station patrols and our wedding in March, 1958. Distance, time, and winter weather, made it difficult. I usually arrived near midnight on Friday. We enjoyed a late Saturday date, dinner and dancing, or a movie. I began leaving later and later on Sunday night. We did work in a little talk of wedding arrangements, but it was clear that Carol and the "Queen Mother" were going to be in charge of that. I told them both, "Ron (my best man) and I would arrive on time in March—just tell us where to stand."

On my last trip before the wedding, I didn't leave Roosevelt until very late. I knew I was in trouble as soon as I hit the Jersey Turnpike. I fought desperately, and not too successfully, to keep my eyes open. I saw two young men hitchhiking, dungarees, and peacoats. I stopped right next to them, not even pulling off the road. I opened my door, yelled over the top of the car, "You guys Navy?"

"Yes, sir."

"You headed for the ferry?"

"Yes, sir."

"Do either of you drive?"

"Yes, sir."

"Get in. Take us to the ferry." I already had the back door open. I slid in and flaked out on the back seat with no idea of even what their names were. I was asleep in seconds. The abrupt bounce of the ferry hitting the pilings and the vibrations of her backing engines woke me at 7:00 a.m. I was still in the back seat, below decks, not a sailor not in sight. The loadmaster mustered me off in time for me to make it to the ship for morning quarters.

I couldn't keep doing this!

When Ross Parker and Hughie Charles wrote the WWII hit song, *We'll Meet Again*, I wonder if they knew how timeless those words would be. Sea duty! They were going to apply to Carol and I for a long time.

We'll meet again, don't know where, don't know when.

But I know we'll meet again some sunny day.

— 12 —

THE WEDDING

RON SAT IN THE SMALL chair at the end of the low finger-painting table with his knees tucked under his chin He was in dress blues, his white gloves smoothed on the corner of the table, his sword balanced across his lap, at the ready, to defend us in this Lilliputian Land. We were two armed Gullivers who had invaded the children's Sunday school classroom of the Roosevelt Methodist Church. It was midafternoon on the Ides of March 1958. Carol and I were about to be married.

Ron and I had already circled the gallery. Cloned artwork of wax crayoned stick-figure families, holding hands, dangled from a string across the top of the blackboard. The families posed in front of a small church that had an oversized steeple with a cross twice the size of the building. A large spiked yellow sun shone from a corner of every paper. Ron and I were shooting toy cars back and forth on the finger-painting shuffleboard. How much more time?

Between the ship's schedule and winter weather, I hadn't seen Carol much since last fall. I had spent the last couple days at the Berlinghoff's helping with what few chores I could. Ron arrived Friday night. He and I trooped off to a motel after a mildly raucous gathering at the house following the wedding rehearsal.

The Ides of March, the date of the infamous assassination of Julius Caesar, was not our first choice for a wedding date. Nana, whose attendance was in question up until a month before, objected because, "No good Catholic would get married during Lent." The date was set by the realities of ship operating schedules and usher availabilities. With three ships and six officers involved, that in itself was not easy.

The ancient Romans, who named the month after their God of War, Mars, celebrated with festive military parades and ceremonies. I thought a military wedding was a perfect setting.

Ron checked his watch as he peeked out the classroom door. Organ music soared into the room. Paul Knudsen, a friend and fellow teacher of Carol's sister, El, had offered to do the music. He was a Harvard music major and occasional concert pianist whose father was the first violinist and concert master for the Boston Pops Orchestra. It was special for us to have him to play.

Ron turned and said, "We'd better get ready. The guys will be seating the families in a minute."

I could see the church was nearly full. There was a light snowfall yesterday that left a lingering chill. Most of the ladies wore open spring coats that displayed their pretty dresses. My seven-year-old twin sisters, Bonnie and Connie, sat in the front row, giggling, stealing the show, with their flaming red hair, patent leather shoes, and toothless grins.

The last few women glided in step on the white gloved uniformed arm of young officers as they ushered them to their seats. Their gold swords jingled like spurs, as they slow-marched to the pews. All four ushers were classmates: De Combs, one of my summer roommates; Hank Harris, a shipmate of De's on the *Ingham* in Norfolk; and Terry Gloege and Don Super, who were shipmates on the *Half Moon* out of Staten Island.

De seated Carol's mother. Then, the other ushers followed with the bridesmaids: Joyce Armbruster, Carol's best friend, and my sister, Pat. When the maid of honor, El, was in place, Ron said, "OK, buddy, this is it." With big smiles, we squeezed off a double handshake and moved into position with the line of ushers.

Paul began Incidental *Music OP61*, which Mendelssohn had written to open Act VI of Shakespeare's *A Midsummer Night's Dream*. We knew it as *Here Comes the Bride*. Commanded by the familiar musical crescendo, everyone turned in unison to watch Carol and her Dad pass in review. Eye contact brought smiles to everyone and tears to many. Her father handed her off to me and took his seat.

Thank God for rehearsals. My mind went into automatic. I just followed the Reverend Cardwell, and presume I said and did what I was supposed to— when I was supposed to. When Paul blasted into the joyful recessional music, and the ushers escorted the wedding party out of the church, I knew it was over.

Protocol demanded that only the newlywed couple be honored by passing under the arch of swords. When everyone was outside, Carol and I stood at the top of the church steps while ushers got into position. We paused for effect, like royalty waving at their cheering subjects, until De barked his commands.

"Officers, draw... swords. "

"Present... swords."

Carol and I moved quickly down the steps, flashing steel blades arched above us, dodging the rice thrown by loving subjects, to a borrowed Oldsmobile, and Ron drove us to the dinner reception at the Coral House in Baldwin, New York.

Cake cutting ceremony

It was a small event with a few relatives and friends. I was pleased that Bob Taylor, my old high school buddy, had made it; he was the only one from Bradford other than my family. Carol and I circulated together, both meeting family and friends we had never met. The twins, of course, circulated well, holding everyone's flowers, having a great time. I think there were as many pictures taken of them as the bride.

I laughed every time I heard Carol's dad tell his story about purchasing liquor from my classmates, Don and Terry, at outrageously cheap prices. They had managed to bring top notch Canadian whisky back from Argentia, Newfoundland, on their last Ocean Station Patrol.

"...there I was standing on that Staten Island pier in broad daylight, next to my open car trunk, catching bottles of Canadian Club, and Royal Crown as they pitched them to me from the deck of the *Half Moon.*" He laughed. "I felt like a bootlegger."

We said our goodbyes, and Ron drove us to Carol's house where we changed clothes and switched to our own car. We stayed in a nearby motel in Farmingdale, Long Island. The following morning we were on our way to Norfolk, Virginia. We planned to spend our first night in our own apartment, and then drive on to Florida the next morning for our honeymoon.

We arrived in Norfolk well after dark. I parked in front of 1615 Alsace Avenue. The white painted lawn sign in front of the office across the street told us we had arrived at *Lafayette Shores,* one of many named housing complexes in Norfolk. They all bore folksy names like: *Aragona Village, Lynhaven Shores, and Pinewood Gardens.* The yellow bug light over our neighbor's doors blended with the night light from the office window casting an eerie glow on the wood framed six-plex. I unlocked the door, turned to Carol, who was still standing by the curb, and said, "Well, here we are, babe...our first home."

"I'm anxious to see it."

I brought the luggage in and went back for our "survival kit" consisting of a few pots and pans, bed linens, and enough necessities to hold us for a few days.

The tour of the apartment didn't take long. There was a bathroom and two bedrooms upstairs. The first floor was one long room with a turn-around sized kitchen squeezed in to the left of the dining area which was furnished with a chromed Formica table and four straight chairs. The under-the-stairs storage space served as a closet. The living area was furnished with a wrought iron day bed with two rectangular foam back-cushions (which never stayed up,) and one nearly matching side chair. They were placed on the edges of an ugly green carpet that served to outline the living room.

We got an early start on our honeymoon trip with a quick breakfast in a nearby diner. We filled up with gas at the adjoining Shell Station. As we pulled away from the tanks, Carol said, "Look at the restroom signs. I can't believe it!" There were three separate bathrooms with painted doors: Men, Women, and Colored.

"Hard to believe, isn't it," I said. "Catch the two outside water fountains: White Only, and Colored. Welcome to the South."

We took the most direct route down the coast. Route 17 passed through small beach towns with gaudy wooden signs pushing swimming pools, beach towels, sun glasses, and easy access to the beach. We cruised through Jacksonville, NC, Pawley Island, and Mt. Pleasant, until we cut inland through Charleston and on to Savannah where we stayed the first night.

Pulling out of the parking lot, headed for another long day, I asked Carol, "Have you driven this trip before with your parents?"

"Only once. I flew down when I dropped out of college. They were in a motel on the west coast. I drove back with them. I do remember this red Georgia clay along the roadway, though."

"Well, I drove it once with three guys the summer after our junior year in high school. I sure didn't remember it as this flat and boring. Maybe it will get more interesting on US 1 and A1A when we cut further out to the coast." It did not. We still had a long way to go.

We finally arrived at *Sea Castle on the Ocean* in Pompano Beach, our honeymoon spot for the week. The motel was a single story off-white stucco building with a three-floor-high tower added to one end. Their post card pictured the small pool and the "tricky putting green." We shared a small private beach with a few other vacationers. *Sea Castle* advertised as "one of the finest resort motels...in a quiet friendly atmosphere...with heat, optional air conditioning, and a television lounge." The post card added that they catered only to "select clientele." Thinking about the dual water fountains in Norfolk, I doubt that that meant "No Canadians."

The first morning at the beach, Carol said, "Do you think anybody knows we are newlyweds?"

I laughed. "Of course they do, Carol. You can pick the other ones out, why not us?" We had only a week before the curtailing ship's schedule would force us back north. We spent most of the time on the beach or sitting around the pool. We did manage side trips to local attractions including the famous water ski show at Cypress Gardens. It was cold the day we saw the show. The skiers performed in wet suits. Carol strolled in the gardens amid the smudge pots in her long gray winter coat.

The week passed quickly. Before heading north, we treated ourselves to a souvenir, a genuine two-humped Florida cypress knee lamp, complete with beige lamp shade. It sat on one table or another in our multiple homes, for the next forty years.

We made it home to Norfolk a week before the *Absecon* sailed on Ocean Station Patrol. That barely gave us enough time to personalize the apartment. Expeditions to nearby shopping centers and a single pass through the center of the city served as our familiarization tour. Carol fleshed out our inventory of housekeeping items, and then led the charge for our first major purchase. "Rich, it's going to be bad enough with you being gone for six weeks. Can't we please get a television set?"

The new Zenith 19" black-and-white TV, complete with rabbit ears, made the apartment more homelike. We bought a small pine bookcase from The Unpainted Furniture Store to serve as a room divider, providing at least the appearance of a dining and living room. After two coats of amber shellac, it was a perfect match for the cypress knee lamp. The lamp cast a warm light through its tan shade. The living room was actually quite cozy, especially with the lava lamp added to the top of the TV.

We took one night to review our financial situation.

I said, "Sorry, but I think we better wait for the washing machine." We had started our marriage with combined savings of a little under a thousand dollars. "I think we had better keep a little in reserve."

"I know. That's OK. I can get along with the scrub board for a while." She never blinked. Carol did all the wash, including the bed linens, by hand with a small scrub board stuck into the kitchen sink. My salary as an Ensign was $355.66 a month. We sprung for a washing machine for her birthday in October.

Carol drove me to the base and stood at the head of the pier with a few other wives to watch the ship sail. My mooring station was on the forecastle, so we could easily see each other. The single long blast of the ship's horn, followed by three short, signaled to ship traffic that we were backing away from the pier. There was something about that mournful blast that pushed all the emotions of separation into your throat. Carol waved until we were out of sight. I thought about how strong she was. I had just left my twenty-year-old new bride in a strange city, not knowing anyone, with two hundred dollars cash, the keys to the car, and a map of the city. "I'll see you in six weeks." It was a tough patrol for both of us.

A lot of families were on the pier for our homecoming; wives wore big smiles, and children shouted, "Daddy! Daddy!" Carol met and mixed with some of the officers' wives in the wardroom while we cleared up ships business.

As we got into the car for the drive home, Carol sidled next to me, misty eyed, and hugged my arm. Talking about the day we left, she said, "I will never, ever, go to see your ship sail away again." She didn't.

"....but you were on the ship and I was on the shore....Harbor Lights."

—13—

WELCOME ABOARD

PEOPLE USUALLY HAVE TIME TO adjust to life changing events. They get through them one at a time. Carol and I ploughed through three major events in one year; we married, moved to a distant city, and embarked on a Coast Guard career.

The engagement period gives couples time to ease into marital adjustments, to make plans, deepen their love, and confirm compatibility. Carol and I were short changed. Our six month engagement was interrupted by winter weather and the *Absecon's* patrol schedule, to say nothing of long distance. We had but a handful of weekend visits.

After we got married, we adjusted easily to the simple things. We negotiated what kind of TV we watched, which side of the bed we slept on and whether the toilet paper unrolled from the top or the bottom. More discussion was required to iron out more dissimilar traditions: when would we put up the Christmas tree? What kind of food do we like? And, more importantly, could either of us cook it? It takes time to build family traditions.

I remember our first Thanksgiving. We had invited our best man, Ron McClellan, for dinner. Carol spent a long day preparing the perfect turkey. Her voice came from the kitchen, "Come see how it looks."

I stuck my head around the doorway. She was bent low to the floor, a twisty turban holding her hair up as she basted the perfect brown turkey breast. I took a deep breath and swallowed the aroma and pronounced, "It is perfect! God that smells good, babe. I'll pour the wine. We're all set."

"Get seated with Ron, and I'll bring everything in."

With a ceremonial flair worthy of a *Saturday Evening Post* cover, Carol paraded the twelve pound bird directly to the prepared spot on the table next to me. I said, "It looks great." After an awkward pause, I said, "Are you going to take it back to the kitchen to carve?"

"What do you mean? I don't know how to carve a turkey. My dad always did it at the dinner table."

"Well, my mom always carved it in the kitchen and brought the platter to the table."

Ron was laughing. He was no help! I picked up the knife, tried to visualize the newspaper's annual turkey carving diagram—and flailed away. When I was done, the bird wasn't pretty, but it tasted great. I reviewed a cheat sheet before the next year's event. I am actually a pretty good carver now.

Like every new couple we faced the big two financial questions: how much money will we have and who's going to handle it? We knew we were going to be on a tight budget. The U.S. Congress established military pay. As an Ensign, my base pay was $222 a month plus a subsistence allowance (for my meals) of $48. Now that I was married, I also received a quarter's allowance of $85.

Technically, I suppose, that was pay discrimination. Given two officers performing equal duties in all respects, if one was married, he made more money. I doubt, however, if anyone ever considered that an incentive to make the trip down the aisle. The government assumed that if you were a bachelor, you could live on the ship. If you chose not to, that was your problem. You were not getting paid for it. We were going to manage our lives on a monthly income of $355.68.

Carol was going to have to manage the daily expenses and keep the check book. The ship' schedule made it impractical for me to handle the household funds. I arranged for her allotment check, which the

Coast Guard mailed directly to her monthly. I kept a minimum of walking-around-money for myself to draw on our once a month cash paydays.

Luckily, Carol had enough working experience and an ingrained conservative approach to money.

We were confident that finances would get better. We lived a happy, however frugal, life. We ate carefully and shopped for the best food prices at the Naval Base commissary. For entertainment, a weekend visit to the Norfolk Zoo was nice, and we watched a lot of TV. We did splurge occasionally when Roy Acres, our Navy neighbor, and I made a midnight run to the new Krispy Kreme Doughnut plant for a dozen glazed, hot out of the oven. Life was good and would get better.

I explained to Carol, "Promotion to Lieutenant (junior grade) is pretty much automatic. I should get that on the first of December. Then we'll be over 2 year's service next June."

"So what will that mean?"

"We should be making $433 a month by next summer."

For our first Christmas, I bought Carol a pair of white sweat socks. I don't remember what she got me. I did make LTJG on the first of December. Carol's mom and dad paid for the new gold striping on my uniform, a much-appreciated Christmas present.

The move to Norfolk, Virginia, proved to be more of an adjustment than either of us had anticipated. While we enjoyed a pleasing southern climate and a welcome touch of big city living, Norfolk was just strange. It felt like there were three distinct cities.

There was Norfolk, the second largest commercial port on the east coast with a population of 200,000. It had cargo and commercial piers, huge shipyards and rail yards sprawled among the peninsulas and islands formed by the tentacles of the Elizabeth and James Rivers. This Norfolk was the hub of Hampton Rhodes, the maritime crossroads of the country. Then, there was the Norfolk of the U. S. Navy, home of the largest naval base in the world. There were over sixty thousand naval personnel and their families serving with the hundreds of ships and aircraft of the Second Fleet. They were the transients, just like us, who lived in apartments and new housing developments for a tour of duty then moved on, or retired and went home to Heartland, USA.

We were a comfortable part of the "Navy Norfolk." There were about a thousand Coast Guardsmen assigned to ships and administrative offices in the Norfolk area. We enjoyed parties and small social gathering with Coast Guard families who we would probably serve with again.

The third Norfolk—the Norfolk of the old south, we never understood. This was home to many who struggled to preserve their Southern image of genteel plantations, peaceful gardens, and magnificent horse farms with gentlemen in gray top-hats and idle ladies in hoop skirts. We were content to live in the naval world and serve the purposes of the maritime commerce world. In two and a half years, I don't think we ever really knew a Norfolk native.

Our first summer in Norfolk, 1958, was one of great civil rights tension. Newspapers, radio and TV were filled with the political battles over ten thousand children who were now receiving no education. It was four years after the U.S. Supreme court ruled in Brown v. Board of Education that schools were to integrated. Norfolk had done nothing. In fact, Virginia had passed a Commonwealth law that permitted continued segregation in the schools. When the Supreme Court overruled the Virginia law and said states could not withhold funding from integrated schools, Norfolk's response was to close *all* their public schools. Combined with our earlier introduction to the three bathroom gas stations, we saw little, if any display of "genteel southern charm."

Adjusting to a Coast Guard career was a bigger adjustment for wives than their husbands. New military wives learned quickly that they had also married their husband's service. The Coast Guard was not just an employer. It was a social mechanism that governs behavior. It was a family imbedded with norms, steeped in history, honored, and respected as traditions. New Coast Guard wives underwent a different experience than a new bride of a University of Michigan engineer who goes to work for Haliburton, or a University of Pittsburgh pharmacist who takes a job with CVS. Neither of them may ever have to adjust to their husband's employer to the same extent as Coast Guard wives need to adjust to the Coast Guard.

The Academy experience did much to prepare me for our military world. It was second nature for me to recognize rank insignias, uniform designations, when to salute, whom to salute, and acceptable behaviors (no holding hands in public). I knew to stop my car if driving on a military reservation during morning or evening colors, or if walking, to stop facing toward the flag location and salute. I knew when to shift sides with my wife in a receiving line for dignitaries and how to make introductions. These protocols were all new to Carol.

Wives did not generally realize that they could be a significant factor in their husband's career. If not in the early years, it certainly was true as you became more senior. It was not unusual to have your superior comment on your wife in your official performance report, particularly as to your potential for promotion or command assignments. One of my reports commented: "Captain and Mrs. Marcott contribute greatly to the development of the CG family. Mrs. Marcott is an active member of the CG Wives Club."

Florence Ridgley Johnson, the wife of a well-known Navy Admiral, had been down this road before. In 1956, she wrote *Welcome Aboard: A service Manual for The Naval Officer's Wife*. Her book was issued to all graduating cadets and was a dog-eared staple in every officer's home. An excerpt:

"Cadets and midshipmen must undergo the transition from civilian to military life; and upon graduation must adjust to a second transition blending both military and civilian social customs, since they will be a part of both. This book will provide guidance for everything from official calls, visits and personal calls, to table manners, weddings, do's and don'ts of conversations, military protocol for ceremonies from change of command to funerals, to boarding ships."

We met our first social obligation when we made our official call on the *Absecon*'s executive officer, Commander (CDR) Ernie Challender and his wife. While I had been aboard for a year, CDR Challender told me that he and his wife would wait until after our wedding and would then be "at home" and wished us to call for dinner.

We both read over the *Welcome Aboard* chapter: Calls, Made and Returned, particularly for the etiquette of calling cards. We both had engraved cards and knew to look for their calling card tray, probably on a side table near the front door. We confirmed that I would leave two of my cards and Carol one. A gentleman calls on everyone in the house; a lady only calls on the lady of the house.

Carol and I call at our formal call on the XO

The social call, actually a pleasant custom practiced in sophisticated society of the 19th and early 20th century, still observable in old movies, had pretty much gone the way of top hats and knickers–except in military society. It was actually a convenient means for military families to meet others and become acquainted with their new surroundings, while still retaining a semblance of a "ranking order."

In a way, I miss calls. There was something civilized and mannerly about them. I dislike how far society has moved away, at times, regrettably, dragging me with it, toward informality. I don't like casual dress for *every* occasion. I'm closer every day to removing ball caps from total strangers who sport them at the dinner table while eating in even the better restaurants.

After one trip around the block to avoid being early, I parked in front of the Commander's house for our social call and dinner. I was wearing my best (only) blue suit, white straight wing tip collar shirt and regimental tie. Carol looked as pretty as ever in a checkered straight skirt and white blouse. With her sparkling eyes and smile, she was going to be an instant hit with the XO and his wife. We moved onto the porch, smiled at each other, took a short breath, and I rang the bell.

The commander answered the door.

"Well, good evening, Marcotts. You must be Carol." He was wearing a blue sport coat, gray trousers, and a plain red tie. Built a little too stocky to cut a neat military figure, the sport jacket fit his grandfatherly image better. He raised one eyebrow, curled his lip into a tight smile and said, "Come in, come in. Welcome."

"Good evening, sir."

"Good evening, Commander," Carol said. "So nice to meet you."

The Commander, his head a little too big and square with loose jowls that bobbled as he talked with his eyes, smiled and completed introductions to his wife, who just entered from the dining room. Mrs. Challender wore an attractive casual dress, her slightly graying hair pulled back in a bun. She flashed a welcoming smile and motioned us to the living room, suggesting cocktails. We all had one. (The book said one was OK.)

The Challenders' homey style and genuine warmth helped us respond comfortably to all the normal get acquainted questions. We enjoyed a pleasant conversation that continued when we moved to the table for dinner. When we were finished, Carol helped clear the table and Mrs. Challender brought out dessert.

Reaching for the coffee pot on the side board, she hovered over Carol's cup, and said, "Of course as a good Coast Guard wife, I'm sure you like coffee."

"Of course, please."

Carol did not drink coffee. Her family did not drink coffee. They never had it in their house. She hated it. It was too late now for me to bail her out. She left her cup until it passed a touch-to-the-lips test while we continued table talk. Then, in a single move, Carol picked up the cup, tipped her head back and drained it to the bottom in several audible gulps like it were medicine.

The always responsive perfect hostess, Mrs. Challender rose and smiling poured her a refill. "I guess you do like coffee."

Carol finished about half of her second cup, in smaller doses this time, obviously feeling it was OK to leave some as a signal that she had had enough.

The Commander escorted us to the door as we thanked both of them for the lovely evening. I surreptitiously placed our calling cards on the small silver tray on the entrance hall table. I had notice several cards on it when we first came in. As we walked toward the car, I turned to Carol with a slight laugh, "What's with the coffee bit?"

"God! That was awful!"

"Hon, you didn't have to do that. You could have just said 'no thank you.'"

"Didn't you hear her? She relates coffee drinking with being a good Coast Guard wife. I didn't want to mess up you career on my first outing. AAUUGH!"

It was all Florence Ridgley Johnson's fault.

Welcome aboard.

USCGC *Cape Knox*
CG 95312

Norfolk, VA

Commanding Officer
February 1959-April 1960

The mission of the 95 foot Cape class patrol boat, was primarily Search and Rescue (SAR) and Law Enforcement (LE). Designed and built by the Coast Guard Yard, in Baltimore, Maryland, there were three distinctive sub-classes that evolved as Coast Guard missions shifted from Anti-Submarine Warfare (ASW) to SAR. The original thirty-five class A vessels were outfitted primarily for shallow draft ASW in the years following WWII. The B class differed by mounting a 40 mm vs. 20mm gun and being fitted with scramble nets, a towing bit, and a large searchlight–all important SAR tools. The C class did not carry the heavy armament.

The *Cape Knox* CG 95312 was a class B patrol boat built in 1955. Prior to 1964, the 95s were simply referred to by their hull number. When named, the CG 95312 became the *Cape Knox*. (For clarity, in the following stories, I have used name and number interchangeably.) The 105 ton steel hulled vessel with an aluminum superstructure had a draft of 6'5" and was powered by four Cummins v-12 engines that gave her a speed of 20 knots. She had a compliment of fifteen, including one officer and two chief petty officers. A limited fuel and water capacity restricted her underway endurance to about a week.

The increased tensions between US and the USSR during the "cold war" added a third mission, Harbor Entrance Patrol (HEP). Every vessel entering a U.S. port had to be identified. It then was assigned an appropriate level of surveillance depending on its connection, and the recentness of that connection, to a Soviet Block nation. The *Cape Knox* shared patrol duties off the Virginia Capes with two other 95s.

—14—

The Calypso

I felt really privileged to get command of the Coast Guard Cutter CG 95312, later named the *Cape Knox*. A seagoing command was a great opportunity. Carol was pleased because the *Cape Knox's* home port was Norfolk, so we weren't going to move. She also had hopes that we might enjoy a little more time together. The *Absecon's* schedule of Ocean Station patrols kept me at sea over 50% of the time.

There were three 95's stationed in Norfolk. My classmate De Combs, who had served on the *Ingham,* commanded one, and the third boat was commanded by D. J. Beasley that I had served with on the *Absecon.* We rotated operating schedules over a three week period: one week underway at the Capes standing HEP, a week of SAR standby at the Navy Pier in Little Creek, VA, and then a maintenance week at our home base in Berkeley. The normal standby status was B2, which meant we had to be prepared to get underway within two hours.

The operational rules during the Cold War in the late 1950's required all commercial vessels bound for the U.S. to provide the Coast Guard Captain-of-the-Port (COTP) at least twenty-four hours advance notice of their arrival. They had to be positively identified, categorized, and placed under the appropriate level of surveillance. A Coast Guard team conducted this mission at the entrance to the Chesapeake Bay, specifically, the underway HEP vessel, a Coast guardsman at Cape Henry Light with long range binoculars, and another man aboard the pilot station where commercial vessels picked up a licensed pilot to navigate the Baltimore or Hampton Roads channels. For the most part, it was not difficult for the team to identify incoming shipping.

However, if a ship did not take a pilot aboard and the weather prevented direct contact, she was classed as "unidentified." She became "unexpected" if she also had not given proper notice to the COTP. Both cases almost always involved the HEP vessel.

Chasing an unidentified ship in dense fog is not for the fainthearted. To intercept, you intentionally establish what is aptly known as a collision course. The U.S. Navy, exempt from reporting rules, rarely reported their arrival or radioed anyone, and they normally did not use a pilot. So, if you couldn't see them, you had to chase them down. On more than one occasion, I had established a high speed collision course with a blip on the radar, only to intercept a fast-moving U.S. Navy destroyer that loomed out of dense fog like a gray ghost pop-up, and the white lettered name of the ship, burst into focus. I have often wondered what the Navy bridge watch was thinking as they plotted my approach.

My "at sea" time on *Cape Knox* was actually greater than the 50% underway time on the *Absecon*, with the added disadvantage of never knowing when you were going out or how long you would be gone. So life was a little hectic, but most of our HEP days were routine.

A notable exception was the day I "arrested" Jacques Cousteau.

We were anchored in Lynnhaven Inlet. The bay was calm with long easy swells. The cook, so happy with the calm weather, was even singing—not the kind of sound we normally heard coming from the galley, certainly not in rough seas. No kicking the oven door, banging pots, and cursing a loud string of creative Southern epithets. Petty Officer Barker, my Quartermaster, was on the bridge making chart corrections, when the FM radio crackled alive.

"Coast Guard HEP, this is Cape Henry. We have one unidentified vessel approaching from the east: dark hull, white superstructure, with exposed deck machinery, approximately 150 feet long. She's crossing just south of Kiptopeke at Cape Charles turning toward the Baltimore channel." That meant she was about fifteen miles away and well outside the normal approach to Thimble Shoals Channel—too far to make a visual identification.

"Roger that," Barker answered. "This is CG 95312 responding from Lynnhaven anchorage." I heard him call away the anchor detail and I left the paperwork on my cabin desk and headed for the bridge. By the time I got there, the anchor was coming up, and the engines were ready to go.

"What do we have, Barker?" I asked.

"Unidentified, heading for Baltimore Channel, Captain. You can barely see her with binoculars because of the haze."

"When we get the anchor up, set up an intercept at two thirds speed for now."

"Aye, aye, sir." It was a simple stern chase. She was plotting dead ahead making only seven or eight knots. I increased speed to full, and the *Cape Knox* responded, pitching slightly into the swells.

As we closed to binocular range, I could see that she indeed had a lot of topside deck equipment, several being small cranes. One of the larger cranes took nearly all the space on the open fantail. I finally made out the name, *Calypso.* I called it in and Group Norfolk confirmed that she was "unexpected." I could see nobody on deck, and as I moved the binoculars to the yard arm on the single mast, a blue, white, and red vertical flag filled my binocular lens. Then it hit me, could this be? <u>The</u> *Calypso*? French Flag?

"OK guys, I think we've got something here. This might be Jacques Cousteau, the oceanographer," I announced. We slowed to match the *Calypso* speed as we came along side, standing off about twenty yards. I grabbed the bullhorn. "On the *Calypso*! This is the United States Coast

Guard. You must stop your engines, slowly move out of the channel, and come to a complete stop. This is the United States Coast Guard."

They responded immediately, and I followed suit, standing clear, but moving out of the channel with them. As we both came to a dead stop and started drifting, a tall gangly man moved from the wheelhouse to the port deck, which was at about the same level as our ship's deck. Now only about twenty feet apart, I could see he was about fifty years old, and had a sharp angular face made leathery from years of outdoor exposure, set off by lightly tinted aviator sunglasses that rested atop his dominant nose. He had a generous amount of swept-back graying hair. I had no doubts now. "Captain Cousteau?" I ventured.

"Yes, Captain, I am Jacques-Yves Cousteau."

"Sir, the Coast Guard did not receive advance notice of your intentions to enter U.S. waters, which is required by our law 24 hours' notice. I am sorry for the delay, but you may go no further until your agent has filed."

"Thank you, Captain. My navigator suspected that may be the problem. This was a late decision to divert to Washington, DC, for a meeting with the *National Geographic* people. We neglected to file. I am sorry. We have already made the necessary contacts and the request should be processed soon."

"Thank you Captain. You may remain adrift if you think it will not take long, or move a little further east of the channel and anchor. Either way, I must stay with you until you are cleared. Your choice, sir." I had seen him enough on TV, that I was not surprised how easily he used English.

We stood on our main decks, chatting in a most casual way about some of the *Calypso*'s equipment and its use for oceanographic research. To my surprise, I discovered that she was built in Seattle, Washington, as a British yard minesweeper, decommissioned after the war in 1947, and refit for Cousteau as a research vessel in 1950.

My crew by now had joined me on the main deck and were taking in the conversation and living in the moment of meeting Cousteau in the middle of Chesapeake Bay. Captain Cousteau explained that the *Calypso* only made 10 knots, and carried a crew of 25. The cranes on the fantail were for moving diving bells, scientific equipment, as well as a small boat.

We received message traffic in less than an hour that cleared them to proceed to Washington, DC. I said goodbye, and my whole crew waved as he pulled back into the Baltimore Channel on his way to the Potomac River. So, maybe I didn't "arrest" Jacques Causteau, but I "pulled him over."

"Let's head back to Lynnhaven Anchorage, Chief," I ordered.

At the end of the day, back at anchorage, the setting sun was building a golden backdrop silhouetting the Norfolk and Newport News skyline. The diehard fishermen in the crew claimed their favorite spots on the deck and made a distant cast, hoping for the best, as they buzzed about the *Calypso* and Jacques Cousteau. Chief Miller and I, both with freshly-filled pipes, leaned against the after rail enjoying the evening and watching the crew. "Well, Captain, I think the troops had a good day today."

"I think we all did, Chief. It's not every day you get to 'arrest' Jacques Cousteau."

—15—
THE MINNIE V.

THE BUZZER JARRED ME AWAKE. It came from the sound powered phone that hung on the bulkhead only a foot from my head. The loud grating tone was overkill! At sea, I never slipped beyond the first stage of sleep. I didn't know any commanding officer who did. The CG 95312 was my first command. At twenty-four, I was the only officer assigned to the 95-foot patrol boat in Norfolk VA, a busy port with lots of Search and Rescue (SAR) action. We were underway near the entrance of the Chesapeake Bay on our second day of a routine Harbor Entrance Patrol (HEP). I grabbed the receiver.

"Captain!" An automatic response. I was already fully awake and alert.

"Captain, this is Barker on the bridge. The *Cherokee* has lost her tow! She's about five miles northwest. She says there are five men in the water. I just changed course to head to her." The routine HEP patrol was about to end.

"Very well, I'm on the way. What speed are you making?"

"I'm bringing numbers 3 and 4 on line now, engines 1 and 2 are running fine, Captain. Coming up to 15 knots."

"Very well." I had just hit the sack an hour ago, leaving First Class Quartermaster Barker on the bridge. He was an experienced underway Officer of the Deck (OOD) and I had confidence in him.

My feet barely hit the deck when I heard the familiar start-up whine of the two Cummins v-12s that roared to life just like the big-rig truck engines that they were. Sitting on the side of my small bunk, I grabbed my pants, which were always at the ready within arm's reach on the chair. As I threw on my shirt, I quickly became aware that the Bay had really kicked up since I'd gone went to bed. The weather report had not been good, but a squall line had moved in more quickly than anticipated. This damned snap-rolling 95 would get the best of me yet. She was sure living up to her reputation for giving you a bouncing ride. Grasping parts of bolted down cabin furniture to maintain balance in the near dark glow of the red night-light, I plowed into my shoes, grabbed my foul weather jacket, and bolted for the bridge.

"Captain's on the bridge!" shouted the young seaman on the helm, feet wide apart to keep his balance, struggling a bit to stay on course as the increased speed now had us porpoising into swells while yawing five degrees to each side. It was like the Chesapeake Bay wanted to deter us from our mission.

"Ever been a bronc rider?" I kidded as I moved behind the helmsman to check the compass.

"No, sir."

"Well, you are now. Just hang on, you're doing fine. Where's the OOD?"

"Starboard wing, sir."

As soon as I stepped outside, I knew this was not going to be an easy night. The swells were running about five feet and the deeply overcast night sky merged into an inky sea insuring damned near total darkness. With no visible horizon, it was like walking into another dimension of total blackness interrupted only by randomly blinking buoy lights as they bobbed into and out of sight in the swells. I knew it was going to take me a few minutes for my night vision to adjust. Had I come out of a white light, it could have taken twenty.

"What's up, Barker?"

"Sir, the *Minnie V.* is a fifty-seven foot fishing vessel out of New Jersey with five men on board. She was 45 miles northeast of Chesapeake Light

Ship yesterday afternoon when she lost power and called for help. The 95 footer from Chincoteague responded and took her in tow at 1730. The *Cherokee* relieved the 95 at 2000 last night."

I glanced at the chart house clock. It was almost 0200. "So what happened?"

"I saw the *Cherokee* steaming in toward the entrance to Thimble Shoal Channel showing towing lights and I couldn't see a tow," Barker continued, showing a flash of humor despite the seriousness of the situation. "Their Quartermaster and I are good buddies and we often practice flashing light when we're in port together at Berkley Base. I hopped on the light, thinking I'd pull his chain about showing the wrong running lights and flashed, 'Where is your tow?' The *Cherokee* answered immediately with an urgent voice message that they needed our help. They didn't even know about it until I signaled them. They're guessing the tow sank with five men on board."

The *Cherokee*, a 205 foot ocean-going tug that the Coast Guard inherited from the Navy, had a stellar history that went back to WW II when assigned to the North African invasion task force. Despite her age, she had been well maintained over the years and was more than up to the task. She was lowering her small power boat now, and was scanning the dark bay waters with her large search light.

"Sound the general alarm, Barker," I ordered. "All hands to search and rescue stations."

The klaxon pitch of the general alarm quickly brought everyone on deck. Despite the ungodly hour, the fifteen man crew, stumbling to gain equilibrium on the pitching deck and groping for their clothes, were at their stations—manned and ready—in three minutes. There were extra men on the bridge, the deck force had dropped a scramble net over each side—several were there to help survivors— the search light was manned, and the engine room crew was at full force. The SAR and man overboard drills we routinely held were paying off.

"It's going to be hell seeing anyone in this sea, Skipper," the chief boatswain mate yelled over the howl of the wind. "It's bad enough seeing anything as small as a bobbing head in daylight with good weather, let alone in crap like this."

Chief Miller was right. The waves were now five to six feet, and the passing squall was blowing rain in our faces. Trying to see anything in the narrow search light beam was like looking for the edge of the road at night in a blinding snow storm through your car's high beams. It was going to take an ordained stroke of luck to save any of these guys.

"Chief, make sure everyone is really concentrating out there. With these water temperatures, any survivors will be exhausted, if not unconscious, in a little over thirty minutes, and they've already been out there awhile."

Then the bow lookout bellowed, "Target in the water, two points off the port bow, 50 yards." He had caught a glimpse of a small object as the narrow searchlight beam swept over it. Our cook, who was manning the searchlight, quickly followed the lookout's outstretched arm, scanning slowly, as we headed in that direction. Suddenly, the light caught the object as it bobbed in and out of sight.

"I've got the Conn," I shouted. I was taking control of the ships movements.

"Cap'n's got the Conn," echoed an unknown bridge voice.

"Barker, take the helm! Come left to the target! Helmsman, go down to the main deck and give a hand."

"Aye, aye, sir. I've got the helm!" Barker instantly responded as he grasped the wheel from the helmsman.

"Aye, aye, sir." The helmsman took off, bouncing off the bulkheads and grasping for his balance as he made his way down the short wet ladder to the main deck. We were heading directly for it now, and I could just make out what looked like a small wooden nail keg.

"All ahead one-third, come right ten degrees." Instantly reacting to reduced speed, I could feel the tenseness in the young crew and see it in their faces. Ignoring their own plight on a wet deck, soaking wet, they went about their jobs. Everybody wanted to get this one right.

"Ahead one-third, right ten degrees," Barker repeated. "Steady course 290."

"Barker, if you can see that keg now, approach slowly and see if you can come along side, But keep it at least 10 yards off to port."

"Aye, aye, sir. I've got it."

As we neared the bobbing keg at a slower speed, we sloughed into the trough of the waves. The broadside swell gave us much greater roll, but the good news was the rescue team was now in the lee of the deckhouse, reducing the wind and rain in their face. With barely enough speed to maintain steerageway, we were taking twenty-five degree rolls while being lifted up and down as each swell passed beneath us.

An excited report from the bow lookout rose through the sound of the wind in the ships rigging, "Cap'n, there's a man holding on the back of that keg!"

Damn, what a break! We were already set up on a good approach. I ordered Barker to keep her so and the deck force to get some life rings to him.

Still struggling just to stand in the wet, slick three foot space between the rail and the deckhouse, the deck crew was at the ready. As we approached, I saw two orange life rings sail into and out of the searchlight beam, over the keg with the trailing lines, landing right across the keg and the man's arm and shoulders. Two perfect throws! He didn't move! As we slipped by, within 20 feet of him, the deck force desperately pleaded across the foreboding water gap to grab the lines. "For God sakes, man, take the line, take the line!"

The chief ran to the bridge. "Captain, he's scared to death. Says he can't swim, and he just knows he'll drown. I can see it in his eyes, Captain, he's never going to let go of that keg. We're going to have to get close enough to help him onto the scramble net." The net, made of sturdy manila line woven into a grid with a heavy wooden 4 x 4 to hold the bottom down, was already in place.

"Right full rudder, all ahead two thirds."

"Aye, aye, sir. Right full, all ahead two thirds," Barker responded.

As we came about, the net 4 x 4 was pounding against the side of the ship like an out of control pendulum swinging in and out from the ship's side with each roll. As we knifed through the swell and waves, our flared bow insured that the now violent pitch would flood the deck with a soaking spray right up to the bridge ports with each diving plunge.

"We've got to go around again, Barker. Make it quick," I ordered. "Chief, keep that searchlight on him and everyone pointing as we come about. If we lose him now, he's done for."

I made a quick check of the chart and the radar. We were drifting closer to Thimble Shoal Channel. Thank God the radar screen was clear. At least for the moment we were alone, except for the *Cherokee* and her small boat who were busy with their own search. If these men drifted into the channel, they were going to be in great danger of being run over by an incoming freighter who would never see them. I had to plan the second approach very carefully. I knew I'd only have one more chance.

As we came about, Barker slowed to one third and centered up on the keg. The approach was good, but we were going to be lying in the trough again and I'd have to let the boat drift down and put the man and the keg right alongside. That worried me. The worst place you could be with a violently moving ship was right alongside. With our quick roll and pitch it was clearly possible to harm (if not kill) him with the 105 ton ship if we couldn't quickly get him onto the net. I did not want to put Barker in the position of making the final approach. "I'll take the helm, Barker, you stand right on that port wing and let me know how we're doing."

"Aye, aye. Cap'n's got the helm."

The approach was going to work. I rang up all stop, then back one third to stop the ship right alongside the fisherman and his keg, about 20 feet away, still rolling a lot, dead-in-the-water. The wind and swell moved us closer, the man clearly hanging on for dear life. I could no longer see him below the deck line.

Barker continued his running commentary. "He's right alongside now, Cap'n. He could grab the net, but he's still afraid to let go of that keg. He's right against the ship!"

Suddenly our most experienced deck hand, Seaman Francesco Lucchese, who everyone called Casey, leaped over the rail and onto the landing net. Grasping the net with one hand and leaning out as far as he could stretch, Casey grabbed the man's thick woolen shoulder. While he held tightly, other men tried to get a line down to him with no success. The man, still fighting to cling to his keg, growing wearier, strength giving out in the cold, was gasping to expel the swallowed cold, putrid seawater.

Casey, along with the fisherman precariously in his grasp, was now getting forced two feet under the water every time we rolled to port. "He's too heavy!" Casey struggled while gasping to take a big breath, shaking the stinging salt water from his eyes as they were both lifted above the surface on the starboard roll. The Chief had plan Bravo. "Get that mooring line on the forward deck—now! Move!"

Seaman Guthrie, not long out of boot camp, jumped at the chief's order and ventured forward. As soon as he stepped out of the lee of the pilot house, he was caught by a gust from the North that I thought was going to sweep him off his feet. Turning to face into the wet wind, weirdly shaping his upper body like a spoon, he leaned into it, defying nature at a Charlie Chaplin angle to the deck. With crab-like steps, Guthrie inched sideways until he could snatch the mooring line. Then, wide eyed with his first seagoing adventure, he practically leaped back to the chief, mooring line in tow.

"Give me the eye," the chief cried, reaching for the line while grabbing Guthrie to keep him from tumbling on the slick deck. He passed Casey the large eye permanently spliced into the 3" nylon line, normally used to slip over a bollard on the pier when mooring the ship in port. "We need to make a horse-collar sling, Casey. See if you can get this over his head and under both arms," the chief bellowed over the persistent howl of wind and the banging 4 x 4.

Somehow, with whatever strength Casey had left, he managed to get the sling in place and convince the man to let go of his keg. "OK. Great! Now, heave around and get him on deck," the Chief ordered as he joined the other three deck hands trying to pull this hulk aboard. Barker was faithfully giving me a blow by blow, with all the excitement of a boxing ring announcer, but there was little I could do now but hold a steady heading and pray for slow, shallow rolls.

Nothing moved! They couldn't budge him. Fatigue was setting in as the rescue team fought against the fisherman's weight while struggling to keep their own footing.

"Get Kirsh up here—quick!" the Chief screamed.

Kirsh, our electrician, was at his SAR station in the engine room. He was big enough to make any NFL defensive line coach drool. He looked like a Kodiak bear crawling out of the warm engine room den. He didn't need to be briefed on his function. Jumping onto the front end of the line, his size and strength gave everyone hope again.

The Chief wasted no time now. "Every time we roll to port, the line goes a little slack, when we do, heave around quickly. I'm going to take a stopping turn around the bit when we start back to starboard so we can hold what we got. We've just got to inch him in." Roll by roll, slack by taut, inch by inch, they moved this giant up the cargo net until Kirsh could reach him. Between Kirsh and Casey they managed to roll him over the gunwale and onto the deck.

Kirsh, gasping to breathe, sounding like a runaway steam engine, dripping wet, knelt over the beached whale of a coughing, spitting, but smiling fisherman. Between gulping pants, Kirsh choked out, "God damned, man, I'm big, but just for the record—how much do you weigh?"

The fisherman tried to raise a hand to shake Kirsh's and smiled. "Three hundred twenty-four pounds, if you don't count all my wet wool foul-weather gear."

Clifford Wescott was a lucky man, as was the rest of the crew of the *Minnie V.*, rescued by the *Cherokee*, now all safe and together in the Norfolk Public Health Hospital. As reported the next morning in the *Virginian Pilot*, the Captain of the *Minnie V.* said, "Once we started to take on water, we sank in two and a half minutes."

They had all struggled, but survived in the cold and stormy Chesapeake for thirty five minutes.

To fish again another day, I'm sure.

—16—

OUT OF THE BLUE

THREE DAYS AGO, THERE HAD been another mid-air collision. The 5th
CG District Rescue Coordination Center (RCC) in Norfolk, Virginia,
had called off the search for survivors. One pilot's body was recovered
along with his plane. Unfortunately, mid-airs involving small private aircraft off the Atlantic Coast were not unusual summertime incidents. Most
of them were spotter planes, hired to locate large schools of Menhaden,
then, guide fishing boats to the catch. It was a competitive business in the
lower Chesapeake Bay and off the coast of Virginia. It was all about fishing
and big money.

It was a late summer afternoon, and the *Cape Knox*, on Bravo-2 status
at the Little Creek Amphibious Base, had just granted liberty. Everyone
except the small duty section was on their way home when RCC called.
Flotsam had been reported fifteen miles off Virginia Beach in the general
vicinity of the recent mid-air. We were ordered to get underway, and
proceed to the reported site and investigate. The OOD started the recall
while the duty section readied the ship for sea. When I arrived home,
Carol had just received the phone call. I headed back into the Norfolk
quitting-time-traffic without even getting out of the car.

I made it back to our pier in half an hour, along with other returning
crewmen. I could hear the quiet rumble of the *Knox*'s four Cummins
engines and barely see a shimmering heat wave rising from the funnel.
They were ready.

As I started up the pier I heard the PA click on. "Captain approaching." At the gangway, I saluted the quarterdeck and the Officer of the Day (OOD) stepped onto the deck. The PA announced, "Captain's aboard."

The OOD returned the salute and reported, "All hands on board, Cap'n. The '312 is ready for sea."

"Very well, let's get underway. Chief Miller, take her out." Chief Miller, the Executive officer (XO), met me at the quarterdeck. He had been aboard only four months, but I valued him as a capable ship handler. When he cleared the pier, he spun the ship expertly to a northerly heading to enter Lynnhaven Inlet Channel that led into Chesapeake Bay. During the slow transit to the Bay, I looked over the chart and planned the first leg. As we cleared the #2 Lynnhaven Inlet buoy, I ordered, "Come right to 090 degrees, increase speed to 12 knots."

I hoped this call was not a false alarm. Nothing plunges crew morale more than being forced to drop dinner, or interrupt an already restricted family life for a false alarm. It was bad enough on a real case, never knowing if you would be back in three hours or three days.

If we had not been on a rescue mission, this could have been a relaxing summer cruise. God knows the normal SAR mission, almost by definition, didn't start with this kind of weather and sea conditions. The sky was clear blue, and the hot summer sun was made tolerable by the refreshing breeze created by our 12 knot speed. The prow split the long slow swells as we peacefully made our way in the flat calm sea. Everybody except the engine room gang was on deck, making preparations for the mission.

I gave the order. "When Cape Henry Light is abeam, Chief, change course to 105 degrees and follow the course to the crash site."

"Aye, sir. Course 105."

"Barker, get this SITREP (situation report) out to the District. SITREP-One: Underway Cape Henry. ETA on scene one hour." When Cape Henry Light came abeam, Chief Miller changed to the new course and I settled in for the smooth ride and started laying out possible search patterns on the chart.

BOOOOMMM!

"Damn, what was that?"

Heads spun toward the sound of the explosion—the sky—and we all knew what it was.

"Cap'n, that jet is in trouble," the Chief said, as he pointed skyward to two Navy fighter planes heading out to sea. There were probably out of Naval Air Station, (NAS) Oceana. One was losing altitude fast. At about 2000 feet, his ejection seat exploded straight up, the powerless plane continued east toward an Atlantic splash down.

A parachute suddenly opened like magic. We watched the pilot descend beneath his white parachute, framed against the blue sky, his yellow one-man raft, tethered to his ankle, bounced in the air beneath him. He was going to splashdown practically at our feet. It was a surreal experience that gave new meaning to "out of the blue." Vacationing hundreds who lined the water's edge at Virginia Beach watched all this unfold.

"If we pick up a little speed chief," I kidded, "I may be able to get right under him. He'll never even get wet."

"Chief, you better get the district on the radio and let them know what's happening," I ordered. "And, see if we can get Oceana on UHF." RCC did not have Ultra High Frequency voice radio, but we did. I thought, *That could be a good thing. I don't need someone in RCC, 15 miles inland second guessing me now.* As the chief managed the radios, I glanced up to see the bailing pilot's wing man circling. I was sure that he had already reported the incident to his home base.

Meanwhile, the chief was struggling to handle two conversations with two separate microphones, one with the district and the other with NAS Oceana. I could hear his frustration with the RCC, trying to make clear what rescue he was talking about—our original mission to examine flotsam from last week's mid-air, or the new one— a man was falling out of the sky! It was just too much. It was turning into an Abbot and Costello routine.

"Chief," I said, "cut the district off, tell them we're too busy right now and we'll explain it all in a few minutes."

He looked surprised, but breaking into a smile, he said, "CG District Five, this is 95312. You do not understand. We are ceasing all communications this frequency now, explanation will follow. 95312 Out!" He loved it, and so did I.

By now, the pilot had hit the water, deftly gotten into his tiny raft, taken his shoes off, and was swatting at flies as if this were all a planned relaxing day at the beach. We had the Navy rescue helicopter visually and were in direct radio contact as I lined up for the approach. The crew had a ladder over the side, ready to assist. The raft was only 200 yards dead ahead. The wing man made a low fly-by executing an impressive wing roll in salute and headed back to NAS Oceana.

"Coast Guard '312, this is Navy Rescue," the chopper pilot's voice shook from the helo vibrations. "When you retrieve our man, we recommend you get underway at 5 knots. Clear your after-deck space and I'll approach from the stern with a sling. Pick-up should be easy."

"Roger Navy Rescue, I'll head 270 degrees, 5 knots. '312 standing by."

I met LTJG Joseph Walter, USN, as he scrambled onto the fantail, wet, but seemingly none the worse for wear. We shook hands. "You OK?" I asked.

"Just a little scratch on the chin, I think from a loose buckle when I ejected."

"Great! What happened?"

"We had just taken off from NAS. I had an explosion and engine flame out at 3000 ft. I tried several restarts, then ejected at 1800. Great to have you guys waiting for me, though." He laughed.

The pulsating thump of the helo blades was getting closer, the approach looked good, the dangling rescue line moved over the fantail. The crew made sure the static line touched the deck first then moved to assist our new Navy friend into the rescue horse collar. Raising his arms to get the collar in place, he shouted over the noisy chopper, "Hey Captain, did you go to the Coast Guard Academy?"

"Yea, I did."

"You don't happen to know Charlie Millradt, do you?"

I couldn't believe it! "Yeah, I do! Charlie graduated in '55, two years ahead of me."

"How about that! Charlie and I went to high school together in Milwaukee. I went to Annapolis, and he went to the Coast Guard Academy." As Joe was being lifted off the deck, dangling like a puppet on a string he yelled, "If you talk to Charlie, tell him I said you Coast Guard guys are OK. Thanks, Cap'n."

Fifteen minutes after his flame out over the Atlantic, LTJG Joseph Walter, USN was back in the NAS Oceana operations center having a cup of coffee.

I turned to the Chief and said, "OK, Chief. Now, where were we when the Navy so rudely interrupted?"

—17—

USS FORRESTAL

IN THE SUMMER OF 1959, Carol and I were looking forward to a rare visit by my mom and dad. He'd managed to get a little time off from chauffeuring his boss, Bradford banker Harvey Haggerty. My mother was a reluctant traveler of the first order. For the most part, family visits happened only if we went home to Bradford. Their trip was timed perfectly. I was scheduled for a one-day underway assignment to escort the USS *Forrestal*, CVA-59, and I knew I could take Dad with me.

I had been the CO of the CG 95312 for four months, and I was looking forward to showing her off. The Navy was moving the 1063 foot-long aircraft carrier from the Norfolk Naval Shipyard in Portsmouth, Virginia, to the open waters of the Atlantic. The first of the "super carriers," the *Forrestal* had a beam over 130 feet, and her slanted deck spanned a width of 250 feet. Her sheer size prohibited anything else in the Elizabeth River channel at the same time.

No small operation, the Coast Guard had already shut down all commercial and private vessel traffic on the rivers until the huge carrier reached the Chesapeake Bay. The *Cape Knox* was to keep all the small boat traffic clear of the evolution all the way to Hampton Rhodes.

It was a beautiful sunny clear day. I parked the '57 Mercury in the CG parking lot at Berkeley Base, and Dad and I made our way to the pier. The crew had the ship ready to get underway as soon as we got aboard.

"Take in lines 1, 3, and 4. Hold no. 2." I ordered as line handlers on the pier went into action and my crew responded.

"Two's holding, Captain."

I kicked the port engine ahead just enough to spring our stern clear of the ship moored close behind us. Dad stood on the starboard wing, taking it all in.

"Take in no. 2." I ordered as I backed the starboard engine a little to begin moving slowly astern. We were berthed in close quarters at Berkeley Base, but after a quick shift of the engines, a little rudder action, we cleanly backed into the Elizabeth River, sounding one long blast on the ship's horn to alert traffic that we were moving away from our pier. When in the center of the channel, I came to a stop, drifting, to await the *Forrestal*. "Take the helm, chief," I ordered, as I moved out to the wing with Dad.

"Aye, aye, sir," Chief Miller responded. "I have the helm. Captain's on the bridge."

The river sparkled in the morning sun. Splashes of light were reflected off the high office buildings of the rebuilding downtown. I glanced at the wide grin and sparkling eyes on my dad who stood on the bridge wing with me, his head on a swivel taking it all in. It was so nice to have him by my side.

He moved, gingerly, into the pilot house, glancing at the rubber light shield sitting atop the radar cabinet like a megaphone. Dad ventured a peek into the open face mask, and then leaned back as if to read all the control dials on the gray slanted control panel. "Is this the radar?" he ventured.

"Yes, sir," Barker answered, jumping to the chance to show off a little. "Let me take that cover off, Mr. Marcott, and I can show you what the scope looks like. It's pretty much like what you see on the weather channel on TV." Barker set the light shield on the deck. "The flashing straight line is our heading that shows the direction we are moving. The ship is at the center of the scope."

I watched Dad, who was intrigued, as the faint green glow from the scope crossed his face each time the sweep hand passed our heading marker. Barker went on to point out ships and buoys on the radar screen, then turned to the chart table.

"Over here, Mr. Marcott, I'll show you how we lay our course out to the Chesapeake."

Dad acknowledged this new information with a few nods and 'ahh haas,' not saying much in response. But, he was soaking it up.

I could see the pride and wonder in his eyes as he put on his sunglasses and moved out onto the open port wing of the bridge, a rogue strand of his slicked down red hair rustling a little in the breeze, he looked pretty cool.

The two CG 40 foot patrol boats, assigned to our mini flotilla to keep the hoard of curious small boaters away, checked in for duty. I made radio contact with the carrier which we could see easing from her shipyard berth further up river, a bevy of Navy tugs along her sides.

"USS *Forrestal* this is Coast Guard 95312 standing by off Berkeley Piers to provide escort and keep the channel clear of ship traffic. I have two small boats running with me."

"Roger Coast Guard '312, we are moving away from the dock. Please take position dead ahead at 300 yards." The blind spot created by the four acre overhanging flight deck made it impossible for those on the carrier bridge to see anything ahead on the surface for a quarter of a mile. The top of the mast on the island structure is 20 stories high. This pride of America's sea strength was an attractive drawing card. The two forty boats, darting from side to side of the channel, were as busy as sheep dogs keeping their curious lambs at bay, protecting them from danger.

As we navigated north in the Elizabeth River channel, the Norfolk cargo piers glided past our starboard side. We could see merchant ships loading and unloading tons of material, their webbed cranes bobbing their long necks, like storks, lifted bundles to and from the cargo holds.

Lambert Point Docks, the largest coal shipping point in the Northern hemisphere, loomed into view. Long rows of rusty coal filled railroad cars inched their way, like a columns of black bugs, to the business end of a funnel where they released their West Virginia coal with a thunderous roar and a rising cloud of black dust.

"I can't believe this whole thing," Dad said. "I've never been on a waterfront before anywhere, I can't believe all the activity." He shifted his weight, knees bent a little, stretching to take everything in. "It boggles the mind."

"Yeah, Norfolk is one of the busiest ports in the country, Dad, and we haven't even gotten to the Navy Base yet. Is the *Forrestal* still with us?" I kidded.

He laughed. "Oh yeah, she's still there. Like a floating city."

"She really is. When they have the flight wing aboard, their population is about 6000 men; that's almost half the size of Bradford."

"Damn! That's hard to believe."

"Wow! What ship is that?" Dad asked excitedly, pointing to starboard at the huge glossy black ocean liner, with its trademark bright red double funnels, slightly canted aft, capped with narrow black over white bands.

"That's the SS *United States*. Isn't she beautiful? She was built right here, only seven years ago, in the Newport News Shipbuilding and Drydock, which we'll be passing in a few minutes. She's almost as long as the gray monster astern of us. I've read she was built with a beam of 100 feet so she'd fit through the Panama Canal with two feet to spare on each side."

We continued the "harbor tour." The 40 footers remained busy keeping small sightseeing small boats clear. We moved past the Naval Operating Base with gray silhouettes of ships of the Second Fleet at their piers.

We began our swing to starboard into the wider area of Hampton Roads. The star-shaped red bricks Fort Monroe came into sight just off the port bow. We cruised over the 1862 battle site of the first ironclads, the *Monitor* and the *Merrimack*. This whole Norfolk, Newport News, Hampton area played such a role in the Revolutionary and Civil War, it was hard not to become steeped in the history. Dad was absorbing it all in his quiet way, a small smile here, a question there, binoculars to his eyes and down again. I knew he was having a great day.

As we made the final turn into the Thimble Shoals Channel, the *Forrestal*, on her final straight shot Eastward to the Atlantic, radioed our release. "Coast Guard 95312, this is *Forrestal*. You are hereby released from escort duty, thank you."

"Roger *Forrestal*, our pleasure. Good Luck. This is Coast Guard 95312. Out." We pulled out of the channel to the South and watched the giant war ship head out to sea to prepare for her upcoming six-month tour in the Mediterranean.

Back at home base in Berkeley, the *Cape Knox* secured, Dad and I crossed the parking lot to the car for the trip home through late afternoon work traffic. We walked slowly over the gravel lot, Dad with a hand on my shoulder to steady himself. I knew the ship movement had taken a bit of a toll on his arthritic feet and ankles.

Neither one of us minded the slow traffic that prolonged our ride back to Alsace Avenue, historic things were happening right in our car. Dad sat tall in his seat, his voice strong, a smile broadening his face. Both our hands were moving, as we relived the day, as if to etch the experience into our memories. My dad surprised me with his depth of interest, genuine, and sincere questions and wonder at it all. Our comments were often punctuated with, "Yeah, how about that."

It had been an incredible day for the crippled chauffeur and his skinny kid from the oil-sodden hills of western Pennsylvania. It was a great day to remember—we never had another one like it.

USCG Loran Station Okinawa

Okinawa, Japan

Commanding Officer
August 1960-August 1961

By April 1945, the United States World War II European Campaign was drawing to a close with Germany on the verge of collapse. In the Pacific, however, the Empire of Japan continued to hold up well against our island-hopping strategy toward an assault on the Japanese mainland. The island of Okinawa, the largest of the Ryukyu Islands, strategically located 400 miles south of Japan, became a major objective of our Pacific campaign. It was expected to serve as a staging area for troops and supplies for our final assault on Japan's mainland.

The battle for Okinawa, the last major campaign and the largest amphibious invasion of the Pacific War, proved also to be the bloodiest. It began on April 1, 1945, and the final surrender document was not signed until September 7th. Long before the fighting stopped, engineering construction battalions were transforming the island into a major base for the upcoming operation. Construction of a Coast Guard electronic LOng RAnge Navigation station (LORAN), was included in that effort.

Construction began in May 1945 on the north end of Ikeshima, the northernmost island in a small chain extending off the east coast of mainland Okinawa.CG LORAN Station, Okinawa, went operational in 1 September 1945 and remained in service until July 1964.

LORAN: A long range system of navigation whereby the position of a ship or aircraft is determined by measuring the difference in times of reception of synchronized signals from two fixed transmitters. It was later made obsolete by GPS.

-18-

KHRUSHCHEV CHANGES MY WORLD

IT WAS AUGUST 1960. CAROL and I sat in the American Airlines lounge at Idlewild Airport (JFK International).We talked quietly, isolated in our morose bubble from the faceless people around us. It was hard for me to look at her when we did talk. We had been married a little over two years and we now faced a one year separation.

After twenty-two changes to my orders in the last four months, thanks to Soviet Premier Nikita Khrushchev, I had finally been dropped from the international political whipsaw. I now held orders to be the Commanding Officer of the Coast Guard Loran Station Okinawa, Japan. My footlocker, however, a victim of the fiasco, was aboard a U.S. Navy transport being delivered to the other side of the globe—Naples, Italy.

The garbled PA announcement sounded like they called my flight. I turned in my seat to face Carol, a strained smile on my face. "Remember, although I'm boarding this plane for San Francisco in a few minutes, you cannot believe I'm really going to end up in Okinawa until you get a post card from there." She smiled back weakly, gave me a publically present-able kiss on the cheek, and said good bye. I turned and walked toward the boarding ramp.

It's not that we didn't know this was coming. Every man in my Academy class, except those first assigned to an Icebreaker, was going to draw Loran duty. There were more Loran stations worldwide than we had graduates in our class. Doing the math was easy. We had talked about this before we got married, of course. It's not the kind of surprise you want to spring on your young bride.

I had received orders in early spring of 1960 to be Commanding Officer of the CG Loran Station, Tarumpitao, Philippine Islands. I was to attend a week school for prospective commanding officers (PCO) in Groton, CT. School schedules were coordinated with station relief dates with one exception. One PCO attended a school one cycle ahead of his stations scheduled relief date to insure a trained officer was ready in the wings, should an emergency relief be required.

My orders read in part, "...*unless relief is required elsewhere earlier, report for duty to...*" It was that little phrase, "*unless,*" that added stress. With seventy-five Loran stations spread all over the world, it was possible that with but a moment's notice I could be headed anywhere, from Greenland to the Caribbean, or from Ulithi Atoll to Attu Alaska. After PCO School, I was administratively assigned to the Group Norfolk office until the normal scheduled relief in the Philippines.

I began to focus on Trumpitao. The station was located in a heavy jungle area on the western tip of the island of Palawan. I exchanged letters with the current CO who shared a few photos and gave me a heads-up as to what he found to be important concerns: keeping the jungle from encroaching on the grass air strip, the station's lifeline; preparing for the inevitable raid from hostile Borneo Pirates (an active tribe of headhunters from nearby Borneo); and avoiding the poisonous cobras that were often found on the station, including one wrapped around the door handle of the CO's quarters.

I could prepare for the first two. Keep hacking away at the jungle, and if the pirates came, give them whatever the hell they wanted. It was the King Cobras that gave me pause.

My first change of orders came two days before I completed Loran school. I was now assigned as the PCO of a new Loran C station that the Coast Guard was building at the site of *Rite 3*. That was the classified code name for a secret location that the headquarters message assured me, "I would know when I needed to know." The people at Loran school couldn't even answer my question, "So, do I pack a fur parka or pith helmet and shorts?"

After all the secrecy at school, however, when I got back to Norfolk, my classmate, De Combs, who had commanded one of the other 95 footers, asked me, "So how do you think you're going to like Spain? You lucky dog." I have no idea how De found out where *Rite 3* was. I was going to L'Estartit, Spain, on the Mediterranean coast in the crescent of the Spanish, French, and Italian Riviera. I was to report during the last phase of construction in July and be the CO when it was commissioned. It would eventually be a family station, a two year assignment, and I could bring Carol over probably for the second year.

That is, until the NY *Times* headline on May 1, 1960:

> "*Soviets Down American Plane;*
> *U.S. Says It Was Weather Craft;*
> *Khrushchev Sees Summit Blow.*"

Lieutenant Colonel Gary Powers, USAF, flying a highly secret American spy plane, the U-2, had left a Pakistani air base to fly over the Soviet Union, take pictures of their Intercontinental Ballistic Missile (ICBM) sites, thence to a safe haven in Norway. The USSR, aware of the existence of the U-2, went on high alert and successfully shot down the American spy plane with an improved surface to air to missile.

President Eisenhower issued statements that this was a "weather observation plane" that had navigational problems and inadvertently drifted over the Russian air space. Then Premier Khrushchev, in one of the great diplomatic "gotcha" moves, revealed that he had in fact captured our pilot and his pictures of their ICBM sites. Colonel Powers was now in a Russian prison. The Eisenhower administration, greatly embarrassed, caught spying and lying, needed to lay low, especially after Khrushchev's speech. "...U.S. must not build another military base on foreign soil...."

As the international situation heated, then cooled, the Coast Guard bounced my reporting date from July to August, then to a "to be announced" future date and back again. Our lives were changing, with every headline a quote from one of the two most important leaders in the world.

At one point, Carol and I had actually completed arrangements for the moving company to pick up our household goods. Our phone was shut off, final rent paid, movers were coming in the morning, and my foot locker had been shipped to Naples, Italy, for further transport to L'Estartit. Then we got another postponement until August!

We frantically manned the phones, putting everything on hold for another month. A week later, another change was the last straw for my Group Commander, Captain Scullion. He phoned headquarters and with a successful plea, "For God's sake, let this poor kid leave. He has been bounced around enough. Let him depart here, take twenty or thirty days leave now, and report in to the Third District Office in New York City until this is settled. L'Estartit is going to operate under the Third District then anyhow." Eventually, the movers picked up our household goods to put into long term storage and my mind shifted to the Spanish Riviera.

Carol and I enjoyed a trip home to Bradford for a visit with my family, then to Long Island to visit with her family in Roosevelt. I was expecting to fly out of New York for Naples in a few days and she would stay with her family until I could send for her. I was sitting in her family's den, reading a magazine when...there was a Western Union Telegraph man knocking at the door.

Of course the message was for me, "Report without delay to CCGD3 (p) for change in orders." Carol and I made the short drive to New York

City without comment. We were oblivious to the hectic traffic on the Southern State Parkway, our minds deep in diverse thoughts. We finally arrived at Battery Park where Carol cooled her heels on a park bench while I seethed my way to the third floor of CG District Office. I opened the door to the Office of Personnel and was unexpectedly greeted by a friendly face.

Sitting at the first desk in the personnel office was Yeoman First Class Ken Gard, who once was an Academy classmate. He had enlisted after leaving the Academy at the end of the first year. (*Ken eventually went to OCS and became a CG aviator, retiring as a Captain.*) We greeted each other like long lost brothers. I know I must have looked relieved to see a friendly face.

"The Captain has your orders on his desk, Dick, I'm sending you right in." Then, with a smile and a supporting pat on the shoulder he said, "Don't worry, he's on your side and really upset with HQ."

"Thanks, Ken. It's really great to see you. Who would have thought?"

I entered the Captain's office and barely got, "Good morning, sir," out of my mouth when he rose, came around the desk, and shook hands. He invited me to sit, and then with great ceremony, held my orders at arm's length in front of him and ripped them right in half!

"I wanted you to see that," he chuckled, obviously amused by my wide-eyed gape. He had no idea how much I would have enjoyed doing that myself. "Mr. Marcott," he continued, "I've been on the phone with Headquarters for most of the morning, and I want to apologize for the way you've been bounced around in this affair. This U2 international incident is not going away, and our building program for *Rite 3* has to be put on hold for an undetermined time and I know that leaves you at loose ends. That's not like the Coast Guard, I hope you know that. We're going to start again."

I breathed a little sigh of relief and managed a grin, "Thank you, sir." Then I thought, *Oh God, I hope this doesn't mean I'm going to be stationed in New York City.*

As if the Captain was aware of my anxiety, he added, "The Coast Guard is sending you to Loran Station Okinawa. My yeoman is typing your new orders right now. You also better check with the supply officer who is working to get your foot locker shipped from Naples to Okinawa."

"Thank you, Captain," I managed a smile and, "I know my wife will be as relieved as I am to get this over with."

"Oh, yes, there's just one little problem, Mr. Marcott."

"Sir?"

"The Okinawa station on Ikeshima doesn't relieve until the August cycle, so you're going to have to take another twenty days leave before you go away. Think you can handle that?"

"Yes, sir," I said, with a big smile. "I know she'll be happy. Thank you, sir." I bounded out of his office, his "Good luck" ringing in my ears, and down the stairs to the bench in the park to tell Carol all the news.

I gazed out my window seat in the Boeing 707 across the tarmac to the large terminal windows knowing that Carol was among the crowd watching the takeoff. Cross country flights with the new jet powered passenger planes, only in their second year, still drew a crowd who cheered each takeoff in amazement.

I had a short stopover in San Francisco and a long flight to Honolulu where I met with a few other Loran CO's for a two day logistics briefing from the 14th District engineering staff. Then on to Tokyo and a short welcome from the Commander, Far East Section. His yeoman handed me a piece of paper and said, "Sir, this has instructions in Japanese for you to show the taxi driver. You'll have to catch a local taxi-boat from Yakina Basin to get to your station. Good luck, sir." Finally, I was on the last leg to Okinawa. I thought, *If our marriage stood up through this transfer, we were meant to be.*

At the Tokyo airport I stopped at the magazine counter, picked up a picture postcard of an Okinawan Shinto shrine and its famous Torii Gate and scribbled a short note, "Finally on a plane to Okinawa for last leg. Wish you were here. See you in a year. Love, Dick."

My footlocker arrived in November!

IKESHIMA ARRIVAL

I FINGERED THE SLIM STRIP of paper with the indecipherable Japanese Kanji characters for the umpteenth time. I was about to step into the foreign world of Okinawa armed with nothing but these instructions for a taxi driver to get me to the Yakina village boat docks.

In the terminal at Kadena Airbase, I still felt comfortable in my surroundings. Uniformed military, dependent wives and children, lounged in plastic chairs, flipping pages of English language magazines, while their kids cried for plastic wrapped toys. They were anxious for their flight home to be announced.

I pushed open the double doors with my B-bag and stepped into the hot August sun and saw long line of yellow taxi cabs. The first cab scooted curbside to a tire squealing stop directly in front of me. The driver bounded out, grabbed my bags, threw them into the trunk, and took the paper strip from my outstretched hand. I watched as he fingered the wrinkled sweat-stained two-inch paper strip. I wondered, "Is the Coast Guard the only service too cheap to provide instructions on a full sheet of paper?"

With a wide smile and quick bow, he greeted me good morning, "Ohayo gozaimasu." He wore a collared T-shirt with the company logo over his left pocket and a yellow ball cap. I returned the greeting and tossed my service dress khaki jacket onto the back seat and slid in for the warm ride to Yakina. I knew it couldn't be too far, the whole island of Okinawa is only sixty miles long and Kadena is located at the pinched narrow center.

We moved past Rolling Heights, a beautiful base housing section, toward the main gate. We could have been in any U.S. suburban development with a golf course, nice houses, and green lawns. We passed through the front gate unto a divided boulevard lined on each side with tall royal and date palms. It looked a Florida highway. *These Air Force folks live pretty well!*

The ambiance changed when we turned east onto the narrow Okinawan cross-island road that intersects with highway 58, the main north south route. We drove past business strips with unattractive two to four story block buildings, whitewashed to an eye squinting white. Some had recessed balconies, New Orleans style, with wrought iron fences. Storefronts displayed garish circus-like banners of bright red, yellow, and green Kenja characters advertising their wares.

Street lamp poles sprouted from the narrow sidewalks, far enough away from the curb to be pedestrian hazards. Their lights hung in arcs over the streets. Sagging wires stretched across the intersections with horizontally hung traffic lights, green to red, left to right. Odd mini trucks and bantam cars filled the streets, leapfrogging each other with every change of the light as if they were in a frenzied race to get out of town.

The driver, totally ignoring posted speed limits on the open highway, struggled in his breathy singsong to point out highlights. Unable to understand a thing, I turned my head in the direction of his pointing finger and grunted enthusiastic sounding, "Oh yeah" or 'Umm."

My mind was clogged with survival thoughts. *How will I ever understand these people? Will anyone from the station be at the boat basin in Yakina? If I miss a scheduled departure, will I have to stay overnight? Where? What kind of shape is the station in? What is Ike village like? The people? God, I miss Carol already! How am I going to make it for a year?*

Finally, resigned that these things would sort themselves out, I turned my attention to the landscape. The patchwork of small, garden-sized farms confirmed the view from the plane. As we came to a larger field, I tentatively asked the driver, "Is that sugar cane?"

"Hai! Hai!" he confirmed with rapid head nods. He seemed excited that I had ventured a question and was about to launch into a travelogue. Just then, we capped a rise that revealed a panoramic view of the east coast of Okinawa, exposing a chain of islands on the horizon, a few miles across the small bay, the northernmost being Ikeshima, my ultimate destination.

A thin line of white clouds joined the low islands to separate the blues of sky and bay. It was a scene like a travel brochure that promised an island paradise. A few red roofs and white houses peeked through the green tree clusters as the road curled downhill toward the fishing village of Yakina.

The paradise image was soon destroyed by the unwelcome smell of fishing docks. The soaring temperature and stagnant air did not help. High concrete walls, some topped with low chain link extensions seemed to squeeze the road even more. Cement-block houses, with no pretense of architectural design, ugly stains bleeding through their bad whitewash, stood squeezed together, uninviting in their protected enclaves. The calming panorama was decaying.

The cab driver pointed me to the taxi-boat dock at the end of the long pier.

The docks were busy. Fishing boats, twenty to thirty feet long, were moored the length of the pier. They had low freeboard and open decks. Some had small cockpits on the afterdeck for the engine housing and an open wheel house.

Workers arranged fishing gear in the shallow well-decks while women, squatting on the pier, knees fully bent, feet flat, repaired damaged nets. They could work in this position with broad-brimmed straw hats providing their only shade, for hours on end. One boat was unloading her foul cargo into a miniature truck for transport to market.

The island hopping taxi boat was filling up with passengers and cargo. Men and women in casual kimonos or shorts hauled their shopping trip bounty onto the boat. Children, typically in student uniforms of black pants, white or black shirts, and beanie ball caps, covered the landscape like Maine black flies. Everyone wore rubber flip-flop sandals. Passengers found space among wooden boxes and unattended cargo of chickens and goats in open crates. I found a bench seat near the stern. I was the only non-Asian, wearing a service dress khaki uniform to boot, and I did not turn a single curious head.

The taxi-boat had wooden poles crudely mounted vertically on the sides with a sagging canvas awning stretched between them like a canopy on a four-poster bed. Passengers pushed, shoved, even stepped on each other, as they found space. The Japanese politeness I expected had, apparently, been suspended. Animated motions and raucous high-pitched Japanese voices filled the air as everyone squeezed into seats on the deck and cargo boxes. Some even perched atop the rail hanging onto the awning poles to keep from falling overboard.

The taxi-boat captain controlled our departure time based on his estimate of the state of the tide, not a clock nor pleas to get moving. Shallow reefs and sand bars between the islands lay in wait to punish those who ignored nature's time. Our captain misjudged it.

We weren't ten minutes into the trip when, with a loud scraping sound of the bottom crunching in the sand and coral, the boat came to an abrupt stop, engine running. Passengers lurched forward, grabbing their flying packages, chicken crates, and each other—we had just run aground. Arguments ensued, everyone talking, the coxswain shouting directions.

Suddenly, four men passengers jumped over the side into water up to their thighs and began pushing the boat backwards. The captain shifted to full astern, engine whining, the churning propellers now making a frothy, dirty sand and coral backwash swirl around the volunteer salvage-assistants. As we slowly moved off the sand bar, the captain cut the engine, and people settled down, accepting the grounding as just another glitch in their crossing. The men jumped back into the boat, their wet clothes dripping on everyone, and we were on our way again.

As we approached the Ike village pier, my spirits lifted at the sight of a gray Coast Guard jeep and a chief petty officer standing beside it. Chief Armstrong, wearing a tropical khaki short uniform with an overseas cap, saluted smartly. He was tall and thin with a deeply lined and tanned face that made him look older than his years. He wasted no time hanging around the village. He grabbed my bag threw it into the jeep and said, "Hop in, skipper. You'll have plenty of time to explore the village. Let's get you out to the station."

WAR GAMES

THE LINGERING BREEZE FROM LAST night's storm threatened to spill the fog from Kin Bay onto the station. Petty officer first class Smith rapped once on my office screen door.

"We're good to go, sir. I just came from the beach. It's damned foggy and the bay is still moving around a good bit, but I don't think we'll have a problem."

"Thanks, Smith. I'll be ready to roll in 10." I had considered canceling the routine supply run, but Smith was an experienced LCM coxswain, and I had great confidence in him. He had cut his teeth driving LCMs on the USCGC *Kukui*, servicing Loran stations all over the Pacific. The weather report called for clearing, and the wind was expected to die down, so getting back from the main Island of Okinawa in the afternoon was not going to be a problem.

The M boat was bobbing a bit, even in our protected cove, as I backed the jeep up the ramp and into position in front of our truck. Smith brought the ramp up, backed out expertly, made the pivot and headed out into the bay. When we moved beyond the cove, the choppy waves pounded the flat ramp like a hammer trying to stop our forward motion. Visibility was less than two hundred yards.

Half way into the seven mile crossing, an offshore breeze from the main island joined forces with the rising sun to lift the veil of fog. I had

Loading the LCM for supply run

been sitting in the Jeep with my eyes partially closed when I heard the coxswain call out, "Sir, we've got a problem here!"

I got out of the jeep, moved aft past the truck to climb the ladder leading to the cockpit. Before I got to the top I could clearly see "the problem." We had blindly moved into the middle of a joint military exercise. We were surrounded by Amphibious Attack Transports, (APA's), with their brood of LCVP's and LCM's circling them like ducklings clinging to their mothers, their assault troops at the ready. The assault task force included a few Navy destroyer escorts and minesweepers. Our uninvited and unexpected black CG utility vessel was the ugly duckling in the middle of a gray Pacific Fleet Task Force! I envisioned Jeff Chandler, in the movie *Away All Boats*, on the wing of the command ship, all squinty eyed and strong jawed, preparing to give the signal to attack.

I grabbed the binoculars, and scanned the beach. A hazy picture of bleachers filled with military observers emerged in the thinning fog.

There was at least one general's flag flying along with two foreign ensigns. It was too late now.

"Smith, take us in slowly, get us unto the beach so we can get the hell out of the way. Then you go back to the station and I'll call on land line to set up a pick-up time. Think you can hold it steady in this surf?"

"Yes, sir. It's not too bad; we can off-load OK."

The ramp splashed onto the beach, the stern rose and fell with the wavelets, but Smith held us steady with his skillful use of engines and rudder. A two foot wide coil of wire, slapping in the surf about 3 feet in front of our ramp, was not a welcome mat. I moved to the top of the ramp. From the front of the bleachers about 50 yards to the right I saw a Marine Corps lieutenant colonel, direct from central casting, a cigar stub in his mouth, sleeves rolled up. He was unperturbed by the sloshing water that soaked his pants half way up his calf. His combat boots cut angry deep divots in the wet sand. He stopped in front of our ramp. "Who the hell are you and where the hell did you come from?" He was steaming.

"Sir, I'm Lieutenant (JG) Marcott, CO of the Coast Guard Loran station on Ikeshima," I saluted sharply and pointed toward the island. "Sir, I'm sorry to break up the exercises, but we received no message traffic about this. Clearly we would have never made our supply run today had I known."

"I don't give a damn about that," he bellowed. "What I'm pissed about is we've held up this exercise for over an hour because the God damned Navy says it's still too rough in here to land their boats!!" (His language throughout this exchange was a little more *Marine-like*.)

When I answered, as soon as the words were out of my mouth, I knew I shouldn't have said them. "Well, sir, we're pretty serious about *our* run— we're after bread, milk, and letters from home!"

I gulped then waited for what seemed an eternity. The Colonel's icy stare burned holes into my head, then suddenly he turned toward the beach and ordered, "Someone—anyone, cut this damned wire and clear a way for this man across the beach—Now! Then tell the Navy to get this damned show on the road!" *Did I detect a slight smile?*

I wasted no time getting across the beach, and up the road, passing units of the "red army" dug in, and waiting for the amphibious assault of the "blue army." The Colonel's war was about to begin.

Later that afternoon, returning to Kin beach to pick up our M-boat, I had barely turned off the main highway when I discovered I was still in the "battle zone." Fierce fighting was taking place in the scruffy growth near the roadside as the blue army made progress against the red defensive positions. I could hear gunshots including machine gun fire all around me.

Suddenly a Marine jumped from the downhill side of my jeep and began running alongside firing blanks over the hood at an enemy he had apparently seen on the uphill side. I was startled, but kept going at a slow pace down the curvy dirt road, the shooter running alongside, until the enemy jumped up on the hill, the two of them now firing at each other and hollering, "I got you."

"No, man, I got you first."

"The hell you did, you can't use that Jeep for cover; it's not part of the exercise."

"Is too. You're dead, man!" At this point an officer umpire, I presumed because of the green arm band, leaped onto the road in front of me signaling everyone to a stop. I hit the brakes, and I think I may have even put my arms in the air a little, as the Marines continued arguing.

The umpire quickly settled the argument. "Although the Jeep is not officially part of the exercise, the blue invader showed Marine initiative taking advantage of changing situations. The red defender is dead, the blue Marine may continue," he announced with boring finality. Without a word, he waved me to continue.

About a quarter mile further, I came upon a roadblock with an armed sergeant stopping traffic and a machine gun nest set up at the side of the road behind a small sandbag bunker. I went through my story, figuring I had an advantage now. From the top of the hill, we could see our LCM coming back across the bay for the pickup, but the sergeant was not impressed. He knew navy vessels were gray and this black LCM approaching could very well be a third country vessel trying to pick up a spy! At his invitation, I accepted the armed guard who road with me while I followed the sergeant to battalion HQ. Oh man! The battalion commander was my Marine Colonel friend from the beach. I felt better when he smiled and said, "So, you're still around here causing trouble, Lieutenant?"

"I hope not, sir."

"I've heard that your LCM was on the way to pick you up, so I'm giving you a non-combat pass that will keep you out of trouble until you get out of here." He was laughing.

"I'm really sorry for the trouble, sir," I apologized again. "We normally get message notice for this sort of thing. I don't know what happened."

"Where you from, Lieutenant?"

"Pennsylvania, sir. Small town in Northwest, called Bradford."

"You go to the Coast Guard Academy in New London?"

"Yes, sir, class of '57."

"You know, there was a lad about your vintage from my home town, Upper Sandusky, Ohio, who went to the Coast Guard Academy, can't remember his name."

"Would it be Tom Matteson, sir?" I ventured a guess. How many more CGA grads around my age could there be from Upper Sandusky? Tom always reminded us that, strangely, it was below Sandusky.

"By God, that is the name."

"Yes, sir, Tom's a classmate. He's in flight school now."

"Well, I'll be damned."

"Yes, sir."

I never had a chance to tell that story to Tom until our 50th reunion at the Coast Guard Academy. He was pretty sure he knew the Colonel's family. Tom retired as a Rear Admiral and Superintendent of the Coast Guard Academy. He was later appointed as the Superintendent of the Merchant Marine Academy at Kings Point, New York.

—21—

VILLAGE LIFE

I DON'T KNOW WHERE THE mule came from nor how it got here, but seeing several of my crew huddled in the field next to it, I was suspicious. I had been invited to this *demonstration* just moments ago. "Sir, you are needed at the crest of the village road." As I approached the hill, I could see a line of onlookers standing in a row facing away from the road and into the sugar cane field. The mule was behind one of the low rock walls that separated the small plots. He had a deep red coat, long ears, and was hitched to a single plow. A young man I didn't recognize was behind him with the reins over his shoulder, and gripping the wooden handles; it was a Grant Wood painting come to life.

I left the jeep standing in the roadway and headed for my men. "OK, guys," I said. "Someone want to tell me what's going on here?"

After a moment of awkward jockeying, they tapped a spokesman who stepped forward. "Well, sir, aahh... we are trying show everyone that there is a more efficient way to get their fields ready for planting." He held his breath and bit his bottom lip, waiting for some response from me. He continued, "Well, you know how these farmers do everything with a short handled hoe and sickle?" He launched into a rapid fire sputter. "They work these tiny plots only to put all the crops together for sale afterwards and if they just took the walls down we figured a plow could save a lot of time—and backs too." Long pause for effect, then. "That's one of our Marine friends from the main island behind the plow, sir. He's from Georgia and he really knows what he's doing. We've got things all ready to go, sir."

So, this was a set up. They had been waiting to spring this little show on me as well as the village Mayor and a group of farmers.

I had never thought of mules being this big. Hell, I had never thought of mules at all. They were never part of my world. Bred for one thing, power, he was destined for a life of pulling plows and heavy farm wagons. He shook his short cropped mane and twitched his large chest and foreleg muscles, impatient for action. Both he and his driver were ready to go.

"So, how did this Marine friend, his mule, and his plow get from Okinawa to Ikeshima?" I asked.

Silence. The whole crew shook their heads, and hunched their shoulders in collective innocence.

"I don't suppose it's possible they were transported here in our LCM?"

A swallowed response from one, still shaking head, "I guess... well... it...it *is* possible, sir."

"Well, these people came out to see... something. You better get this show on the road."

The young Marine in civilian clothes, grabbed the plow handles and tossed me a casual salute. I could tell he was back in his element. I returned the salute, he yelled out some "mule command" and the pair of them took off. They move at a steady pace, plowing a single furrow that ran the length of what was formerly three separate plots.

The size of sugar cane fields on Ikeshima was deceiving. What, at first, seemed to be a few large fields were, in fact, many small plots. Each was farmed by a single family and separated by two foot high hand-built stone and coral walls. The fences were hidden deep in the tall canes, but you could see them from the air. The bamboo-like clusters poked skyward, as if they sprouted from ice cube trays to form a quilt of green.

When harvested, the entire production of the island is pooled and sold at market in Okinawa for the benefit of the whole village. The fishermen do the same thing with their catch. The village was governed as a commune. The fruits of individual labor were willingly shared. Everything for the common benefit of all.

Two inner walls had been removed, leaving a rectangular plot about fifty yards long and twenty yards wide for the Marine and his mule. The villagers were suitably impressed. They bowed, hands folded prayer fashion, at their chests. They clapped politely and engaged each other in animated conversation. They seemed amazed and thankful. No more back breaking effort for Papa-san and Mama-san. Planting would be much easier and probably ten times as fast. My crew was back-slapping the Marine, and smiling at each other. I was proud of them, and told them all, "Great job, men. It looks as though you have made a major impact on the people of this village."

The following day—the walls were back in place. The farmers worked their separate plots, bent low, putting the finishing touches on the plowed furrows with hand-held hoes. We had not made a single difference.

It was the culture!

Centuries have molded the religion and culture of Okinawa. The people of the Ryukyuan Islands had suffered through often violent regimes of Japan, Korea, China, and then Japan again in 1850. The religions of Shinto and Buddhism flowed from the Japanese to mix with local beliefs and practices.

Our house-boy, Seiji, told stories of how the Japanese had treated Okinawans as conquered people rather than citizens of Japan. He said that during WWII the Japanese soldiers were mean, and made the Ikeshima young people drill with wooden sticks as make-shift rifles. The Ryukyuans generally consider themselves Okinawan rather than Japanese.

In Vern Schneider's novel, *Tea House of the August Moon*, he mocks the early occupation of Okinawa by the American Army. One of his characters, Colonel Wainright Purdy III, declares, "My job is to teach these natives the meaning of democracy, and they're going to learn democracy if I have to shoot every one of them." His first order of business was explaining democracy to them and that it was now in their hands. Everyone cheered. He was delighted until his interpreter explained that during 800 years of foreign occupation the Okinawans had learned to cheer whoever was in charge, no matter what was said. Perhaps this scenario was repeated at our mule-plowing demonstration.

The 1958 book *The Ugly American* by William Burdick and Eugene Lederer was required reading for prospective Loran station commanding officers. It is a book of short stories that were serious critiques of American's ability to win the hearts and minds of a foreign population. At the time, their target was our policies and actions in the Far East before the peak of our Vietnam involvement. They maintained that our arrogance and ineptitude along with making no effort to understand the language, culture, or the true needs of the people we were trying to help, contributed to major failures.

While their book was about the Far East and our fight against communism in the late fifties, I believe their message has a timeless appeal. When I think about our decade plus of Near East involvement, I can't help but think, "Maybe it's time to break out the Ugly American again."

Every man on our station learned from cross-cultural experiences. The most dramatic examples for me were the O-Bon festival and Thanksgiving dinner.

In mid-July, I was invited to share one of the major Japanese holidays with a village family. The *O-bon Festival* marks a reunion of the living with the spirits of the dead family members who return to the world of the living to visit. This "Feast of the Dead" originated in India and was introduced to China and Japan with the introduction of Buddhism. In Japan, the celebration lasts for eight days; in Okinawa the festival is limited to three.

The eve of the first day was a time to visit family tombs. Every family has one. Some as simple as a small cave dug into the hillside, others were no more than an open jar of bones placed in a marked natural alcove in the side of the hill. The wealthy often built a concrete structure that might have been more expensive than their house. A standard design had a turtle-shaped dome and a small door similar to the tunnel entrance into the more familiar Eskimo Igloo.

The remains of departed family members lie inside. In olden days, it was the job of the youngest unmarried woman of the family to enter the tomb and cleanse any remaining flesh off the bones of dead relatives. The bones were then placed in decorative vases in the rear of the tomb, cleansing the spirits for their visit to the earthly world as well as making room for more family members. Reportedly, cremation has begun to eliminate this ancient practice, although I have heard that some traditional families in rural areas might still practice this. On Ikeshima? I don't know.

It was the first day of the feast, one on which the family gathers for a meal in their shrine room (*chashitsu, a small formal tea room*) in their home. I arrived in the afternoon and was welcomed by my host with gracious bows as she pointed for me to enter. She wore a beautiful kimono of colorfully patterned silk, her hair meticulously piled high on her head, held there by several large combs. A broad sash, *obi*, circled her waist several times. I bowed in return, thanked her, *"Domo arigato gozaismasu."* She smiled at my attempt to use the more formal "thank you very much" not just "thanks."

I placed my white bucks (I was in tropical white long uniform) alongside the row of *getas* (Japanese wooden sandals) on the single step leading into the raised *chashitsu*. The formality of the occasion did not permit the cruder rubber flip flops that were normally worn. I was invited into the small four-and-a-half tatami room. A *tatami* is a two-inch-thick 6' x 3' straw-mat floor panel. In this case they were placed like a puzzle around a half-size tatami in the middle making a 9' x 9' room of eighty-one square feet. With no furniture except the low table in the middle, the room seemed larger.

The simple purity of the atmosphere was enhanced by the pale off-white light that filtered through the rice paper sliding doors, and the strong odor of incense burning in a small dish in the *Tokonoma,* The *Tokonoma,* a shrine like recess in the wall, was beautifully decorated. A simple vase with long pussy willow-like branches that were arranged high above its rim stood on one side. A low candle was burning on the other, the only artificial light, along with the low brass dish that held the burning incense. On the back wall was a vertical scroll with large hand-painted Japanese Kanja characters. Nobody explained what it said except it was "something suitable for the season." The Tokonoma was unquestionably the focal point of the room.

I was seated at one end of the table facing the shrine. Four others were seated with two on each side of the table. The guest of honor's place was opposite me where he would be framed by the Takonoma at his back. Others, when looking at him, would then see him as if he were included in a three dimensional religious scene. In this case, of course, the seat remained empty, having been reserved for the expected ancestral spirit. There was a small dish of cut fruit set at each place—including the empty seat of honor.

There was subdued conversation including faulting attempts in half-Japanese, half-English to teach me the key points of the holiday. I had a basic idea what to expect, but when the moment came, I confess that I entered a whole new dimension.

One of the women at the other end of the table suddenly thrust her arms out over the table, palms down and let out a loud SSSSHHHH. Everything stopped. She continued the SSSHHH-ssshhh gradually lowering the volume as well as her hands until they were touching the table. There was a long silent pause, and then she whispered in a barely audible voice, "Ghosto come." When I saw the intensity on the face of the others as they directed all their attention toward the empty seat, I just *knew* that all of them they felt a new presence. For a moment, I wasn't sure about me! The rising hairs on my arms sent me into a physical shudder.

Part of me wanted to get out of there, part of me wanted to stay. Low level conversation in Japanese continued for a while as we ate the fruit on our plates. I was no longer involved. I found myself thinking, "Are they talking *about* the spirit— or talking *to* him?"

After an eternity of ten or fifteen minutes, the ceremony seemed to be over. We thanked each other for the opportunity to share the O-Bon, and I returned to the station. Alone to ponder my thoughts for days, I found myself comparing the religious rapture I saw on the faces of the Japanese ladies at O-Bon with that on the faces I remembered on kneeling old Italian ladies in St. Bernard's church at home as they said the rosary. Though each communed with her very different Great-Spirit in a different way, they both seemed at peace in their own serene world.

The second day of O-Bon was more like a family reunion, where they exchanged gifts and payed homage to their ancestors. The final day was a time for gay festivities, shows, and dances that lead up to the final send-off. Sugar canes were cut to length and placed outside the tomb as walking sticks to assist their ancestors in their return journey to the land-of-the-spirits.

In return for the wonderful O-Bon experience, I wanted to share an American holiday with the people of Ikeshima. I had always considered two holidays unique: Halloween and Thanksgiving. Clearly Halloween was out. I thought it was too close to O-Bon, they might think we were "making fun of it." So, I invited the Mayor and several villagers to our "Coast Guard Loran Station Thanksgiving Holiday Dinner."

Our skilled cook took pleasure in preparing a traditional meal. We had a huge carved turkey, ham, mashed potatoes, dressing, the whole works. While the mess hall lacked traditional decorations beyond a centerpiece of fruits and nuts, the aroma of roasting turkey and pumpkin pies stirred hints of homesickness in many of our young crewmen who were thousands of miles from homes they would not see for a year. We had prepared a head table for our guests to join our key petty officers and me.

The Mayor arrived with his party of six. The four women were dressed for a special occasion in their colorful formal kimonos. The men wore suits and ties. The women looked nervous as they watched and copied the mayor's every move. After the round of normal bows, they shook hands, and then giggled with their fingers appropriately covering their mouth, lest they offend.

Our guests seemed overwhelmed with the abundance of food, and confused by the complications of using knives and forks. Everyone was intrigued. They all enjoyed the taste of turkey, ham, and all the veggies, but they *loved* the pumpkin pie. Their animated expressions and rapid Japanese chatter told me they understood and enjoyed Seiji's rendition of the "Story of American Thanksgiving."

When cigars were offered as a ritual at the end of the meal, the women, seeing the Mayor take one, did the same. By the time I noticed, they had already followed the mayor... and lit up. I didn't want to embarrass them, so I said nothing. After three or four puffs, lots of smoke, and a few coughs, one lady ceremoniously placed her cigar in an ashtray, the others followed. They very graciously took it all in stride.

I spent a year discovering cultural differences. Although the people of Ikeshima lived under the principles of Socialism, they were not governed as a Socialist country. They happily shared the collective benefits of individual effort. That was true not just with fishing and farming, but they even shared electricity (a recent luxury) furnished by the single Island generator, on a rotating daily schedule.

They were a culture that respected the elderly and revered their ancestors. They were a culture that raised their children with total freedom, and no discipline. They let them *be children*—until they were six years old when the heavy hand of discipline and work ethic descended upon their lives. The school children wore uniforms, (there were no status symbols to fire competition.) They were serious about school and demonstrably grateful for little things we took for granted like the apples, oranges, and walnuts that they stood in crowded lines to receive from the men at our station who were trying to share a little pleasure at our Christmastime.

—22—

THE WEDDING PORTRAIT

THE RAMP OF THE M-BOAT clanged into the frothy surf on Kin Beach. It had been an easy seven mile trip in the WWII amphibious landing craft (LCM). The sea was calm; the weather was pleasant; it was a good January day for Okinawa. It was our weekly supply run with an added personal mission. I needed to find an Okinawan portrait artist.

I eased the jeep down the ramp and across the soft wet sand, the trip made short by the morning high tide. Our first-class hospital corpsman drove our 2 ½ ton-truck down the ramp behind me. He and a seaman assistant would pick up commissary supplies, go to the bank, and run by the Navy machine shop at White Beach to pick up a repaired motor. We would meet back at Kin beach at 1600 for the return trip to Ikeshima.

I have never been clever in coming up with unique gift ideas, and with our third anniversary approaching, I really wanted to surprise Carol with something special. Fortunately, one of the Marine pilots who had been practicing landings at our station had a great suggestion. "Why don't you look up one of the Okinawan portrait artists to do a painting?"

Okinawa had a lot of fine artists who worked in oils, watercolors, lacquerware, wood carvings, and other media. I knew there were art shops along the highway north of Naha. I had been there before to purchase popular handmade Okinawan Shoji screens that I then shipped back to the senior officers in Honolulu. The screens were the latest thing in Hawaiian decor. The Coast Guard C130 cargo plane that made a supply circuit of the Pacific LORAN stations every month rarely returned without several of these beautiful three-fold open patterned wooden screens.

The Jeep climbed above the sand line to the dirt road that had been bulldozed years ago by an American movie company who needed access to the beach to film a war picture. The aging road, pock-marked with boulders and holes, was a minor challenge even to our WWII hand-me-down vehicles, but it was usable. Low scrubby pine-like plants, still wet with morning dew lined the road like squat green sentinels keeping us on the s-curved path to the paved highway 58. The faint smells of Kin Beach gradually faded as I moved further inland.

I enjoyed the pleasant ride in the open Jeep. As I passed through sugar cane fields, I noticed that the green 7-8 foot high bamboo-like plants were nearly ready for harvest. During the war most of the crop had been processed into alcohol to fuel torpedoes for the Japanese navy.

Approaching the outskirts of Naha, I passed between rows of small tin-roofed storefronts with crudely painted signs advertising their wares. I passed stores with beautiful lacquer-ware bowls, and painted silk screens—half of them of Mount Fuji. Other classy storefronts displayed bolts of *Bashofu*. The highly prized thin, natural banana fabric was unique to Okinawa. Spun, woven and dyed, the material was artistically transformed into popular informal Kimonos. I found the corner with the Shoji screens, turned right, and parked on a dirt side street, and walked the arty lineup.

I stopped at a small shop that displayed nothing but oil paintings. There were landscapes, cityscapes, and a lot of portraits. I was glad to see American as well as Japanese subjects. I entered the battered wooden entrance. The shop had an open showroom that doubled as a studio. In progress paintings were spread on easels throughout the room. A small, slightly bent older man smiled at me and said good morning. "*Ohayo gozaimasu.*" He gave a slight bow of his head and shoulders, his hands straight down, resting on his thighs.

"*Ohayo gozaimasu,*" I returned with an awkward attempt to imitate the bow. (There was a whole body language encompassed in bowing. How deep the bend, how low the head, the placement of the hands—everything sent a message.) "You Higa-san?" I asked, in halting pidgin talk, taking the signature name from an oil painting on a nearby easel.

"*Hai,*" he affirmed.

"You do painting for me, *kudasai?*" (Please). I fumbled for my only wedding photo, a wallet sized picture of Carol and me.

"*Hai, hai, hai.*" His head was bobbing in quick little yes-nods while making that slow sucking sound, drawing air between his closed teeth. That could mean, "yes," or "I'm thinking about it,"...the equivalent of our American "Ahh...."

Higa-san studied my wallet size photo then and asked, "How big you want?"

"*Saymo-saymo,* this one," I said in international GI talk while pointing to a portrait of a beautiful Japanese girl. Higa-san lifted the 17" X 14" painting from the window and asked "Frame?"

"*Hai.* Frame, too. How soon you make?"

"Two week." he answered taking my snapshot, studying it within inches of his thick round glasses. "*Hai,* two week."

I thanked him, and we shook hands. We had a deal. I left the shop with its pleasant lingering odor of oil paint, and returned to the jeep and made the trip back to Kin Beach.

Two weeks later, it was the end of January. Higa-San, on the sidewalk outside his door, smiled as I approached. "Good morning, Higa-san," I said with a wave.

"Good morning, how are you?" he smiled as he shuffled to open the door. He invited me in with a sweep of his arm while he bowed.

"*Dozo,*" he said, inviting me in. He barked in excited Japanese for a clerk in the back room to bring the painting out. I couldn't wait to see it.

Higa-san and the clerk dropped their smiles as they read the obvious disappointment on my face. I could tell they were upset and embarrassed. They had wanted so much to please me. For the most part, I was happy with the picture, but how was I going to tell him—my wife's breasts were too small and flat?

"*Sukoshi,* (small) too *sukoshi,*" I said, pointing to Carol's breasts on the painting.

"You want a' more bigga?"

"*Hai,*" I smiled until Higa reached for a larger painting holding it up for my approval.

"This one more bigga, OK?" This was not working! I did not want a larger painting; I just wanted more normal breasts on my pretty bride.

An older Okinawan woman, drawn by the raised voices, scooted in from a back room. Her wooden geta sandals clacked across the floor. She joined the confusion, speaking with Higa in an animated, but low tone. I mentally translated her words into something like, "What the hell are you doing here Higa-san, this man is our customer?" They stopped and both looked at me.

I knew I was on thin ice here, but had to give it a try. I slowly approached the woman, both arms extended straight in front of me, index fingers pointing from my closed fists, ever so closely, directly at her withered breasts peeking from behind her loosely tied kimono, and choking whispered, "*Okusan sukoshi chichi.*" Then putting my hands on my own breast as if I were juggling C-cups. "Make my *okusan more okii kudesai.*"

I hoped I had said, "Your wife has small breasts; please make my wife's larger." I did not know the proper term for woman's breasts. I knew *chichi,* commonly used by sailors, was probably not polite. There are also Shinto religious figures called *Shishi*. Known as lion-dogs, their sculptured figures are often mounted on roofs to keep out bad spirits and welcome good spirits. The spoken inflections of *chichi* and *Shishi* were too close for me to differentiate.

I could only hope I had not said, "Your wife has tits like a small dog. Make my wife's bigger like a lion's," or something equally offensive. Thank God, everyone laughed, including Higa-san's wife who, like all Japanese women, permitted only a giggle, covering her mouth with one hand as if to protect me from offending teeth.

Higa-san laughed while he made circle gestures toward his wife's breast and then Carol's in the photo. Everyone understood, thought it was funny, and nobody was offended. We shook hands, and I left feeling I had this under control.

On my way back to the beach, I stopped at Machinato, the Army base that served as headquarters for United States Civil Administration Ruyukus (USCAR). I parked in the reserved Coast Guard parking space right at the front entrance to the administration building. I was so glad my predecessor had made this arrangement. Parking was always tight, and it made the mail run a quick in and out. This had been a good day.

I made a return trip to the main island the first week in February. There was still enough time to ship the painting to Carol before 15 March, our anniversary. I stopped to get mail first before going to pick up Carol's portrait.

I swung into the parking circle at USCAR headquarters. Someone had taken our Coast Guard parking spot. I continued around the circle, upset that I would now have to scrap for a parking space. As I passed the offending car, I was shocked to discover it was an Army staff car with a 3 star flag flying from the front fender. This car was waiting for an Army General.

Then it hit me—there was only one Commanding General and High Commissioner of the Ryukyuan Islands. The "CG" painted on the curb did not mean Coast Guard! I parked a long way from the entrance, not eager to have my gray Coast Guard Jeep seen anywhere in the vicinity. I got the mail then got out of there. I could only wonder how I had been lucky for 7 months.

Entering Higa's shop, I knew something was wrong. He did not greet me with his usual friendly smile. "I'm sorry, Lieutenant, your picture not done. Need more time." I'm not sure how I reacted or what I said, but I'm sure it was not nice. Higa-san went on, "Ryukyu get new High Commissioner on 12th. Spent week painting family portrait for go-away present for old General." I couldn't believe it. Damn!

I now knew three things: (1) I had picked the right artist if he was good enough to be painting the High Commissioner's family, (2) I sympathized with the pressure Higa must have felt, and, (3) I really didn't like Lt. General Donald P. Booth, High Commissioner, Ryukyu Islands, who was, thank God, leaving on 12 February. First he steals my parking place, now my portrait artist, and I didn't get an invite to his Change-of-Command ceremony. After all, I was the senior Coast Guard Officer in the Ryukyu Islands. Damned Army.

With much bowing, head nodding, and teeth sucking Higa-san assured me with a sad-eyed expression on his face, "Next week. I promise Lieutenant, you number one." I left before saying anything, my ears wringing with advice I'd heard somewhere, "Okinawan culture insures you will always get a yes—it's considered impolite to say no."

This third trip to Higa-San's studio had better be the last. It was the end of February, I was hanging at the end of my thread for shipping time. With General Booth gone, and Higa-San's heartfelt promise, I was more confident that this time was going to be the charm. I parked the jeep nearly in front of the art studio and entered congratulating myself for this clever idea. Carol is going to love this.

As I opened the door, Higa-San and his assistant, in the back of the room, turned to me with big smiles. Now I knew it was going to be my day! He ceremoniously led me to an easel with a draped cloth covering the painting, his assistant, like a magician's side-kick, on the other side, unfolding her arm as an invitation while Higa-San undraped the framed oil painting.

"Oh my God, Higa-San, what in hell did you do?" I was furious! He ruined it! Both Higa-San and his assistant knew when I threw my hat on the nearby table, that I was more than a little upset, shriveling into their kimonos like frightened armadillos into their shells. Raising my voice short of a scream, "What the hell is that on my uniform lapel? Is that a flower? That can't be a flower! Is that a damned flower? This was a military wedding. You can't see I'm wearing my uniform?" I stopped to catch my breath. Higa-san was obviously deeply hurt, and his assistant nearly melted.

A little shaken, Higa struggled, "I so sorry, Lieutenant," sucking air, head down, avoiding eye contact, he pointed to my single lonely gold ensign stripe on my uniform sleeve and nearly whispered, "I think maybe only one stripe, you no able afford. I cause you too much trouble, so I try make you more important. *Gomennasai.* (I'm sorry)."

After a long, long silence, feeling like a complete ugly American jerk, I was sorrier than Higa-San. He had a heart of gold and this was his way of apologizing. How could I have hurt this sensitive and wonderful man? "Higa-San, *Gomennasai*, I am the one should be sorry. I understand you only wanted to make me more important, but it is my Coast Guard uniform and we don't wear white flowers. It's going to have to come off. The painting is beautiful, my wife looks perfect, but the carnation must go."

Taking a pallet knife from the nearby table, he immediately began carefully scraping off the obvious recently added offending boutonniere. When he finished, there was a smooth, now off-color, blue scar remaining on the lapel. He said, "One more day, I fix blue be same as uniform."

Wedding Portrait by S. Higa

"No, Higa-San, I must take it now to get it to my *Okusan* in time. I'm very happy. *Domo arigato gozaimasu*," I thanked him, paid him, bowing humbly to show respect, repeating, "*Domo arigato gozaimasu*." To this day, I am so thankful I took the flawed painting. Now, when we share our wedding portrait with friends or strangers and I see them silently staring at the off-blue spot, I can enjoy retelling the story of my Okinawan friend, S. Higa, Artist.

That evening, the sun lowered herself in the west, pulling the orange curtained sky behind her until the silhouette of the distant hills faded into the blackness of an Okinawan night. In the morning, she rose in the east, a bold yellow, and climbed her way into an overwhelming blue sky.

It had been a good day. They cycle continues.

One less day to go.

USCG Reserve Training Center

Yorktown, VA

Instructor
September 1961-May 1965

The U.S. Coast Guard Training Center Yorktown, Virginia, is one of the service's four major training centers. It occupies the site that was once the U.S. Navy Mine Warfare School. The base sits on the southern bank of the York River, a few miles from the Chesapeake Bay, at the end of the historic Yorktown Battlefield. The Moore House, where British General Cornwallis surrendered to General George Washington, ending the Revolutionary War, is just outside the main gate.

When the Navy closed its Mine Warfare School, it was a perfect location for the Coast Guard to centralize its reserve training, including Officer Candidate School (OCS) and a large number of two week schools for reservists to attend on their annual two weeks active duty for training (ACDUTRA). This was in addition to their monthly weekend drills near their home towns.

The Coast Guard took possession in 1959 and commissioned the Reserve Training Center that same year. In the early years, RTC convened two seventeen week OCS classes each year, commissioning the graduates as Ensigns in the U.S. Coast Guard Reserve. Summers were filled with thousands of reservists attending ACDUTRA courses.

RTC also provided training to other U.S. military services, government agencies, and foreign country Coast Guard equivalents. Later its missions expanded to include basic and advanced occupational training for petty officer ratings, and mission specific schools such as: Search and Rescue, Merchant Marine Safety, Boarding Officers. The name was changed to Coast Guard Training Center, Yorktown.

—23—

RETURN TO THE COLONIES

ROTATING OFF A YEAR'S ISOLATED duty I rather expected my assignment request would be honored. I thought that I had given Headquarters assignment officers a lot of latitude; I asked for shore duty at a district or group office, anywhere on the west coast. I felt a little disappointed when I received orders to the Reserve Training Center, Yorktown, Virginia. In the first place, Carol and I hoped to see more of the country; Yorktown was thirty miles away from Norfolk, Virginia. Secondly, I didn't know what a Reserve Training Center was, nor what type of duty that would mean for me.

So, I didn't get what I asked for. But, what I got—proved to be a wonderful career-defining assignment that both Carol and I have cherished as our favorite duty station in a twenty-eight year career.

We enjoyed short visits with both families, before heading south. We were anxious to look for a house and to begin a new chapter in my yet young Coast Guard career. We did not mind the area, actually. When we were stationed in Norfolk, we had ventured to Yorktown-Williamsburg as day-tripping tourists. This time was different. We were digging into what was probably going to be a four year assignment.

When headed south on US17. We crossed the peninsulas made by the great rivers that raced from the mountains of Virginia toward the Chesapeake Bay: the Potomac, the Rappahannock, and the York. We drove through villages with homey names like *White Marsh*, and *Ordinary*. The landscape morphed into a rural postcard. Flat sandy soil dotted with scrubby clumps of grass stretched from the narrow highway. White farm houses sat sheltered in an oasis of trees protecting families from the hot sun of clear-cut farm land. You could almost see them sitting on the wrap-around porches waiting to offer lemonade or a pint of stout to friends arriving by carriage up the long circular drive. Roadside signs every twenty miles reminded us we were traveling the George Washington Memorial Highway. We knew we were in the south again, but one that, somehow, seemed more honest and pure than Norfolk.

When we came to a sign that pointed the way to *Gum Fork*, we knew that the George P. Coleman Memorial Bridge was not far. The bridge took us across the York River at the pinch point between Gloucester and Yorktown. From the middle of the bridge, Carol pointed down river to the East and said, "Do you think that is the Reserve Training Center?" We could see a large two story house, white with green awnings sitting on a prominent point forty feet above the river, and a few nondescript gray buildings sprawled to the left of the house.

"It seems about right. It might well be." I pointed up river and added, "The Naval Weapons Station is up there with twelve miles of riverfront. There's also a naval supply center, and a more secretive place, generally known as the 'farm,' at least to the CIA agents that go to spy school there."

Nick's Seafood Pavilion sat at the foot of the bridge in the village of Yorktown. Built in 1944 by Greek immigrants it was a featured "must-stop" for east coast travelers. It was famous for its Greek paintings and armor-plated, helmeted statues that you had to weave among to be seated. It was a thing of beauty run by the friendly gods, Nick and Mary Mathews, who swallowed their guests with their bodacious hospitality. They had been known to open their doors at midnight to help lost Coastguardsmen, and sailors trying to find their newly assigned base or ship. Over the course of our tour we would enjoy many evenings there, and while tempted to stop now—the timing was not right. We were anxious to get to Newport News and start house hunting.

We wanted to buy a house. A four year assignment made that a reasonable alternative to renting. We also had managed to save some money in the last year. I had spent hardly any of my salary on Loran duty in Okinawa, and Carol who stayed with her parents in Roosevelt, Long Island, worked as a teller at the Meadowbrook National Bank. In addition, within a year, we could expect a big raise as I went over four years of service as a lieutenant. My income would be double what I made since we last managed a household in Norfolk, Virginia. It was time to buy.

We had contacted a realtor before we left Roosevelt who was ready to show us options. Newport News was 10 miles south of the base. We quickly settled on a three bedroom rancher on a cul-de-sac in a new development at 721 Roslyn Road. Offer made and accepted—our first home cost $15,500. The following day, we were ready to move in, except we had no furniture.

Our realtor recommended a large furniture store on the north end of town. Carol and I had a great shopping day and the salesman an even greater one. We bought furniture for every room in the house in one day from one store. Dining room table, chairs, china closet, buffet, two complete bedroom sets, desk and bookcase for a den, and a roomful of living room furniture highlighted by a curved sectional, coffee tables, and end tables. We furnished the whole house. We had a ball doing it.

We sat watching the salesman filling out the sales slip with a big smile he couldn't hide.

I said, "You know, we bought a lot of stuff here today. Are you going to throw in at least a couple of lamps?"

"Rich!" Carol visibly gasped as her eyes darted soundless messages at me.

"What?" My response was a slow, whisper-like sing-song above hunched shoulders.

"I'll have to check with the manager," the salesman broke in, as he disappeared with a quizzical look.

"God, Rich! My mother would die if she knew what you just did." Her face was still red. Her mother was a furniture adjuster in Abraham & Straus, a well-known department store on Long Island.

"What do you mean? Everyone does that. It's standard practice in Bradford." I continued, "After all, nobody's going anywhere, the buyer or the seller. Bradford sales clerks know they sell to generations, and they know how to keep customers. A new suit would always get you a free tie. An expensive one would net you a shirt and a tie."

The salesman returned. "The manager will be glad to add two living room end-table lamps to your order, sir. No cost, of course, and thank you." He looked as surprised as Carol.

Who raised these people?

The furniture was delivered in a day. We took another two to get it arranged then our attention turned to the back yard. We needed a fence. The back yards of all the houses were open to each other, including those on the next street. Carol was already hinting for a dog. We decided on a three rail board fence, nothing fancy, 1 x 6s between 4 x 4s.I thought it would be a do-it-yourself project until I attempted the to dig the first post hole.

The "sandy soil," was but inches deep. Beyond that was clay—hard packed, battleship gray, shovel sticking, back-breaking clay. I didn't have the time, nor probably, the energy to do it. We asked the realtor for suggestions for a fence contractor.

"I'll tell you what," he said, "you can get that done a lot cheaper just hiring a couple day laborers to dig those post holes then nail the rails up yourself, or you can let them do it. Can you be around to supervise?"

"Yea, I guess, but how do I get them?"

"Well just drive down to the lower end of Jefferson Ave, toward the water. You'll see a bunch of niggers standing around on a street corner, just jiving with each other while 'they look'n fo' work.'" His tone was mocking. "But, those who are really serious will have a handkerchief tied to the parking meter and will be standing nearby it."

"Are you serious?"

"Yes. Just pick out a couple of big bucks and ask them if they'll give you a couple of days digging fence-post holes. They'll give you an honest day's work, but you gotta be there to tell 'em what to do and keep an eye on 'em." That was 1961. It was obvious there was not much progress in racial attitudes from the three-bathroom (Men, Women, and Colored) filling station we encountered three years ago in Norfolk. They were nice guys, worked hard, and I had my fence in two days, including a redwood stain. As someone once said, "The past is never dead—it ain't even past."

I stood outside the office of CDR Orland D. French, the Training Officer. I was an instructor in Officer Candidate School (OCS). My first OCS Class had just graduated and he was reviewing instructor performance on the student poll.

"Come in, Richard." I was barely in the door and he continued, never looking up. "You are aware, of course, that we ask each class to rate instructor performance."

"Yes, sir." The commander pushed his glasses down onto the end of his nose, scanned the papers in his hand for what seemed like a long time.

"We didn't have a chance to get you into the Navy instructor training school before this class, did we?" It wasn't really a question. I began to feel a little anxious.

"No, sir. The plan was to schedule me before the next class convenes. I'm looking forward to it."

"How do you feel about your classes?"

"I really enjoyed the teaching experience, sir. I actually had fun and I think the OC's did as well."

"Well, we are not going to send you to IT school. No need to waste the time you can use to get geared up for the next class after the holidays."

"Yes, sir. Perhaps before the next summer ACDUTRA season."

"No. I'm not going to send a man to IT school who polled as the no.2 instructor his first time out of the box. The students' comments are great as well. You did remarkably well." He rose with a big toothy grin and shook my hand. "Welcome to the training business."

I walked out of the Commander's office, so glad to get the good news. I felt confident in the classroom, and had such fun. I knew it in my bones—I loved being a trainer, and wanted to continue to grow in "the training business."

Officer Candidate School was a seventeen week program for civilians who held a college degree, and for enlisted men with a year of college plus active duty experience. Therefore, the program did not include academic subjects. It was crammed full of military indoctrination (marching, drilling, small arms training, leadership, CG organization), and specific subjects that prepared officers to take on a new ensign's duties. They included Navigation, Damage Control, Seamanship, and Operations Training. In my first class, I taught Combat Information Center (CIC) operations with Lt. Bob Larose. We operated a sophisticated ship simulator that realistically recreated the environment for navigating in fog, defending against air attacks, avoiding ship traffic, assisting distressed aircraft to a safe ocean ditching, and conducting submarine warfare. I guarantee that the experience was real enough. Many students filling the key evaluator position broke a sweat in the dark noisy atmosphere trying to put it all together; some broke down.

We made sure students stayed grounded in reality. If, during the class after-action briefing, an evaluator seemed to "strut his coolness," we reminded him, "Remember, if you remained calm when those about you were excited—maybe you didn't understand the situation."

(During WWII, the Navy's nickname for CIC was "Christ, I'm Confused.") It was a good test of initiative, skill, and leadership, under high tension action.

After several OC classes, I moved up the hill to teach Navigation with Jon Uithol. Jon was in the Academy class of 1958. I loved teaching with him, and I loved teaching navigation. We became close friends. We worked together during the summer also when the Reservists flooded the campus. My resolve to remain teaching became stronger with each year.

More importantly, Carol and I had matured into a real Coast Guard family. The experience of living closely with people you liked, worked with, and played with daily went a long way to cementing career intentions. We were in it for thirty.

—24—

THE GOOD LIFE

YORKTOWN OFFERED CAROL AND ME a different world than the one that shaped the first three years of our marriage. The Reserve Training Center never got underway, and Carol never spent nights worrying if I were coming home in a few days or a few weeks from a search and rescue call. It was certainly better than our thirteen month separation while I was on Okinawa, and she had to revert to living with her family, after three years of independence.

Those experiences made us stronger, and hardened us to life's little bruises. We learned that we could handle whatever was thrown at us. But, sharing the four year Yorktown assignment with a great group of officers close to our age and rank, assured us that we could look forward to a Coast Guard career and still live ordinary lives. We were regular people. I was an OCS instructor, a *school teacher,* who went to work every day, and came home every night. I was not that different from the neighbor who taught school in Newport News. With the Coast Guard as a common de-nominator, we became part of an extended family who loved each other, and what we were doing.

When we first moved into the house on Roslyn Road, we had only one neighbor, a car salesman with a wife and two young children. We were never close. Toni was friendly enough, a good across-the-fence neighbor. Her husband, Lou, was a caricature of a southern used-car salesman. He was easy to talk with, and could be fun, but in a buffoonish kind of way.

Most nights, after dinner, he sat in his car in the driveway, his slob-bering bull dog next to him, listening to the stock car races on the radio. Lou knew cars, the ones he sold and the ones raced in circles by men who wore jump suits splotched with patch-ads. Harmless, Lou at least served as comedy relief from some of the more unkind images we had of the south—like three-bathroom gas stations and tips on how to hire "a few big buck" post-hole diggers.

I had just finished planting a row of clematis trees at the curb line, and the redwood stain on the fence rails was hardly dry when Carol said, "I want a dog." I was not surprised; she had always had a dog. As far as she was concerned we were out of an apartment and into a house with a fenced back yard—what was there to ponder? My only input was, "I don't want one of those scrawny little yappity-rat-tailed-terriers like Grandpa Boyd always had. If I'm going to have to live with a dog, I'd rather it be a big one."

Her name was *Ruby*. Collies were a favorite breed of the Hampton Rhodes area. Ruby was a tri-colored lady who already carried a registered kennel name, Lisettes, which I could not change, only add to. With a July birthday, we registered her as *Lissettes Royal Jewel*. Her call name, Ruby, of course, is the July birth stone. We thought that was pretty clever.

We were delighted to get news that three officers that I knew from the Academy, all grads of the class of '58, would be joining the OCS staff. We became close to the Uithols, Parkers, and the Gruels; we remain lifelong friends. We shared the advantages of Yorktown together for three years. Jon Uithol and his wife, Nan, lived in Williamsburg, but Frank and Gail Parker, and Carl and Donna Gruel bought homes on our street. That gave us a Roslyn Road car pool and the wives many opportunities to get together.

With just one house between the Parkers and ours, Carol and Gail got together often. They watched soap operas and folded clothes together, talked about children, husbands, and of course, base gossip. There was always gossip. The new doctor and his wife who painted their kitchen black; the toddler son of an OCS instructor who experienced the joy of building a fire under their porch; the security officer who roamed the housing area in the middle of the night with his flashlight; the CO who got the dentist out of bed at 2 a.m. to treat his tooth ache (jalapeno pepper between his molars); or the Arab foreign nationals in OCS who had drunk too much of "the milk of lions" at the officer's club.

We were never at a loss for things to do. The base provided many opportunities. We had a gymnasium, swimming pool, intramural softball, and a mixed bowling league. Halloween costume parties at the O'Club, and New Year's Day traditional *call* on the CO were annual events. There were wine and cheese tasting, movies on the base, and picnics. We were a self-supporting community with our own police force, fire department, recreational facilities, even a small store for necessities and gifts.

At the end of one bowling season, I entered the Hampton Rhodes Bowling Tournament with Gary McManus, a fellow Navigation instructor. We were eligible because we bowled in a sanctioned ABA league, albeit on "barely certified lanes." We registered for the singles and doubles competition. The Hampton Rhodes Tournament stretched over two weekends with bowlers from hundreds of miles away. It was a handicap tournament and both Gary and I, with our 150 averages, would get the maximum handicap. Like all 150 bowlers, we experienced crazy good (and bad) nights, which made us dangerous.

The tournament ran all day Saturday and Sunday for two weekends. Bowlers in the first flight on the first day (that included us) were at the lowest end of the totem pole. Most of us didn't even have bowling shirts, the fancy rainbow colored silks with script names embroidered on the back.

We wore khaki pants and a T-shirt. We both went crazy. I bowled one of my highest sets ever (585 scratch), and Gary did about the same. When we checked the leader board at noon we were surprised to see we led the pack: "McManus and Marcott 1310." We grabbed a beer and laughed about our short lived fame and headed home. At the end of the day, someone called us and said we were still on top.

We went down on Sunday to watch the higher tier bowlers. When the first week of the tournament was over, McManus and Marcott were still in the lead. We could hear murmurs in the lobby as people stood around and looked at the standings. Lots of, "Who the hell are McManus and Marcott?" and "Hey, anybody know those guys in first place?"

The following week was the same. But by now, it was the crowd of the hot-shot teams, with uniform shirts and cheerleading wives that still couldn't believe the leader board. Gary and I, a little intimidated, stood amidst the non-believers, chuckled to ourselves, and said nothing.

Two weeks later, at the banquet, we were crowned Hampton Rhodes Doubles Champions. When we were presented our trophies, and the $200 cash prize ($1500 in 2015) we were not overwhelmed by the isolated one or two person applause. We allowed ourselves to be a little smug returning to our table.

As young Lieutenants, we had reached the financial point where investing or saving a little money became possible. When I taught with Bob LaRose, he was into the stock market. With a huge investment of $200 in Oakmont Mining (Philippine Gold,) you would have thought he was a Wall Street trader. He drove his broker crazy with phone calls several times a day. "Taylor, how's the market doing? Do you think I should be making a move?" When even he felt embarrassed he would ask me, "Dick, Why don't you call Taylor Darden and see how the market is doing? I just called him this morning." I had opened an account with the same modest amount invested, minus the broker harassment. The poor guy must have been glad to see us move on.

Jon Uithol and I became great friends when we were teaching Navigation together. Jon was the outdoor-man from Michigan who knew everything about guns, knives, bows and arrows, and scuba equipment. He was an inveterate story teller. He told jokes in the first person present tense. He could suck you into two-thirds of the joke before you realized this was not something real that had just happened to him. He enjoyed his own stories, with foot stomping laughter and loved telling them. Jon was my story telling icon. I tried to model his style, and still do. Carol has said to me more than once, "Now you sound just like Jon Uithol." I took that as a compliment.

When we discussed investments, Jon was all into land, particularly waterfront property. He had a lot on a canal in a new development in Placid Lakes, Florida. I bought the adjoining lot. Our idea was that when the property became scarcer, we would make more money going together to sell a double lot. Development slowed, and we both sold our lots separately a few years later. Nothing loss, nothing gained.

Now, land in Canada was a different ball game. Jon knew this area, his family having made trips to the Upper Michigan Peninsula for the annual harvest of their Christmas tree farm. They had watched the section of Canada just north of them gradually grow and felt it had long range potential.

I came into the office one morning, and Jon had a deal.

"Dick, listen, there's this great chance for good property in Canada. It's not far north. Big tax sale. Back taxes plus 10% is the norm. I'm sure we could get this hundred acres for eight hundred dollars." He pulled his Canadian government land sale newsletter out of his desk drawer. "What do you think?"

We commiserated about the buy for a week. Finally, we both got practical.

"I don't know Jon," I said. "If the payoff is too far away, I don't know if I can afford to have $400 tied up for too long."

"Yeah, you're right. I don't want to tie up $400 either. Let's put it away for now, something else will come along."

It wasn't a month later that I came into the office in the morning with the folded *Newport News Daily Press* in my hand. I threw it on the desk.

"Morning, Jon."

"Morning, Dick."

I grabbed a cup of coffee and sat down. Jon was quiet.

After a few minutes I said, "Did you see the paper this morning?"

"Yeah."

"Well, is it or isn't it?"

"I don't know. I've been afraid to look."

He reluctantly pulled the Canadian land map out of his drawer and I spread the front page of the *Newport News* paper beside it.

Headlines in the *Daily Press* read something like: "Major silver strike near Timmins, Ontario sparks land rush at $1000 an acre." There was a large inset map with a big X marking the spot. When Jon and I compared the map and the newspaper insert, we both groaned. The one hundred acres we were going to buy a month ago for $800 was smack in the middle of the silver strike and was selling for $100,000 that morning. We made a pact, which lasted a few years, to never tell anyone how we blew that one. We laugh at the story today, but it wasn't so funny then.

We enjoyed a lot of good times with our friends. We went tent camping with Jon and Nan Uithol at Big Meadows in the Blue Ridge Mountains. We spent several weekends with the Donna and Carl Gruel at their cabin in Bayse, Virginia.

In the great stretch of fall weather, Carol and I often camped alone for the weekend on the Rappahannock River, about an hour away. She would have the car all packed when I got home from work on a Friday. We piled our 10 x 10 umbrella tent and our Collie into the Mercury and headed out.

Gail Parker's father had a large wonderful summer place on the Eastern Shore. It was always open to Gail and Frank, and they were most generous to include us as well as the Uithols, and Gary and Marian McManus, and others. We spent hours enjoying the huge great-room fire place, and day-tripping to interesting remote eastern shore towns. We also usually got in a little rifle and pistol target practice. Our collie, Ruby, had a ball playing with the kids.

Jon and I took advantage of the Coast Guard Tuition Assistance program by enrolling in the George Washington University's off campus program. Lieutenant Commander Jack Smith, the Officer-in-Charge of OCS, joined us. The three of us trudged off to the Army base at Fort Monroe in Hampton, Virginia, two nights a week for two years, summers included. We had to take a final comprehensive exam that covered the entire two years on the GW campus in Washington DC. Jon and I had joined a comp study group in our last semester at Fort Monroe. We both passed the exam and received our MA in Personnel Management. Jack, who had not been able to join our study group, took the exam and received his degree the following term.

At the end of each two-week summer ACDUTRA session, a newly promoted flag officer (Rear Admiral) was often the graduation speaker. It made a nice occasion for him to receive his first honors, complete with musical "ruffles and flourishes" and an eleven-gun salute.

We rotated lieutenants through the job of arranging for the honors with the Marine Corps detail stationed at the Naval Weapons Station. It was my turn, and I had left a message for the Sergeant in charge to call me back.

"Sir, this is Sergeant Kimick at Naval Weapons."

"Good morning, Sergeant. Did you say Kimick?"

"Yes, sir."

"Interesting. I grew up with a Jerry Kimick in my home town of Bradford, Pennsylvania."

"I wondered when I saw the name, Marcott. Dick, I'm Jerry Kemick from Poplin Avenue."

We were neighbors! We'd grown up together. He was two years younger than me and had joined the Marines right out of high school. Here we were working together nearly twenty years later.

In my last year at Yorktown, Capt. Mark A. Whelan, our CO pulled me out of OCS to replace the base security officer who had been transferred. I was reluctant to leave teaching, of course there was no option, but the move did have its advantage. Since the Captain required the security officer to live on the base that meant that the government moved me from Roslyn Road. That let me sell my house on at a leisurely pace.

We moved into the large two story duplex next to the Captains Quarters, high on the bank above the York River. Carol loved the view. She could watch the Navy ships moving under the bridge to and from the Naval Weapons station all day. It was a comfortable house, the second best location on the "Officer's Circle," and we enjoyed the peace of mind of a longer time frame to sell the Roslyn Road house. We managed to break even on the sale, which was not bad for a three year ownership.

In April of 1965, the war in Vietnam was escalating. At the Navy's request, the Coast Guard assigned seventeen 82 foot patrol boats to the effort to stop interdiction of enemy men and supplies from North Vietnam to the South. Our boats were well suited for the shallow draft operation.

They carried a weapons suit, and could be self-sustaining with live-aboard crews. President Johnson signed the order committing the Coast Guard to active service in the Vietnam under the Operational Control of the U.S. Navy as Squadron One.

Our 82 footers normally operated with an all enlisted crew led by a chief petty officer. But, because of the nature of the anticipated boardings, the Coast Guard was assigning Lieutenants, those with a good record as CO of a 95 foot patrol boat. Turnaround time was going to be fast. The crews would only have a two or three weeks' notice before reporting to CG Base Alameda, CA for the first part of their training. Personnel plans were being developed in secret, so orders were going with no prior discussion.

Former 95 foot WPB skippers were spread throughout the service. Two of them were Jon Uithol and me. We had both been ashore for over three years, and met the qualifications, so we were ripe for transfer. The HQ assignment officer, Stanley Walden, told me a year later that he had literally flipped a coin to determine our fate. One of us was going to go to Vietnam; the other was going to be assigned to Headquarters. The good life was coming to an end.

U.S. Coast Guard Headquardters

Washington, DC

Chief Training Branch, Training and Procurement Division Office of Personnel

June 1965-June 1966

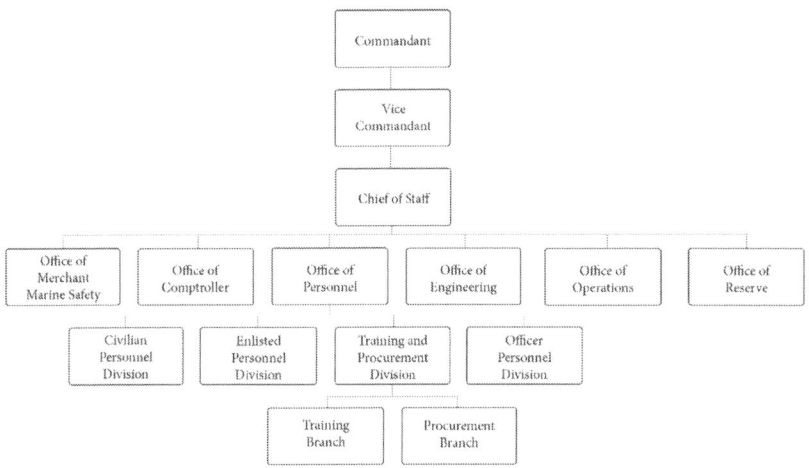

Coast Guard Headquarters in 1965 was located on Pennsylvania Avenue, directly across from the National Theater. The top officer in the Coast Guard is the Commandant, a four star Admiral. In the broadest sense the Commandant with the assistance of his primary staff, six office chiefs (Rear Admirals) directs the administrative activities of the Coast Guard. They direct the policy and program development, legislation, and administration of the entire service. They insure legislative compliance with statutory obligations and requirements and establish and maintain liaison with other government agencies. In general, division chiefs hold the rank of Captain.

Historically, the Coast Guard was founded by Alexander Hamilton in 1790 and functioned under the department of the Treasury from that time until it became part of the new Department of Transportation in 1967. It later moved to the Department of Homeland Security where it currently resides on a new campus in southeast Washington, DC.

−25−

HEADQUARTERS I

JON HAD ONLY A COUPLE of weeks to report to the Coast Guard Base in Alameda, California, for training and further assignment to Vietnam. He deserved a proper send-off. Several of us reported for duty at Jon's house with a bottle of tequila. Our objective was to say goodbye, and help dismantle the swing set in the back yard, a task we didn't get to until nearly midnight. We must have been successful because the next day, the swing set, the bottle of tequila, and Jon were gone.

Within a few weeks, I had my orders to report to Headquarters in Washington, DC, for duty as Chief of the Training Branch in the Training and Procurement Division in the Office of Personnel.

In 1965, parking was so limited at CG Headquarters on Pennsylvania Avenue, that I was advised to report first to an assigned coordinator who would advise me as to available car pool vacancies—then I could look for housing in that area. Carol and I ended up renting a small rancher, outside the beltway, sixteen miles southeast of DC in Clinton, Maryland. Anything closer was cost prohibitive. Car pools ruled.

Our five members drove individually to the Marlow Heights Shopping center, and we pooled in from there to the small lot behind HQ where an attendant stacked us in bumper to bumper every morning. The whole building had to leave work at the same time each day so we could be peeled out one at a time. The building emptied fast. Anyone who dared to tarry, blocking hundreds of fellow commuters, did not curry favor.

Travel distances limited social contact with others assigned to HQ. People were spread out on all sides and beyond the beltway. A simple dinner invitation could mean a seventy mile round-trip. We pretty much stayed home. Carol got a job as a bank teller at the Bank of Upper Marlboro in Marlow Heights We did occasionally get together with one interesting neighbor, a Syrian Arab who worked at the Library of Congress. He and his wife were both graduates of University of Michigan. He invited us to a number of always interesting social receptions at the Syrian Embassy in DC. The people were weird, but the baklava was to die for.

Finding a car pool first, then your house was not the only unusual aspect of this assignment. Military men and women of all services assigned to Washington DC, had to wear civilian clothes instead of uniforms. Hundreds of men and women in military uniforms on the streets of DC might lead visitors to think that the U.S. government was run by the military.

That created a new decision-making process every morning–what to wear–as well as an extra expense of maintaining a business wardrobe as well as uniforms. Men could get away with a few suits and a sport jacket or two. Thank God for the one-dollar-tie store across Pennsylvania Avenue from HQ. A new tie could create the illusion of an expansive wardrobe. It was also fun to buy one. The shop attendants were pretty young women who would go to the sidewalks to entice window shoppers into the store. A five minute shopping-buying event in the middle of the day lifted the spirits. It was a great stress breaker. I never bought just one tie. Nobody did.

In April 1968, following the assassination of Dr. Martin Luther King, the nation's capital became an armed camp. Widespread rioting, fires, and looting, turned the city into a war zone. Egged on by activist Stokely Carmichael for several days, twelve hundred buildings were destroyed. Over 13,000 federal troops were activated. Marines with machine guns manned the Capital steps and the 3ʳᵈ Infantry Old Guard protected the White House. Rising smoke from the nearby business district could be seen from our offices. HQ shut down.

Our carpool drove home in near silence sickened by the disgraceful scene of armed soldiers spread along Pennsylvania Avenue, yards apart, to protect the city and its citizens. It took days to regain peace. Over one thousand people were injured, a number were killed. Six thousand rioters were arrested. Damages in DC alone were in the millions of dollars, as riots spread through other major U.S. cities. It took decades to restore the destruction in Washington. It was a sorry thing to witness—the middle sixties.

On a brighter note, there were good things that happened. I was promoted to Lieutenant Commander on July 1, 1976, setting me up for a potential afloat assignment as Executive Officer. I requested assignment as XO of one of the new 210' WMECs. Carol and I both wanted to expand our horizons with a west coast assignment. Classmate Ron McClellan was XO on the USCGC *Resolute* when it was under construction at the Coast Guard Shipyard in Baltimore. MD. Her scheduled home port was San Francisco. The Commanding Officer was CDR Paul Yost, who had been a math instructor when I was at the Academy. The timing was right for me to relieve Ron in two years.

With our stunted social life, and no duty nights to stand, both Carol and I found time to enroll in a continuing education class offered by the Prince Georges County schools. She took a sewing class, which eventually increased our household inventory by one sewing machine. I took a ground school aviation class just because I had always been interested in flying. The class was intended to help students prepare for the FAA written exam for a private pilot's license. I had no intentions of actual flight training.

My first solo flight was on January 28, 1968. I had joined the Andrews Air force Base Aero Club, and flew out of Hyde Field in Clinton, only two miles down the road from our house. Jerry Rochet, a club flight instructor had just told me, after my third good practice landing, to pull in front of the club house. I knew what was coming. All instructors made the first solo a surprise. They thought it reduced stress.

I tapped the breaks on the little Cessna 150, a workhorse trainer for thousands of new pilots, and made the second turn-off. I taxied to the club house, stopped, and Jerry got out.

He read the lump in my throat. "Don't worry, you're ready. I'll be in the tower. Call me if you need me."

The prop-wash billowed his light jacket as he backed away on the tarmac while giving me a toothy grin and thumbs up. I taxied for my first solo take off. I had had seven hours of dual instruction. The flight went well, and the landing was great. I taxied back to the clubhouse and everyone there cheered me. Then following a long tradition, they cut my T-shirt off, wrote the name and date on the torn shirt and nailed it to the ceiling, where it hung like a limp cloth stalactite with those that had belonged to pilots who reached this milestone before me.

There was still work to do after soloing. I had dual instructions in maneuvers and cross country navigation. Eventually I made solo flights to Newport News, Richmond, and Leesburg, and one at a large controlled field, Dulles Airport.

Meanwhile, time for a transfer grew closer. Stanley Waldon, the assignment officer that brought me here, would greet me in the hall with, "Good morning, Dick. Are you feeling resolute today?" After a month of his not-too subtle hints, the assignment slate was approved and I received orders to report to the *Resolute* as Executive Officer.

The timing was going to be close. I wasn't sure if I was going to get my pilot's license before having to leave for California. But, on June 7, 1968, I smiled at the FAA Flight Examiner in Manassas, VA as he shook my hand.

I had passed my flight test. I was now a certified private pilot, SEL (Single Engine, Land). I had only one day left to fly in Clinton. I rented a plane and Carol was my first passenger. We celebrated the occasion with a short local sightseeing trip. I didn't fly again until November when a got a check ride in a Piper 180 out of Buchannan Field in Concord, California.

Two days after Carol and I flew, we watched the moving van pull away. We plunked Ruby onto her "dog shelf" in the back seat with her bowl of water, and headed home to Bradford for a short visit. Within a few days we were off on our first Cross Country trip. California, here we come. We were happy.

USCGC *Resolute*
WMEC 620

San Francisco, CA

Executive Officer
July 1968-June 1970

The Coast Guard Cutter *Resolute* (WMEC620) was built at the Coast Guard Yard, Baltimore, MD, and commissioned on December 8, 1966. The new 210 foot cutter was one of sixteen *Reliance* class medium endurance cutters built to replace the old 165 foot Patrol Crafts. The new class of ships also ushered in a new era for the Coast Guard—helicopter decks. To give more space for helo operations, the *Resolute* had exhaust vents in the stern, rather than a conventional stack. This eventually proved to be a problem and stacks were installed during a 1980 class overhaul.

The Resolute carried a crew of seventy-five who enjoyed comfortable above standard crew accommodations. She had a beam of thirty-four feet and a draft of eleven feet. Her two sixteen cylinder, 2500 HP Diesel engines gave her a top speed of eighteen knots and power to tow ocean vessels up to 10,000 tons.

The Resolute drew standby duty for Search and Rescue (SAR) including scheduled weeks at the pier in Monterey Bay to better cover the southern region. Her primary calling, however, became patrolling the U.S. Fisheries Zones, which included two month patrols in Alaska. The Coast Guard is the only agency able to conduct at-sea enforcement of fisheries laws, and its afloat presence was necessary to enforce the international treaties.

Eventually, the resolute served in several home ports including Alameda, California, Astoria, Oregon, and her current home port of St. Petersburg, Florida. Her primary duties now involve drug and migrant interdiction as well as SAR.

—26—

CALIFORNIA

"I'VE NEVER BEEN THIS FAR west before," Carol said in a wide smile as she spread the roadmap open on her knees, ready to navigate. We had just turned onto Route 17 at Seneca Junction, ten miles north of Bradford; we had been on the road for twenty minutes.

I laughed. "Well, when we get to Cleveland, I can say the same thing."

I had a reporting date to meet, and we needed time to house hunt, so we left Bradford after a two-day visit with my family. House hunting advice from people who had been stationed in San Francisco was, "Decide what kind of weather you like and go twenty-five miles in that direction." That was something we never knew about the area; it was a city of micro climates. The San Francisco peninsula was foggy until noon, then gray and overcast the rest of the day. Marin County north of the Golden Gate Bridge was nice, but too expensive. We opted for the mild winter, hot summer, blue sky valley east of the Oakland Hills in the Lafayette/Walnut Creek/Concord area. Our realtor, Dan Azmus, who I had contacted earlier, was already working on finding a house.

Navigation was not hard. Once we hit I-80, just over the Ohio border, it was 2600 miles straight ahead. The trip was not conducive to sightseeing: A fleeting glimpse of the Golden Dome of Notre Dame University as we breezed through South Bend, IN; an hour at the Des Moines Airport to watch small planes do touch-and-goes after dinner; and a quick run through Buffalo Bill Cody Museum in North Platte, Nebraska.

We traveled all Holiday Inns because of their guarantee to take pets. Ruby was terrific the whole trip. Our eighty-pound collie moved gracefully in and out of the car at each rest stop. By the third day, she recognized the big Holiday Inn signs. When she felt she had ridden enough, she would whine at each one we passed, telling us it was time to stop. With all HI's built the same, when we did stop, she knew right where her food and water was going to be and where she was going to sleep.

Just as Carol and I were growing bored with the flat miles and miles of corn and wheat fields from mid-Ohio on, the landscape changed. The green crops gave way to desert-like flats with dusty rock outcropping. We were on the long slow rise to the eastern edge of the Rockies.

We had been on one barren stretch for a long time. Carol had to pee.

"Rich, I mean it. I really have to go."

"Well, Carol, there's not much I can do about it. Do you see any place?"

"No, but I don't think I can hold it."

I hit the brakes and moved off the road to the right shoulder, kicking up a little dust as I slid to a stop. I was more irritated than I had any reason to be. "So, get out. Go right here."

"Rich! I can't do that. What if somebody came by?"

I got out of the car, slammed the door, and looked up and down the highway.

"For God's sake Carol, I can see fifty miles in both directions. If there's anybody else on this highway with us, it's going to take them an hour to get here. Now, get out, open both doors and go in between them. Trust me, nobody's here to see you."

Reluctantly, she got out; I could hear the sigh of relief. Actually, it seemed like a good idea. So, Ruby and I got out, too. All three of us felt better after our little walk-around unscheduled rest stop—"facilities not available." Carol was good, the dog was good, I was good—on to Laramie, Wyoming.

We stopped at a drug store on the outskirts of Laramie. Carol had a developed a bothersome rash on the top of her foot and ankle that she said

232

"itched like crazy." She held her foot out for the druggist, who squatted down to get a closer look.

He looked up at her. "What part of the East did you come from?"

"Washington, DC, actually. But, how did you know we were from the east?"

"You've got poison ivy. We don't have that here, only back east." *Micro climates and no poison ivy. What other weird things did we not now about the west?* He gave us some ointment, and all was well.

Laramie is a dusty small town west of Cheyenne that historically had been a frontier town with saloon fights and vigilante justice. Now it was home to thirty thousand people, many of them cowboys and college kids. After dinner in the motel, we took a short walk to stretch our legs and experience the local color. After a few blocks, we stopped for a beer one of the local watering holes.

Cowboys—real cowboys— lined the bar. They all wore jeans, western shirts, cowboy boots, and sweat stained Stetsons, either tipped back on their head or pulled low over their eyes. They stood with one foot on the brass rail, and talked above the background honky-tonk music about the price of cattle, who was moving their herds, and joked about stale biscuits. There were no young college kids in here. It was as though we had invaded the movie set of *The Westerner* or *Wyoming*. Where were Gary Cooper, Walter Brennan and Wallace Berry? It could have been *Old Cheyenne* with Roy Rogers and Gabby Hayes. We finished a beer and strolled back through the time machine to our modern hotel. "Damn, Carol, that was a trip. From now on, I'll believe every western movie I see."

"Me too. This *is* cow town. Now I know why their football team is named 'Cowboys.'"

On I-80 heading into Salt Lake City, the six lane road lies at the bottom of a deep V cut in the Wasatch Range. The sides of scraggly rock and mixed greenery are so steep you can't see the top without bending to peek up and out of the side window. It felt like we were wee people in the pit of God's prayerfully cupped hands, and only he could peek through the tops of his outstretched fingers to judge our progress. *Are we protected or are we prisoners?* Intermittent splashes of sunlight across our windshield hinted that an opening was ahead.

As we emerged from a long curve, it was as though He had rotated his hands to expose the magnificent view of the Salt Lake Basin. If the Mormons had come upon this scene after their arduous journey from the east, I could believe they must have felt that God had truly shown them where to build their temple. Today, the city was there, all pristine, and white. Tall buildings reflected a golden sun about to dip below the western peaks. It is an awe inspiring sight.

We pulled into Oakland, California, at the end of the sixth day. I contacted Ron, and we enjoyed a mini-reunion and met his wife Ryoko for the first time. After dinner, we found a small motel with good weekly rates a couple miles south of them to serve as temporary quarters while we looked for a house.

That night I came back from waking the dog, excited, and said to Carol, "Don't get too settled, we're moving in the morning."

"What are you talking about?"

"Well, Ruby and I got a few blocks away, she did her thing, and then I saw eight or ten uniformed and plain clothed cops across the street with guns drawn, crouched behind bushes and car doors. They were obviously about to raid a house. I didn't wait around to see the action."

We wasted no time getting out of there in the morning. We had heard nothing during the night. We found a new motel north of Ron and contacted Dan Azmus to begin our house hunt.

Dan had done his homework. Working from our wish list he had several homes to show us. By the end of the first day, we had narrowed our preferences to live in Walnut Creek, in an "Eichler" home.

Dan had shown us a number of Eichlers. They were named after the architect who had over ten thousand homes of similar style in Bay Area housing developments alone. His modern, but not too crazy, design appealed to us as did the layouts of the developments. With curved streets, tall greenery, and "privacy fences," you hardly knew that you were in a development.

Eichler wanted his homes to connect with nature. He designed straight-lined open floor plans with glass-walled vistas that opened to patio gardens or internal atriums, or both. The flat roofs were supported by huge open beams that ran the length of the house. There were no street views from inside the house. Internal walls were mahogany panels.

Our side patio had a fifteen foot high bamboo patch, islands of geraniums and flowering bushes, and a solid fence with espaliered pyracantha that blocked the view of the street.

The fermented berries in the fall were an attraction for the birds that Carol often found drunk, staggering around the patio, unable to walk, much less fly. She would pick them up and set them next to a pie tin of fresh water. They complacently sat beside it and drank, sometimes for hours, even a day, until they were sober enough to fly away.

Our back patio had planted squares of Japanese maples, and assorted flowering bushes. The six foot high privacy fence separating us from our back neighbors' swimming pool, was made two feet taller by a huge blanket of thick flowering clematis that draped over the fence top like the blanket of roses worn by the Kentucky Derby winner. We especially loved the sense of peacefulness created by the evening view of a garden from the glass back wall of our bedroom.

Dan told us that despite the near hundred degree days, the evenings were cool and we could enjoy our patios with no bugs.

Carol looked at me then back to Dan and said "What do you mean no bugs, Dan?"

"We have no flying gnats or mosquitoes, and you really don't even need screen doors. Also, it may be hot in the afternoon, but you'll need a light sweater most evenings." *That's the third weird California factoid.*

Carol glanced at Dan and said, "OK, Dan, if the summer afternoon is so hot that you have to hibernate inside the house, this one has no air conditioning, that's an added expense we'll face."

"No, you don't need air conditioning."

"What?" Carol and I responded together.

"Come on, Dan," I said. "This flat uninsulated roof that is also our ceiling, with hot direct sun beating down on it, has got to be hot."

Dan laughed. "Not really, a little tar paper covered with white gravel reflects a lot of the heat, then your *swamp cooler* takes care of the rest."

Carol asked, "Swamp cooler? That sounds like you're adding humidity, Dan. Why on earth would you want to make the house more humid in the hot summer?"

"Carol, we have very low humidity in the summer. It really helps to cool the place."

Dan explained the swamp cooler. Picture a square box, with no bottom, mounted on the roof over a cut out square in the ceiling. The sides of the box are stuffed with exposed straw and water is pumped from a trough at the bottom of the wall to the top where it then drips through the straw back into the trough. A down-blowing fan mounted in the ceiling hole, sucks the outside dry air through the wet straw, cooling it, and then blows into the room. It actually cools a fairly large space ten or more degrees. It is a great substitute for an air conditioner, and it is a lot cheaper to run.

Carol and I laughed and told Dan we felt like rubes from the east. "What else don't we know about California?"

"Well, the weather in San Francisco is nearly the same all year. All summer it is fifty five degrees with a twenty knot wind from the northwest blowing through the Golden Gate.

The "Golden Hills" of California are burnt grass because it does not rain from May through November. Then, it rains nearly daily during January and February, plushing the hills to green again starting another cycle. The hottest month is October and the coolest is July."

Walnut Creek was an attractive community of thirty-five thousand that sits sixteen miles east of Oakland at the foot of Mr. Diablo, a 4000 foot mountain that dominated the valley that stretched four hundred miles south to Los Angeles. We bought the house at 2620 San Benito Drive in Walnut Creek for $39,000.

Ron and I had three days together on the ship before I relieved him as XO. The *Resolute* moored at the U.S. Naval Station, Treasure Island. TI was a flat four hundred acre land-fill attached to the natural island of Yerba Buena (YBI) in the middle of the San Francisco Bay. The city of San Francisco had originally built the island as the site for the 1939 Golden Gate International Exposition to celebrating the completion of the Golden Gate and Bay Bridges.

The city had planned to run the exhibition for two years, and then convert the island into a civilian international airport. When World War II interfered, the island was turned over to the Navy. It served as the headquarters of the Twelfth Naval District, and a receiving, training, and shipping center for personnel heading to the Pacific Theater.

Three thousand military and civilians who worked there got on and off the Bay Bridge from YBI. Getting onto the island was not bad—getting off was the trick. At the end of the work day, cars waited in a long single lane for their turn to merge into the fast moving lanes of San Francisco commuters rushing to the East Bay. There was neither an entrance ramp nor merge lane.

Cars sat at a dead stop, at the ready, angled toward the eastbound lanes. Drivers did not watch the traffic, but rather glued their eyes on a very brave shore patrolman who stood with his whistle in his mouth and hands at the ready on the white line separating the traffic whizzing by either side of him at fifty miles an hour. When *he* judged that you should be able to make it into the traffic flow, he blew his whistle and waved furiously—you had best be ready to peel out! It added an element of excitement to every workday that I could have done without. The Coast Guard still has some facilities at YBI. The Naval Station Treasure Island was closed in 1997.

The Resolute Commanding Officer, CDR Paul A. Yost was a lieutenant math instructor and company officer at the Academy when I was a cadet, but I had had little interaction with him. Ron had served with him since the ships commissioning, and he gave him a good report card. All XO's share their accumulated wisdom on how to get along with the "old man." The CO-XO relationship is special. They are a team and must present a single and consistent image to the crew. The CO defines the roles. A seagoing urban-myth tells of a Navy Destroyer CO who told his newly reporting XO, "There's only room for one SOB on this ship, and it ain't gonna be me." The XO knew what his job was.

Captain Yost came across a little straight laced and all business *when he should have been*. I found him to be a friendly, open man, with a pleasant personality. He had been a wrestler and coach at the Academy, and still looked like he could get into the ring with anyone. It was a pleasure to have served with him. I never hesitated to give advice or comment, and, when I did, I always felt they were duly considered. His wife, Jan also had a winning personality, and Carol and I always enjoyed the few social occasions we shared with her and the Captain. I was not at all surprised when ADM Paul Yost became the eighteenth Commandant of the Coast Guard in 1986.

The *Resolute* had a light Search and Rescue load in the Bay area during my tour as XO. That was also true of the several two week stand-bys we stood in Monterey, California, where we shared the city pier with more than a hundred barking sea lions who never slept and smelled badly.

To keep up with our military preparedness, we periodically got underway for drills and exercises. That effort paid off when we logged pretty impressive scores when we underwent Navy Refresher Training in San Diego.

Alaskan fisheries patrols dominated our at-sea time. Former classmate, Ed Grace, and his wife Betty were a wonderful support for Carol while I was gone. Ed had started in my class at the Academy, but graduated with the class of '58. He was assigned to the Twelfth Coast Guard District in San Francisco as merchant marine inspector. He and Betty lived in Concord.

We had known them for a short while at Yorktown. Ed reported to teach in Merchant Marine Safety School when I was shifted to security officer in my last year at Yorktown. He was one of the infamous crew that dismantled Jon Uithol's swing set. We became very close during my tour on the *Resolute*. Betty was then, is now, and always will be the epitome of the mother hen taking care of her friends, or anyone in need, for that matter. She adopted Carol when I was on patrol.

She had her for dinner every weekend when I was gone. She checked on her often, was a shoulder to cry on, and a shopping companion. You could count on her to be there if you needed her, and she would tell you to "just get it together," too, if that was what you needed. We are fortunate to count Ed and this talented nurse-wife as best lifelong friends. Their four kids grew up calling us Aunt Carol and Uncle Dick, (and still do today.) Kimberly reciprocates the honorary title with them. When I shifted to Alameda, Ed was transferred to Boston as the Engineering Officer on the Coast Guard icebreaker, USCGC *Edisto*. Our paths didn't cross again until we both retired. Now we still try to get together at least once a year. We are lucky people.

My first Alaskan patrol was during salmon season, and the Japanese fishing fleet included a huge factory vessel that was served by ten or more 125 foot gill net catcher-boats. Our main interest was the size of the net's mesh, how big the catch was, and where did they catch them. Salmon migrating north to their spawning grounds split at the 180th meridian. Those that went east belonged to us; those that went west were fair game for the other nations.

The gill-netters dumped their catch on the ship's main deck where they were sorted to conveyer belts that delivered them to the factory below decks. Four to six hundred workers, mostly women, prepared and packaged the salmon. By the time the fleet went home at the end of the season, the ship had a whole cargo of canned tuna, cooked, labeled and boxed for delivery to Japanese grocery stores. The factory ship then underwent an amazing three week transformation in a shipyard where the salmon factory was completely removed and replaced with a whale processing plant. The fleet then headed to Antarctica for the whaling season. It was an impressive and efficient operation. I doubt if we could do an environmental impact statement in three weeks.

I boarded only Japanese vessels. The cold-war tensions with the USSR had made any boarding attempts with them impracticable. The Japanese were most congenial. It was important to them to honor the international seafaring tradition when ships who met at sea exchanged gifts. That was awkward for us because they always had gifts while the U.S. regulations forbid expenditure of government funds for such purposes. We avoided embarrassment with a creative over-order of fresh fruit for the crew's mess. The Japanese loved fresh grapefruit, a rare and expensive treat for them. For a more personal touch, a coffee cup and saucer officially marked as Coast Guard officer wardroom china was a big hit. Our "bad weather breakage" qualified for replacement. To top the gift package off, our crew donated a couple of Playboy magazines— possibly the biggest hit of all.

In December, CDR Jack Smith reported aboard as our new Commanding Officer. He was the same Jack Smith I served with at Officer Candidate School in Yorktown. I always liked Jack, and I looked forward to being his Executive Officer.

The following summer Jack planned his first Alaskan Fisheries Patrol with port visits to, Vancouver, British Colombia, then Ketchikan and Juneau, Alaska, via the inland passageway. The diversion added a little to the time away from home, but I think most of the crew welcomed the adventure. I know I did.

The 1969 summer Alaskan Fisheries Patrol took on a whole new meaning. The U.S. and USSR had entered a new period of detente, and for the first time in many years, the U.S. was going to conduct "courtesy boardings" of the Russian fishing fleet.

I soon found myself right in the middle of that adventure.

—27—

THE RUSSIANS ARE COMING

THE TALL RUSSIAN CAPTAIN, HIS four gold stripes tarnished by years of salt air, smiled at our Coast Guard boarding party. I was on a factory vessel in the middle of the Bering Sea. It was my thirty-fourth birthday, July 20th, 1969. The four of us had just made the long climb up the pilot ladder, and stepped through the bulwark of the four-hundred-foot converted cargo vessel. Now we stood before the Captain and two civilian men who greeted us. The Captain smiled, saluted, then shook hands all around, stood back then pronounced, "Gentlemen. Congratulations! Your man has landed safely on the moon."

This was our first news of the success of the U.S. Apollo Eleven Mission.

From a Russian!

The *Resolute* was mid-tour on a sixty-day Alaskan fisheries patrol. We knew this one would be different. We may have entered an official period of détente, but that didn't mean we were all that trusting. The U.S. suspected that Russian factory vessels, with far from typical antenna arrays, were engaged in electronic eavesdropping. An Army Intelligence Officer (AIO) out of Anchorage had been assigned to the *Resolute*. Though he spoke Russian, he was not aboard as an interpreter, but as a man with his own mission. He joined us in Juneau, wore a Coast Guard crewman's uniform, and he was part of the boarding party when we boarded Russian factory vessels.

Also joining us in Juneau was Sid Morgan, an agent of the Alaskan Department of Fish and Game, Our "Fin and Feathers Guy." Sid had years of experience accompanying Coast Guard aircraft and cutters on fisheries patrols. He had boarded Russian factory vessels in the past. We counted on him for the details of the treaties and, above all, identifying the various species. Sid was a well-known Alaskan character. An inveterate story teller, and his catalog of adventures was about to grow by one.

We left Juneau, passed through Stephens Passage and Frederick Sound, into the Gulf of Alaska. Half of the crew was on deck capturing pictures of the Fairweather Range before it got out of sight. The four jagged peaks were among the highest mountains in North America ranging from twelve to fifteen thousand feet, and you could frame them all in one 35mm slide.

When we entered the Gulf, we were officially on patrol. Our first stop was Kodiak Island, seven hundred miles across the Gulf. From there we would move on to Dutch Harbor, another six hundred miles out the Aleutian Chain.

I had always enjoyed Jack's sense of humor. His room-stopping boisterous laugh that I knew at Yorktown was now a more subdued command-like chuckle, more of a soundless bouncing of his shoulders. He still smiled with his eyes first, but they were now beneath thick graying eyebrows.

We stood together on the bridge wing enjoying the unusually smooth Gulf of Alaska until the mountains faded astern. We moved inside and Jack boosted himself into the CO's chair, which, through its own Karma, projected a command presence. The young messenger of the watch moved quickly to hand him a cup of coffee. I stood next to him to chat about the possible boardings.

He clutched the hot mess deck coffee cup in his right hand, and with his chin musing on the coiled fingers of his left he said, "You know, this could be a pretty significant event. You may be the first Coast Guard officer to conduct an enforcement boarding on a Russian ship since the Cold War."

"I hadn't really thought about that, sir." He had already informed me that I would be in charge of the boarding party.

"I figure as Executive Officer, and with your rank of Lieutenant Commander, you will be senior enough to show proper respect to the Russians."

"Yes, sir."

"But more importantly, it will leave me a bit remote, but on scene, should we need any fallback position."

"Yes, sir. In case I screw it up, you mean?" I smiled, knowing he'd take it as intended.

"Yeah, well that, too." We both laughed.

"Anything else, sir?" I said, serious again.

"Even if the weather is good, I plan to lay off a few hundred yards and send you to them in our small boat. I want any and all transfers made only in our boat."

"Aye, aye, sir."

As it would turn out, his strategy was prophetic. A year later, on the East Coast, when a CG vessel nested alongside a Russian ship for a similar boarding, the Coast Guard CO acted as boarding officer. A Lithuanian sailor leaped from the Russian ship onto the CG vessel, seeking political asylum. The incident ended with a team of Russians boarding the American ship and physically removing their deserter. With the Coast Guard CO directly involved, there was no American on scene senior enough to keep the issue local. It quickly escalated to an international incident to the embarrassment of the Coast Guard and the U.S.

The trip across the Gulf was uneventful. We enjoyed the overnight at the CG Air Station in Kodiak. A few of the men had a chance to link up with old shipmates, and buy a few souvenirs at the CG Exchange Store. Jack and I joined the CO of the CG Air Station for dinner. CDR Bill Black, was an academy classmate of Jack's, but also happened to be one of the few Coast Guard officers from my hometown of Bradford.

A dark flat base of heavy clouds hung low when we left Kodiak, smothering the smooth gray ocean. With a slight breeze and temperature in the fifties, the foul weather jacket felt good. It stayed that way for the two-day trip along the southern coast of the Aleutian chain. It was mid-July, but by now I knew this was just a summer day in Alaska.

As we approached the pier in Dutch Harbor, the bombed out wooden buildings of the former Fort Mears and the Naval Operating Base lined the shoreline to the east, then up a slope to the top of a small hill. Their shattered remains, still identifiable as buildings, were now pock- marked and graffiti covered. Once alive with American military, they stood in silent testimony to the Japanese bombing attacks on Dutch Harbor in WWII.

Before the next day was out, a CG patrol plane, a C-130, reported a Russian factory vessel, processing king crab on the western end of Bristol Bay. Her fleet of catcher boats was working their tangle nets near the Pribilof Islands. This portion of the bay was known as home to the largest cash crop of Alaskan Red King Crabs. It was the season, and the Russians were here. We got underway, heading for our first boarding.

As we set out of Dutch Harbor on a southerly course, the onion dome of the Russian Orthodox Church in the village of Unalaska receded astern. The village, founded by Russian fur traders in the late 1700s, had come alive for the fishing season. Unalaska's normal population of four hundred ballooned to many times that, with rugged men who came to make their fortunes at sea or in the packing plants.

The *Resolute* then pushed north through Unmak Pass into Bristol Bay, that portion of the Bering Sea that separates the Alaskan Peninsula from mainland Alaska. It was not long before we spotted the Russians on the horizon, a catcher boat, about a hundred feet in length, alongside. The factory ship cranes were unloading her catch of king crabs.

As we closed the distance, the deck force readied our port side small boat for lowering. The ship slowed to five knots. The Captain stood with me at the boat davits on the main deck. I saluted him and turned to get into the boat. Returning my salute, he said, "Good Luck!"

"Thank you, sir." I stepped aboard to join Sid, and the AIO, along with one of our Ensigns. The Captain had added the fourth member to provide experience for our younger officers who would rotate through the assignment. We motored the two hundred yards to the Russian ship.

The large converted cargo ship swung easily at anchor. As we got closer, we could see the indecipherable name of the ship and home port emblazoned in bold white Cyrillic letters across the black rust-streaked transom. I asked, "Everybody ready? Any questions?"

Our Ensign spoke up, "Sir, check out the women at the rail."

Sid, the AIO, and I all smiled, but he was right. There were clusters of sailors, and more than a few women, peeking over the bulwark. Like the Japanese factory vessels, most of the six hundred workers processing the king crab were women. In addition, some served as ships officers in communications and administrative duties.

I led the climb up the narrow pilot ladder; flat narrow hardwood rungs braced between vertical manila lines. I gripped the lines tightly as the ladder slapped the steel sides of the ship in rhythm with the slow rolls. It moved more than I expected.

We were all a little taken aback with the Russian Captain's Apollo Eleven news bulletin. We had been following the space mission since take-off on July 16, but given the fickle communication Gods of the Bering Sea, had not received word on Astronaut Neil Armstrong's landing. I thanked the Captain for his kind words, trying to act like this was old news, but Indeed, their antenna systems were better than ours.

246

The Captain introduced himself as the ship's master and the heavy-set civilian next to him as the fleet commander. The thin man in the background was not introduced, but also never left. I presumed he was the ever present party representative that I had been briefed about.

The open deck amidships was piled high with squirming Red Alaskan King Crab. The smell filled the air as we watched the ship's crane swing overhead, the operator expertly lowering its large wicker basket to the catcher boat alongside. It soon reappeared, dumping a new load of live crabs atop the pile already struggling to regain their freedom. The purple and white crabs, which can reach twenty-five to thirty pounds, a leg spread of as much as six feet, their shells encrusted with sharp spiny bumps, tumbled over each other like bizarre outer space creatures playing king of the mountain.

We were struck that the main after-body of the ship, looming four decks above us, bore a giant portrait of the former Premier of the Soviet Union. The stern face with pinched brows made his eyes more penetrating. With his bald head and familiar goatee, Vladimir Llyich Lenin stood like a ghostly watchdog. The leader of the Bolshevik revolution was a constant reminder to everyone onboard of their roots.

The Captain gestured us toward a door inviting us into a narrow, dimly-lit passageway that led to the wardroom. As a crew member held the heavy steel door, I noticed that Sid, just before he stepped over the shin-busting threshold, caught a glance back at the crab pile. He made mental notes of the size, species, and estimated numbers of the catch. The AIO, I'm sure, was making mental notes of a different nature.

As we snaked out way to the wardroom, the Captain suddenly took my elbow and quietly said, "Come with me, please." The rest of the party moved on while I turned to follow the Captain down a side passageway and up to the next deck. Stopping at a beautiful mahogany door with a polished brass name plate, he turned and said, "Please step into my cabin." My mind struggling for a scenario, I stepped inside. He followed and closed the door. Before I could say anything he pointed for me to sit in a small leather chair at the side of his desk and, in perfect English, he asked, "Do you own a car?"

"Do I own a car?" I had no idea where this was going.

"Yes, do you have an automobile?"

"Yes, Captain, I do."

"What kind?"

"A Toyota Corona."

The Captain leaped out his chair, a huge grin on his face, extended his hand to shake mine, pumping it vigorously. "So do I!"

I got the feeling he now saw us as some sort of kindred spirits. He sat down and leaned back in his chair.

"How long did you wait?" He steepled his hands, tapping his fingertips in anticipation of my answer.

I must have looked confused. I had no idea what he meant.

"You know. How long did you have to wait to get your car?"

"I'm sorry, Captain. I don't understand."

"Well, in my country, as Captain of a fleet factory vessel, I am highly ranked. I got my new car after waiting only three months. How long did *you* wait?"

"Captain, in my country *anyone* who wants to buy a car makes a trip a car store. There are usually several in a row on the same street. When I bought mine, I knew I wanted a Toyota, test drove a few models, decided, then bargained for the best price. I drove the car home the same afternoon." From the look on his face, I feared I had embarrassed him. Damn!

He said nothing for a while, then, "I like the U.S. Coast Guard. They are not like the Navy or Army. You and I are just men who go to sea." After a slight pause, he added, "I don't like our Army or Navy either." Before I could recover, he placed both palms flat on his desk, pushed out of his seat and pointed to his cabin door.

248

"We should probably be joining the others in the wardroom." To this day, I imagine an old Russian sea captain sitting around a fire, stoking his pipe, downing a vodka, dramatizing this same event to his grandchildren, "...yes, that's what that crazy American tried to get me to believe—he buys his cars in one day!"

It was a short trip to the wardroom. As we maneuvered the passageways, the deck rose and fell just enough to remind me we were at sea. We entered the plainly decorated wardroom, a few pictures of dignitaries and maritime scenes on the bulkhead, reading lamps bolted to the deck beside comfortable lounge chairs, light tan square lampshades. The bulkheads were pale, relaxing green. It was like I had been there before. There must be a worldwide pact that requires this standard decor for naval officers to eat and lounge at sea.

The rest of our group was already seated at the table along with two Russian officers I had not met before. Everyone rose as the Captain entered. He moved to the empty seat at the head of the table and indicated the chair at his left for me. As I took my place, I turned to face the shoulder of the giant officer next to me. I tipped my head back, took in his scraggly face, large nose, and unkempt black hair that hung a little over his ear, and smiled hello.

"Gentlemen," the Captain spoke the single word of greeting as he took his seat followed by all others. Set at each place, there was a dessert-sized plate with cut fruit and a small stack of nondescript neatly quartered cold-cut sandwiches. There was a large filled water glass to the right of the plate, and next to it an empty one about the size of an I-Hop juice glass. A single line of Pepsi-Cola sized bottles extended the length of the table. They were clear glass, clear liquid, tops off, standing shoulder to shoulder, like a centerpiece of crystal towers. I couldn't read the label, but, I figured that the bottles didn't contain water.

For a few moments, we engaged in a babble of awkward introductions, struggling with unpronounceable names. But, congenial sign language set the atmosphere for a friendly meeting.

Then the AIO gave a prearranged signal. We were being bugged. So—friendly yes, but be careful what you say. I had no idea how he discovered that, and I probably couldn't have found out if I had asked him later.

Before long, the Captain stood in place, stopping the chatter, and everyone pushed their chairs back in unison and stood at attention. He reached for his juice glass and the closest bottle of vodka. He filled his glass, a good four plus ounces, set the bottle back on the table. Extending his arm in front of him, elbow straight, he said, "Gentlemen!" Everyone followed his lead, charged glasses all, arms extended, awaiting the next move. Lifting his glass as if it were an Olympic torch, he intoned in a solemn bass voice, "A toast. To all the men who go down to the sea in ships."

"To all the men who go down to the sea in ships," we echoed like a practiced chorus, we all raised our glass high. Then with a single bend of the elbow, heads tossed back, the Russians drained their glass to the bottom in nearly one gulp.

Fortunately, I was prepared. Briefing notes from past boardings, before the cold war, warned that the Russians might try to get you drunk. So, in a perfectly polite gesture, I took a small sip from my glass, smiled, and returned it to the table to await the inevitable next toast. Our boarding party did the same. Then, from the corner of my eye, I saw the bear paw of the giant officer next to me, long hair on the back of his hand, a finger twice as big as my thumb, pointed at my glass.

"What's this?" A heavy accent, but I understood.

I turned, faced his blue shoulder, then peeked up at his unsmiling face and continued with my prepared speech. "Sir, in my country, when we are so honored to share such fine whisky, out of respect for its quality, we sip it to ensure its endurance."

"Bullshit!" The bear was roaring now! "In my country, we drink like this!" Refilling his glass and inhaling it in one tipping, he then ceremoniously slammed it upside down on the table, rattling the centerpiece, bottles clinking in tones like wind chimes.

"That's the way we drink to honor a country! You drink like the stuffy British!"

Oh crap!

What do I do now? I thought. *Détente—first American boarding— what could happen? International incident?* So I raised my glass with equal flourish and drained it to the bottom, then slammed it upside down on the table to great cheers, applause, and laughter of the Russians as I choked back an embarrassing cough, my throat burning. My team gave me a questioning glance, then dutifully followed my lead.

After the toast, we did a little business. Sid asked about the size, species, and origins of the crab catch. The Russians described their use of tangle nets on the ocean floor to capture the creeping formations of king crab. (The U.S. claim that all king crabs were ours, and therefore subject to the treaty, was based on the fact that they do not swim—they crawl. Therefore, even beyond the protected two hundred mile fishing zone, in international waters, they are *our creatures of the continental shelf*.)

It became obvious that protocol dictated, unlike at casual dinner parties at home, no drinking during the conversation. I began to fear interspersed bottoms-up chug-a-lug moments.

The fat Russian on the other side of the table in the ill-fitting double-breasted suit and yellow-stained teeth that matched his soiled white collar, open at the neck, no tie, lifted his bulk to stand at attention. He charged his glass in a repeat of the Captain's ritual, all stood and followed.

"Gentlemen! A toast to the men of the U.S. Coast Guard." Hell, I couldn't deny that one. Down it went, burning my throat again. No mistakes this time. Upside down and empty. Now it was obvious there had to be another toast, and it had to be mine.

Official business continued: display of fishing charts, examination of logs, and discussion of Russia historical fishing grounds dating to before Alaska was an American territory. At one lull in the proceedings, the Captain turned to me, placed his elbow on the table, open hand pointing straight up, pushed his coat sleeve back and poked repeatedly at his wristwatch. He said, "Do you know Ratti? Coast Guard Ratti?" Now a Rear Admiral, stationed in Washington, I knew that when he was a Commander he had been the CO of the *Storis*, out of Kodiak, and surely a veteran of fisheries patrols.

"Yes, sir. I do know Admiral Ratti. Not well, but I know of him."

"This Ratti's watch! I beat him." He chuckled, slamming his closed fist to the table. So, they had been in an arm wrestling contest and the Russian captain now wore the prize. I could not get into this. I turned to Fin and Feathers. "Sid, are you comfortable with what you have?" When he nodded, I rose and charged my glass. Everyone followed.

When all glasses were filled, arm extended, I said, "Gentlemen, we thank you for your hospitality. Our business is done. We appreciate your cooperation. We must return to our ship. But first, a toast." With all arms raised to the overhead, I continued, "Gentlemen! A toast. To all the mariners at sea working hard to bring food to their countrymen." God! That really sounded stupid! But the vodka went down the same. This time, however, it only warmed my throat. No burn.

As we wove slowly back through the passageways, I thought about how dumb that toast must have sounded. Besides, none of their catch went back to the USSR. The factory processing on board was complete to the point of packing the crab in labeled cans and boxing them in cartons, ready for overland transport. All labels were in English, French, and German.

As we emerged onto the bright open deck, which had been cleared of the small mountain of crabs, I began thinking that the climb back down the pilot ladder was going to be more dangerous than the climb up. The Captain must have had the same thoughts as he motioned with his arms and yelled something in Russian. The cargo crane whirred and swung toward us, expertly placing a large wicker fish basket on the deck in front of us. "This will be easier," the Captain said as he shook all our hands and assisted everyone into the clean basket.

We shot straight up, a rocket-like takeoff, and then swung quickly across the deck like a giant pendulum. A crowd of factory women, gathered for a last glimpse of the Americans, laughed and waved to us as we flew over them. Then, like a Coney Island parachute drop we came to an abrupt hover over our small boat which had been standing by. The boat crew grabbed the tether which dangled beneath our gondola and guided us to an easy landing. The carnival ride over, we all got out of the basket, without incident, and returned to the *Resolute*.

I made my way to the bridge and reported to the Captain. "Sir, the boarding went well; Sid has all the information. I'll get together with him and prepare a report."

He leaned close to me, smiled, and quietly asked, "And how are *you* doing?"

"Actually, Jack, I'm good right now, but I could use a little cabin time. The full force of that vodka hasn't hit me yet."

"Yeah, I agree. You better get some sack time, because we've got another boarding about five hours over the horizon."

USCG Training Center

Alameda, CA

Training Officer
June 1970-June 1974

The land fill from the dredging of the Alameda Estuary in the late 1800's created Government Island, which sits between the cities of Alameda and Oakland, California. The estuary gave the two cities a sheltered deep-draft port. It was administered by the U.S. Government for the benefit of several agencies. The Coast Guard established Base 11 on the island in 1926 on fifteen leased acres. Later, to meet expansion demands of WWII, the Coast Guard established a training and supply depot as well as piers and support facilities to accommodate major cutters. Eventually, the Coast Guard Training and Supply Center was the only occupant of the sixty-seven acres island. There were several smaller schools, but the primary mission was recruit training.

The TRACEN Alameda was one of two Coast Guard Recruit Training Centers, the other at Cape May, New Jersey. Alameda trained recruits from the western half of the contiguous states, Alaska, and Hawaii.

Once a twelve week program, the nine week "boot camp" provided training in basic seamanship, first aid, survival training, and military conduct as well as customs and traditions, and rights and benefits. Recruits, at pay grade E-1, in 1970 were paid $138 per month plus quarters and subsistence. Today, basic pay is $1450 per month. Graduates are advanced to the grade of Seaman Apprentice and receive $1756 per month. From Boot Camp, they move to operational commands as non-rated apprentices or go directly to advance occupational specialty schools to become petty officers.

The TRACEN Alameda closed in 1982, when all boot camp training moved to Cape May, NJ. Government Island, now Coast Guard Island, is home to the Eleventh Coast Guard District.

—28—

RECRUIT TRAINING REFORMS

THE BREEZE FELT GOOD. I had the top down on my new Fiat 850 Spider convertible. The bright blue two-seater responded well when I moved off Treasure Island into the early bridge traffic. I was still getting used to the standard shift, and I left a little rubber when I popped the clutch when the Navy shore patrolman gave me the signal. He flashed me a quick thumbs up and smiled as I pulled past him. I shifted up to speed as an eighteen wheeler pulled past me in the adjacent lane. I was riding lower than the top of his tires.

I was headed to the CG Training Center, Alameda (TRACEN) for an interview with the commanding officer, Captain Walter Curwen. When I told my assignment officer a few days before that I was really interested in the TRACAEN, he said, "You'll have to meet with CAPT Curwen first. I can't assign anyone as Training Officer without his approval."

I had called the Captain, and he suggested an early afternoon meeting on a Friday. "That way we can talk for a while then you can go to our recruit graduation with me." Sixty or seventy new recruits graduated every week. I was looking forward to meeting Captain Curwin; I felt I knew why the interview was necessary.

I crossed over the narrow causeway from Dennison Street in Oakland, the only access to the Government Island, and parked in the visitor's space in front of the red brick administration building. Captain Curwin's office was on the second floor. He was expecting me.

"Good afternoon, Mr. Marcott. Glad you could make it." He came around his desk to meet me. His natural smile and warm welcome made me feel good about him right away. He wore the wings of a Coast Guard aviator on his blue blouse.

"Good morning, Captain, I'm pleased to meet you, and thank you for seeing me about your open training officer position." The Captain gestured me to a chair, drew one up near me and ordered his yeoman to bring us both coffee.

"Well, Mr. Marcott, you'll see in a minute why it was necessary. This is a key position at TRACEN, and frankly, I have reasons to be sure we get the right man."

"Captain, I think I have a good idea why. Before I came to the *Resolute* two years ago, I was Chief of the Training Branch in PTP." Rear Admiral Scullion asked me in my exit interview how I felt about Alameda. I gave my opinion that we were getting too many complaints of mistreatment of recruits, and when I contacted the TRACEN for comment, I was uncomfortable with their response. Their "investigation" of incidents seemed perfunctory, if not contrived.

The captain, relaxed back in his chair, took a sip of his coffee, and with a smile on his face he said, "Good. Then let's talk about recruit training."

What followed was a philosophical discussion of training methods we each felt appropriate for boot camp. Clearly we were on the same page, and I felt it was the only way either of us would have continued with the plan to assign me as the new Training Officer.

I speculated that he had been assigned to "clean up" the boot camp operation. The old training officer had been transferred and, LCDR Bill Hudson, Captain Curwin's personal choice, had replaced him. Bill had been doing a great job, but the captain was concerned he was getting burned out after a tough year and a half.

I met Bill at the recruit graduation that afternoon, and then the three of us continued our discussion after the reviewing officer reception in the officer's club. We all felt we had a match, and Captain Curwin asked Headquarters to assign me as Training Officer. I left the Resolute and reported directly to Alameda TRACEN on 16 June 1974.

The relief process with Bill Hudson took a few days. As soon as I relieved him, I spent priority time meeting with the company command-ers individually and in a group, and particularly with the assigned Navy Chaplains and Dr. Dennis Short, a Psychiatrist, and a Commander in the Public Health Service Commissioned Officer Corps, and Chief of the TRACEN Medical Division.

I learned two key things from these meetings: (1) Conditions had been much worse than I had suspected, and (2) With very few exceptions, the people directly on the firing line, the company commanders (CC'S,) were ready and willing to embrace change. They respected Bill Hudson, and knew that Captain Curwin had his back. I assured them that I was in com-plete agreement with the changes they were instituting, and we needed to work together to keep making progress.

The meetings did wonders to improved relationship, particularly between the CC's and the Chaplains. The CC's, who used to think the Chaplains would "just mollycoddle" the recruit, seldom referred anybody for counseling. They expected chaplains to stick to conducting Sunday services. The chaplains, on the other hand, had considered CC's as uni-formed street hoodlums.

Recruits who were in trouble had become very adept at working one against the other. By sharing their perspectives, the "good guys" began to trust each other and often devised a mutually agreed upon course of action. The CC's were, at times, surprised with the "tough line" of the Chaplains. Dr. Shorts' professional observations and advice was welcomed by both CC's and the Chaplains. He began to hold separate sessions with the CC's to teach them observations techniques, what behaviors to look for, and how to describe them in terms beyond "the kid just doesn't have his shit together."

The meetings helped me get a feel for the type of boot camp Alameda had been running. Although all military boot camps had much in common, there were differences in training methods. I can't find fault with anyone who was trying to do right by their recruits and still meet the demands of their service. The Marine Corps boot camp methods, *which worked for the Marines,* for whatever reason, appealed to the Alameda Training Officer. He had established a similar system and, in my personal opinion, had carried it well beyond the Marine Corps model, as though he needed to out-Marine the Marines.

It appeared to me that poorly performing recruits were *all* dealt with as *disciplinary* problems. Placed in a separate X-Ray Company, they had undergone demanding physical fitness routines, marching drills, sleep disruptions, inane work details, and constant harassment. When the X-Ray company commander felt they were ready to "square away," he returned them to regular training. I doubt if any recruit had left X-Ray company feeling better about himself or the Coast Guard.

There is no magic source of young men 17-20 years old. They reflect the norms of our society as a whole. The men who answered the call of their country in WWII, draftees and volunteers alike, expected boot camp to be tough, and they knew it had to be, for their own good, even survival. They were part of a total national effort where everyone wanted to do their part. They were scared, yes, but proud of their effort as well.

The young men who entered into boot camp in the decade of the sixties and seventies were different. They entered from a society that had grown weary of the Vietnam War. They were from a society of youth protests, and anti-war militants who were openly hostile to most of what their fathers and mothers knew as middle class values. Instead, they embraced the norms of counterculture groups. They demanded individual freedom, from dress to personal grooming, and flaunted their disdain for all authority figures.

The men who reported to Alameda came from troubled urban centers, pleasant suburbs, and quiet patches of remote countryside. The last sound heard by some of them was the gavel of a judge, who told them their choice was the military or jail. Others heard their fathers telling them to get out and not bother to come back, or the cries of their mother who reluctantly gave up their youngest, but glad they would be saved from the gang warfare that threatened all her children.

On the other hand, some of them had enlisted to get the GI Bill that would pay for them to go to college later, others didn't know what they wanted after high school, but thought the service was a good place to learn a trade. Some came because having received their master's degree they had lost their student deferment and they reasoned that joining the Coast Guard would be better than being drafted.

There were the few that hated the military, but could not bring themselves to escape to Canada. So they enlisted in the Coast Guard, then immediately tried to disqualify themselves through rehearsed description of medical maladies. Our location on the door steps of Berkeley gave easy access to such guises, but our USPHS doctors were on to them; they could recite the memorized complaint along with them.

Every week seventy or more of these young men were dumped into the caldron of open bay living in double-deck bunks, and gang showers with yelling company commanders who made sure they could do nothing right. Survival depended on pleasing their CC and the mob soon discovered it would take teamwork to succeed.

I remember one particular recruit from a ranch in Montana. He had graduated from a small one-room school and the twenty friends and relatives who had attended his graduation were the most people he had ever seen in one place at one time. The Coast Guard Recruiter had driven him to the airport, and put him on a plane for San Francisco.

I can only imagine what he must have thought coming into the air terminal at SFO. Somehow he managed to get a bus to Alameda and worked his way to Government Island, only to be dumped into the mob scene with more weird people than he had ever seen in his life. He was not a discipline problem! He was overwhelmed. We pulled him out of training for a week for counseling until he was ready for a regular company. When he was ready, he performed well, graduated and moved on to the active fleet, a proud Seaman Apprentice.

In addition to struggling with hippie counterculture, experimental drugs, and anti-Vietnam protests, the whole country was engrossed in efforts to eliminate entrenched discrimination against minorities. Responding to public pressure, federal, state, and local institutions, as well as civilian corporations struggled to develop solutions. While many were helpful, there were some that, in my experience, aggravated the problems.

A few weeks before I had left the *Resolute*, a young black seaman apprentice, not long out of boot camp, entered my office to complain of prejudicial treatment.

I'm sorry to hear that," I said, "but I'm glad you came to me. Take your time and tell me what's happening."

"Well, sir. You know I'm on the deck force and we do a morning washdown every day."

"Yes, I'm aware. So, is something happening there that makes you think you are being treated unfairly?"

"Yes, sir. I never get to hold the hose."

Only the sincere look in his eyes kept me from laughing. This was a real problem for him. "I'll talk with the first lieutenant, I'm sure he'll straighten this out."

"Thank you, sir." Then as he moved to the door, he turned back to me. "Actually, sir, I'm not assigned in the right department. See, I'm an engineer."

We met again alone the next day along with our Engineer. When asked, he explained his engineering training, "Sir, I went to the Job Corps Training Center. I had a lot of training there and graduated an electrical engineer."

The EO spoke up. "Tell me about the kind of work you did as an engineer."

"Well, sir, I made rounds and read gages to see if the machinery was running OK."

"Can you explain that further?" I said.

"Sir, if the needle was in the green, I knew things were OK and if it were in the red section, I had to go tell my foreman."

The Job Corps, which was started in 1964, as a resident training program to improve the economic self-sufficiency of disadvantaged youth, had done nothing for this young man. And, when he met reality, because the Corps had brainwashed him as to his capabilities, when he didn't achieve, he "knew" it must be because he was prejudiced against.

The Job Corps program has been much maligned as one of the most wasteful, least effective programs in the field of government. It has appeared on the "chopping block" of more than one president. Yet, it continues today with one hundred twenty five resident training centers nationwide providing training in one hundred career technical areas as well as GED instruction. I hope with improved performance.

The weekly meeting with Chaplains, Company Commanders, and a Medical Department representative bore fruit and led to changes in the overall training process. To begin with, we adopted the underlying philosophy that recruits had, like any new employee, joined the Coast Guard voluntarily and wanted to succeed. We no longer assumed they were all recalcitrants who needed to be subdued before we could build them back into one of us.

The greatly improved sharing of behavioral observations led to better solutions that addressed core problems. Those that needed help or adjustment time were assigned to "Special Company" and assigned a CC who could deal with them appropriately.

While we retained X-Ray Company for the hard core problems— there were always a few that were disruptive enough to be dealt with separately— we greatly reduced the crazy night time drills and nutty work like digging huge holes only to be ordered to re-fill them as soon as they were done.

We focused the company competitions, an important part of building esprit-de-corps, toward a practical "Nautical Skills Field Day," and written tests on Coast Guard knowledge.

I learned quickly that if there was an element of training I was concerned about that I needed to figure out a way to make it part of company competition. The CC's strived to be Honor Company and they would be all over any deficiencies. When the short knowledge quizzes became a problem, CC's quickly identified the root cause. "These damned kids can't read!"

I discussed this problem one morning with Captain Curwin. That afternoon second class petty officer Joseph Streufert, who was a yeoman in the front office, was at my door asking to see me.

"Come in, Streufert. Well, this is an honor," I kidded. "What brings you to the realm of the action?"

"Sir, I heard you talking to the Captain this morning about recruit reading problems. I think I can help, but I don't know how, or if, I can be transferred from the Captain's office."

"Sit down, Streufert, tell me about it."

"Well, sir, I have a master's degree in remedial reading. That's what I want to do when I get out in a couple of years. I'd love to develop a remedial program, if you agree."

In less than an hour, Captain Curwin's office was short one yeoman, and I had set Streufert up in a classroom, put him in charge of Special Company, and told him he could have whatever he wanted in the way of supplies. The Captain had quickly agreed, of course, and Streufert was off and running. He established what proved to be the most successful answer to the recruit reading problems. He was their Company Commander, instructor, and counselor. Within a few months he was running one of the most successful reading programs in the country.

While he had total control of the class 24/7, an advantage from the public school, who still only saw their pupils 5 days a week for a relatively few hours, his accomplishments were nevertheless recognized at the national level. He had written several articles for literacy journals, and we received phone calls from hundreds of people (military and civilian) who were facing the same problems.

He used the California Reading Test (the gold standard at the time) to measure progress. We were routinely raising recruits two full grade reading levels in a few weeks of "phonics" training. It worked, and I believe we may have been the only institution in the country with that kind of results.

I felt that two other government institutions had failed to help one young man—the Coast Guard and a school district. Like the Job Corps, they actually aggravated the situation. He was a Native American recruited in Albuquerque, New Mexico. He was one of four boys in a family of proud Marines. Three brothers had enlisted before him. He was turned down by the Marine Recruiter. He was hurt because he couldn't follow, as his brothers had, in the footsteps of the famous Native American who helped raise the flag on Iwo Jima after that World War II battle.

He found a Coast Guard recruiter, who, unfortunately, was under great pressure to meet his minority quota, and had fudged his Qualifying (AFQT) score to 41. (The minimum for all services was 40.) We had learned that all scores of 41 were suspect. We called them New Orleans

41 per-centers. New Orleans, headquarters for the Eighth CG district, which included New Mexico, was a frequent offender.

Streufert had also tested him as reading at the fourth grade level on the California reading test. Yet, he was carrying a valid HS diploma and believed he had earned it. His school district was guilty of blowing smoke at this poor man the same as the job corps made my seaman on the *Resolute* think he was an engineer. Everyone loved this recruit. He had a gung-ho attitude, was polite, never any trouble, and a hard worker. We worked with him far longer than others. He was in special company over four extra weeks.

I received a phone call directly from his congressman, a highly unusual event in itself. He made an impassioned plea that we keep him in the service.

"Sir, I wish we could," I answered. "Please understand that with this young man's scores, he would not even be drafted in time of war. He needs much more help than we can give him. The Coast Guard did him wrong, for which I'm sorry. But I think you need to do something also to discourage the social promotions in high school. Giving a man a certificate when he has trouble reading at the fourth grade level is not helping him." The Congressman fully agreed, and he was thankful for the talk. We sent the young man home with an Honorable Discharge.

Recruit training was a challenge. The military services were expected to bring young men with diverse backgrounds, motivations, and abilities into a cohesive unit ready to function as contributing team members of an operational unit. And they had to do it in nine weeks.

Boot camp could be a perfect laboratory for group and behavioral psychologists. But, I doubt if they could perform the miracles that the first class and chief petty officer company commanders did. These dedicated enlisted men, were hated by everyone for the first two or three weeks. But, in the end, they were loved by all. Every recruit felt proud and grateful that his CC had helped him meet the demanding standards, and, for many, had given him a direction in life. Ask any man who went to boot camp, and although he may not remember a lot of the people he served with, I'll bet he can name his Boot Camp Company Commander, and he'll remember him fondly.

Ironically, Dr. Joseph Streufert momentarily reentered my life twenty years later. After I retired, I was serving as a director of the Bradford Area School District. The Superintendent reported that the teachers were enjoying a two day in-service training program led by him. Shocked, I called the local Holiday Inn, and discovered it was indeed Petty Officer Streufert. We met at the motel that night and rehashed Alameda days for more than an hour. Dr. Streufert was a reading professor teaching at an eastern Pennsylvania University. I tried, unsuccessfully, to contact him while I was preparing my memoir.

I loved every moment of my job as Training Officer at Alameda that gave me great sense of accomplishment. Carol and I enjoyed living in Walnut Creek for the two years I was on *Resolute,* and we continued to enjoy California living for the four years I was stationed at TRACEN Alameda. Early in that assignment we experienced a personal change.

It was the most welcomed—it changed our lives forever.

—29—

IN THE SHADOW OF DIABLO

"THE RABBIT'S DEAD!"

I stared blankly into the phone. It was one of the doctors in sick bay, I couldn't speak.

"Dick, did you get that?"

"Oh, sorry. Yeah, I got it all right, Doc, you're not kidding about this, right?"

He wasn't. I hung up the phone leaned my office chair to full tilt and laughed to myself. I fought the urge to call Carol right now; I wanted to see her face when *I* was the one to tell *her*, "Babe, after thirteen years—we're pregnant!"

My little blue spider made the twenty mile trip home in jig time. I pushed the seventy mph speed limit, bobbing and weaving kept me from getting sucked into the draft of the semis. I opened the door and spilled the news to Carol. We hugged, smiled, cried, then laughed, then cried again. I said, "Oh, man....now what?"

Carol had not been feeling well for some time. She had finally said, "Rich, I've either got cancer or I'm pregnant. Take a sample in to Alameda and get the doctors to test it. Let's get through the easy one first." After thirteen years with no children, I think we both had been silently dreading the answer. Needless to say, we were ecstatic.

On that wonderful three day weekend, Valentine's Day, February 14, 1971, at the Oak Knoll Naval Hospital in Oakland, California, Carol gave birth to Kimberly Ann Marcott, a perfect Irish redhead.

Carol and I left the hospital alone. Kimberly was fine, but she was slightly jaundiced and remained in the hospital for a few days. We called the new grandparents right away. I had the right answer to the first question from my Nana, now a first time great-grandmother. "Yes, Nana she has red hair." My dad and I both had red hair, and his mother was one of twelve siblings–all with red hair. *The dominant gene continued; both of Kimberly's children are red heads.*

Carol and I were more mature than most first time parents. She was 33, and I was 35.We didn't succumb to youthful panic when we weren't sure about things. We had prepared for this event all during Carol's pregnancy. When we did make goofy little mistakes, we were still able to laugh about them and move on. Carol's parents flew out to see their first grandchild within a month. I was proud with how well Carol handled her mother. No clash of wills or debates on parenting practices. Carol was confident and in charge.

The baby did well until mid-summer when she couldn't shake a series of infections. Several visits to the doctor and the tests that followed revealed the bad news. Kimberly had a congenital blockage of one ureter. The kidney was enlarged, and already damaged to some extent. It was serious, and she needed surgical repair. Time was of the essence, so at five and a half months old she underwent a *pyeloplasty*. The doctor explained it as a surgical repair to the kidney. The blockage was in the ureter close to where it entered the kidney. The ureter would be removed from the kidney, the blockage snipped off, and the ureter re-implanted into the kidney at another location. I knew how small Kimberly was, I could only imagine the size of her kidney, much less the ureter. I couldn't see how anybody could possibly work this miracle on an infant.

Oakland Naval was the place to be. The hospital, originally built in 1942 to care for Pacific War victims and Naval personnel stationed in the Bay Area, had closed after the war. It was re-opened and expanded in 1968 to serve Korean and Vietnam War victims. Its specialties with large departments were, fortunately for us, Orthopedics and Urology.

Kimberly was operated on in the late afternoon. The staff finally convinced Carol and I to go home, and come back in the morning. They had assigned a corpsman to sit at her crib side all through the night. Exhausted, we did go home. Early the next morning we were moving quickly down the corridor to the room she shared with a young Filipino baby.

What the hell was happening?

The Filipino baby's crib had been rolled into the corridor. Red lights were going off over the doorway. The PA was calling doctors by name to answer some code— in her room.

We rushed through the door. The scene was chaotic. People in whites were hovering over her crib. The oxygen tent she had slept with was removed. The corpsman was there along with several nurses and at least two doctors. Seeing us, one nurse came quickly to move us to the window. She tried to assure us things were going to be OK but did not ask us to leave, just stay out of the way over by the window.

Carol grabbed my hand and we stood silently looking out the window, hardly able to watch the horror going on behind us. I caught a glimpse of Kimberly's tiny face; it was turning blue-gray. She wasn't moving. Shouldn't she be crying? Her eyes were closed. A white uniform was reporting to the open room, "I'm getting nothing."

Everyone was talking; they were loud, but controlled. I looked at Carol, both of us had tears. I'm sure she was thinking the same as I was, *Oh, God, not now, not now. Please, not after all this!* The staccato voices continued.

"Oxygen deficient."

"Airway."

"Cyanotic."

"Pedes trach kit. Stat!"

My mouth was going dry, I tried to look through Carol's teary eyes, but there was nothing to see. It was as if we checked out, put the action off as unreal. Carol was holding her stomach. Our stares were confirming to each other that this was real. We squeezed each other's hands in an unspoken gesture of "I'm with you."

A new doctor entered the room. Suddenly a nurse yelled, "Hold it! Hold it! Hold it!"

The new doctor dove to the crib, "Extension, more extension." Finally—"She's OK, she's got it." Everyone relaxed; the medical crowd congratulated each other, wide grins on their faces. They all patted us with reassurances that she was OK now. She survived the operation itself well, but during the very long surgery, the anesthesia tube had rubbed her throat raw, closing it to breathing. Something in one of those packages of loose paper strewn all over the room had worked to reopen her airway.

Carol took a deep breath, let out a whoosh through her gapping mouth as she slid against the window sill. A smile was building again on her face. My thoughts were jumbled, but I held her hand tightly as I let the reality slowly creep back into my soul. Five minutes of hell were over. It seemed like thirty.

A mother daughter moment on Mt. Diablo

Richard Marcott

We got through the real infant years and began living the good life again, this time with Kimberly. We made the best of the great California central valley weather. We lowered the convertible top on the Spider 850, stashed Kimberly onto the short shelf behind the seats and explored the flavor of the Bay Area. We didn't miss much. We tripped from Fisherman's wharf, and Ghiradelli Square in the city, to the Giant Alameda County Fair, the Coast Guard Day picnic at the Training Center, and to the Nut Tree Inn on I-80 toward Sacramento. One of our favorite weekend drives was to the peak of Mr. Diablo. With the top down, and Kimberly sharing the shelf with a picnic basket, we shifted our way up the curvy climb to the 3500 foot summit.

The view was spectacular. The massive volcano shaped mountain rises from the north end of the famed California Central Valley. It sits alone; it tapers to the low foothills and the city of Walnut Creek. The view from the top covers forty counties, and we could see the Farallon Islands, thirty miles beyond the Golden Gate. The park at the summit is the second best place on earth at which you can see the most land from; it is second only to Mr. Kilimanjaro in Africa. The sun shines three hundred days a year in the Valley—it's hard not to have a good day.

Kimberly was doing fine. She had periodic checks in Nuclear Medicine at Oak Knoll so the urologist could see the plumbing and re-assure us that all was well. She was adjusting to the presence of other small people in the world at the Wile-a-way Nursery in Walnut Creek, while continuing to explore the world around her.

Kimberly was christened in the chapel at Alameda by our Chaplain friend, Dick MacCullagh. Don Morrison, classmate, and my old housemate from New London stood in as a phone proxy for Carol's sister Eleaner who was Kimberly's godmother. Don had reported to the USCGC *Gresham*, homeported in Alameda, as Executive Officer around the same time I had reported to the *Resolute*. Conflicting ship schedules didn't allow for a lot of time together, but when Don was transferred to the District Office in

San Francisco, and I was at the TRACEN, our families got together quite often. Don and his wife, Gil, who was a sister of classmate Buddy Morris, and their two children lived just beyond us in Concord.

I had missed being able to fly much since getting to California. Other than a check ride and a short flight or two, the ship's schedule just didn't make it very possible. The shore job at Alameda changed that.

I took advantage of the VA program, and enrolled in flight training for my commercial license. I flew out of Navajo Aviation at Buchanan field in Concord. Buchanan was a very busy regional airport. I took commercial Ground school, duel flight lessons, and I flew often. One of the major requirements for a commercial license was experience. I needed two-hundred hours, much of it cross country. That changed the way the family explored California.

It was not unusual for us to decide on a Sunday afternoon to go grab a hamburger—in Monterey. I'd check out a Piper 180 from Navajo Aviation, get the family aboard, and we flew the hundred plus miles, viewing the magnificent coast from a thousand feet ten miles off shore.

Then it was back north over the inland valley, head for Mr. Diablo, which was always easy to pick out. We would be back home for the evening news on TV.

Kimberly's favorite short hop was to fly to the Nut Tree Inn, the fly-in restaurant near Sacramento. She flew enough to take it for granted that everyone flew in for lunch. She liked the trip because she got to ride the miniature railroad from the airfield to the restaurant. When we drove there one day, she was disappointed and whined until we paid for the train ride from the restaurant to the tarmac and back.

We made one long cross-country trip to a fly-in resort in Bend Oregon for a vacation. We had to get out early on the last day because of weather, but made it home with a short stop in Marysville, California, to wait for the valley fog to lift before getting back home to Buchanan Field.

My mom and dad flew out for a visit and a chance to enjoy their granddaughter. We made all the usual tourist rounds, then one afternoon I said, "Come on, Dad. I'll take you for a plane ride. It's a great day for it." We'll just trip down the Oakland Hills and back. You'll have a great view of San Francisco Bay and the Mountains to the east. It'll be getting near dusk soon, a great time to fly." We left the rest of the family at home and drove to the airport.

I explained every step of the walk-around. He was involved with my banter, asked a couple of questions and we got aboard and called for taxi instructions. Dad was quiet, just taking it all in.

The radio squawked, "Piper November Eight Eight One Six Papa... you are cleared for takeoff."

I replied "Roger, Six Papa rolling." As soon as I was straight on the center line, I went to full power and just past mid field, I eased back the stick and we were airborne. I looked at Dad whose head was on a swivel, looking all around.

I climbed to 4000 ft. brought the plane to straight and level and said, "OK, Dad, I'm going to give you the airplane." I explained the basic operational controls, he took them, I coached him through a few easy turns, all made with a big smile on his face.

When we landed and came into the house, Mom asked, "Well, how did you do, Joe?"

"Ginner, I actually flew the plane! It was great."

Mom later explained that he had not done well on the commercial flight from Pittsburgh. He was a white knuckle flier all the way. His explanation, "Two things, I could see out front and it seemed to make me more aware of what was happening, and two, my son was the pilot."

A personal first for Dad, a treasured moment for me.

I logged another treasured moment while at Alameda, my first and only World Series: The 1973 World Series between Oakland A's and the NY Mets.

I tried to get Carol to go. She did not like baseball. After I moped around the house for a few days she finally said, "Rich, get in your car and go in and buy you own ticket. You'll be mad at yourself if you miss this chance."

It was two days before the opening game. I stood in the long line and watched people ahead of me walk away empty handed. But I was not going to leave now. When I got to the counter, the ticket seller stunned me. No problem sir. Since you only want a single...you even have a few choices, but you have to buy tickets for all four home games. You'll get a rebate if the series doesn't go seven." Like that was going to be a problem.

I sat in the second row of the upper deck nearly behind home plate, struck up a relationship with my seat-mates on both sides, and was thrilled the series went seven games. I saw the first two and last two, an exciting series that Crowned the A's World Champions.

I cheered with all 50,000 fans at the Oakland-Alameda County Coliseum for exciting games, and great players, in the days when they all had great names: Rollie Fingers, Regie Jackson, Vida Blue, Catfish Hunter, Blue Moon Odom, and on the other side; Tug McGraw, Willie Mays, and Rusty Staub. A memorable day for me, and I would have missed it had it not been for Carol.

Carol had her own first, and one that surprised me. She announced one day that she was going to be the president of the San Francisco Officer's Wives Club. She had always been an active member, attended most meetings, served on committees—but president? Carol was an introvert, although many people did not see this, and this was one of the largest clubs in the Coast Guard. She presided over the club from 1973-1974.

She packed Kimberly up and took her to the nursery on Treasure Islands until the meeting was over.

She had a great year, which she attributed to her experience as the Worthy Advisor of the West Hempstead Assembly of Rainbow Girls in high school. She knew how to run a meeting, picked good committee chairs, set the strategy, gave them what they needed to do their job, and let them do it. I was really proud of her. She also enjoyed those occasions to have lunch with the District Commander. Our Commanding officer at Yorktown, Captain Mark Whelan, had been promoted to Rear Admiral, and he was now the District Commander of the Twelfth District. She was always comfortable with him because of the old Yorktown connection.

I had mixed emotions when I was ordered to command the USCGC *Chilula,* in Morehead City, NC. I was pleased that I was getting a sea-going command, but after serving as XO on the *Resolute,* which meant I was really comfortable with that class, I had asked for command of a 210 anywhere in the country. The *Chilula* was a WWII relic handed down from the Navy. We also had loved California, but orders were orders and we prepared to move.

We packed up our station wagon that we had bought as a more reasonable family car after Kimberly was born, and I sold my Fiat. We sold the house for $42,000, three thousand more we had paid for it six years before. Unfortunately, our timing was bad. One year later in the middle of the big housing boom, the house sold for $100,000. That missed opportunity was not as bad as the Canadian silver strike that we missed out on in Yorktown, but it would have been nice to have had that extra year.

When Mr. Wheeler parked the immaculate new North American Van in front of our house, he was so proud that he insisted that I check out the wooden deck before he loaded a stick of furniture. He had waxed and buffed the hardwood floor with bowling alley wax. It was a thing of beauty.

I was comfortable that our household goods were in good hands. It was a direct move, so he was going to be the only one in charge of loading and unloading the truck. Not much over five feet tall, the strength of this elfin man surprised me. He lifted and bullied our furniture and awkward boxes into place, stacked and protected, with the precision of a professional load master. He and Kimberly had struck up a great relationship.

We slept our last night in Walnut Creek, and when the sun peeked over Mr. Diablo the following morning to take us out of the shadows, we headed south, then east on old U.S. Route 66, the southern route.

USCGC *Chilula*
WMEC 153

Morehead City, NC

Commanding Officer
July 1974-October 1975

The U.S. Coast Guard Cutter *Chilula* was originally a U.S. Navy Fleet tug (AT-153). Built in 1944 at the Charleston Shipbuilding and Dry Dock, Charleston SC, the 205 foot oceangoing tug was assigned to the Asiatic-Pacific Theatre in World War II. Following the war she served on Occupation Duty until 1946. The *Chilula* was decommissioned in 1947 and shifted to the Atlantic Reserve Fleet in Texas. Transferred on loan to the U.S. Coast Guard in 1956, she was re-outfitted at the Coast Guard Yard and commissioned as WATF-153. That designation was changed soon after commissioning to *Medium Endurance Cutter* (WMEC-153).

The *Chilula* served as a search and rescue vessel for the duration of her Coast Guard service from her home port in Morehead City, North Carolina. Her capabilities as an ocean-going tug particularly suited her for duty just below the bight of Cape Hatteras, an extremely dangerous area known for hurricanes, strong storms, and turbulent water. With the large number of shipwrecks throughout history, the Cape Hatteras area has earned the nickname, *"Graveyard of the Atlantic."*

The single-screw ship is powered by four GM 750hp Diesel-electric engines and has a deep draft of over fifteen feet. The *Chilula* is manned by a crew of five officers and eighty enlisted men. The ship was berthed at Fort Macon at the entrance to the Port of Morehead, one of the deepest draft ports on the U.S. East Coast.

The *Chilula* was decommissioned in 1991, returned to the U.S. Navy and was eventually sunk as a target ship in 1997.

30

MOREHEAD CITY

MR. WHEELER OPENED THE SIDE cargo door of the huge North American furniture van parked in front of 110 Gull Harbor Drive. Kimberly bounced on her toes at the top of the driveway, her tiny fists quivering against her chin, watching his every move. He hooked the off-load ramp into place then disappeared into the van. In a moment he reappeared at the top of the ramp holding a red tricycle high over his head. "Well, lookie what I found here, Kimberly."

"Oh, Mr. Wheeler, you have my bike! You have my bike!"

He had understood how a move could affect a child, and had made a production of loading her tricycle last. "Now see right here is where I'm putting your bike, and when you see me in a few days, it will be the first thing I get out of the truck." For five days, every North American van we passed on the cross country trip triggered a peep from the back seat, "Do you think that's Mr. Wheeler, and he has my bike?" We had no idea so many North American vans existed. Finally, after 3000 miles, she was a happy camper again. He had beaten us in the cross-country race despite having to unload two other houses on the way.

It was only 8 a.m., but the rising summer sun and North Carolina humidity would soon overcome us. You could rub your thumb and two fingers together and feel the air. The odors wafting from Bogue Sound at low tide settled over us in what would become a new twice-a-day experience. Three independent workers, hired in much the same way that I had hired my post-hole diggers in Newport News, Virginia, had arrived in their pickup truck. They wanted to make quick work of it if for no other reason than to get out of the heat. They worked hard and we waved goodbye to Mr. Wheeler as his van pulled away shortly after noon.

I had been fortunate to parlay a training conference in Washington, DC into a house-hunting trip to Morehead City. I had bought a spec-house, a two-story light tan stucco, from a builder with the iconic Southern name of Holden Ballou. It was in a new development on Bogue Sound, just off NC24, called Gull Harbor. There was one other occupied home and one empty one.

The town of Atlantic Beach, which was squeezed onto a narrow sand-spit across Bogue Sound, had seen their ocean front resort, Emerald Isle, build up in the last few years with new condos, motels, and vacation cottages. Maybe there was hope for Gull Harbor too.

We had to make the 3000 mile trip in five days just to keep up with Mr. Wheeler who had agreed on a date to meet us. Fortunately, we had great weather, drove long days, and for a three-and-a-half-year-old, Kimberly suffered the trip like a champ. We had one unwelcome delay in Albuquerque, NM, to replace all four tires on our Mercury station wagon.

At a motel stop in Memphis, Tennessee, Carol and I welcomed the fresh smell of rain in the air as we got ready to go to dinner. The first sharp bolt of lightning lit the room like a flash bulb, followed by a tremendous thunder clap. Carol and I looked wide eyed at each other for one second— then shouted together, "Kimberly!"

Thunderstorms are extremely rare on the west coast. We lived in Walnut Creek for six years and had never seen one. "Kimberly must be scared to death." She had never seen a storm, and, of course, we had never felt the need to explain them. She was on the balcony, staring into the darkening sky. She had jumped a little—startled by the flash-bang attack—but her wide-eyed grin said she wished for more. We brought her into the room and explained thunderstorms. She was fine, we went to dinner and then we all got a good night's rest.

The final stretch of US 17 from New Bern, NC to Morehead City was thirty-five miles of straight barren highway through the Croatan National Forrest. Two-hundred foot tall pines lined the highway on both sides. Hints of civilization appeared in the form of tall water towers. Their flattened-onion-shaped tanks looked like the heads of alien creatures peeking above the pines from deep in the forest.

As we neared the U.S. Marine Corps Air Station, Cherry Point (MCAS) trees gave way to shabby roadside businesses: gas stations, pawn shops, massage parlors, fast food joints, and small storefronts, with big signs for quick loans and cheap jewelry. The perimeter of every base we knew in the country looked the same— *a paycheck dump for GI's and sailors.* We stayed on the base overnight in the visiting officers' quarters (VOQ). It was only a few miles from Gull Harbor where we met Mr. Wheeler the following morning.

Following Mr. Wheeler's departure, Carol and I unpacked boxes, set furniture in place, and managed to get the kitchen to the point we could at least eat meals. At one point, I needed to find a hardware store. I checked with our only neighbor, Tom, who lived in the other occupied spec house.

"Well, if you want a real hardware store, you are probably going to have to go to Beaufort. I don't think there's anything in Morehead that will help."

"Thanks, Tom."

"It's easy to find, can't miss it. It's right on the main street." Then he added, "By the way, Dick, that's pronounced *Bow'-furt (long o)*. The Beaufort in South Carolina is *Byou'-furt*. Folks will know you're not from here if y'all get that wrong." He laughed and waved me on.

"Thanks, Tom."

That trip to Beaufort revealed more about the place we would call home for the next two years. On the outskirts of Morehead, the highway was lined with small businesses set back twenty yards from the road. There were ice cream parlors, beach souvenir shops, insurance offices, sundries, and dress shops—most in single story buildings that looked more like homes than retail shops. They were painted blue-gray with porches that held white painted rocking chairs that invited you to "sit a spell afore y'all move on. Thanks for comin' by."

The dominant feature of Morehead's central business district, if I can call it that, is a single railroad track that runs like a boulevard the full length of the main street to the crossover bridge to Beaufort. The intersections with crossing streets were sparsely landscaped with a few bushes plopped into jagged red lava stones in what I took as a vain attempt to distract you from the depressing view of rusted rails atop a mound of gray stone chips.

I crossed over the bridge to Beaufort. Tom was right. The hardware store was obvious. I parked directly in front; I was the only car. When I got to the front door, I knew why. There was a gray cardboard sign scotch-taped to the door. The neatly blocked out red crayon letters read, "BLUES ARE RUNNING–BE BACK TOMORROW." It was the middle of the afternoon on a regular weekday—the owner had gone fishing. For the fourteen mile drive back home, I mulled over other thoughts about Morehead City.

With one of the deepest ports on the East Coast, and decent storage and cargo handling equipment, I was surprised by the lack of industrial growth. The port was a leading exporter of phosphate, but there was no evident push to expand the commercial port. The "boulevard railroad track" seemed to serve a single purpose—to transport aviation fuel from tanker ships at the Morehead piers to the Marine Corps Air Station at Cherry Point.

The permanent population of 8000 seemed content to let Morehead remain a summer respite for the people from Raleigh, New Bern, and the North. During the season, vacationers nearly tripled the population, and when they went home the locals fell back to their parochial roots of fishermen, farmers, and small business people.

After two days of living among boxes and staring at piles of things that still needed to be done, Carol said, "Why don't we just leave things where they are, go home to visit your folks, and we can take our time finishing this up when we get back?"

"That sounds like a plan to me." We were packed and on the highway the following morning. Thinking about our experience, I said to Carol, "You think somewhere down the road, ol' Holden Ballou is sitting in a rocker on his porch, sipping lemonade, and chuckling, "Ha. Got me another one o'them Yankees?"

We had a wonderful time at home. It had been a long time since we had seen the family. Everyone enjoyed the visit. Kimberly, to say the least, stole the show. After a pleasant uneventful trip back to Morehead City, we pulled into the carport in the late afternoon. I stopped dead at the side door into the kitchen. I turned to Carol, "There's a note from the realtor: 'Stopped by, found the storm door forced open. Sorry, you've been broken into.'"

"Carol, we've been robbed!"

We called the police, who arrived shortly. The thieves had stolen a .22 cal rifle, and had dumped Carol's jewelry box into a pillow cover they had stripped off the bed. Fortunately, they had missed the still-boxed silverware and silver service set, which would have been a sizable financial loss. Carol's jewelry was not expensive, but some pieces had sentimental value. All she had left was what she had taken on our trip to Bradford. The police were not encouraging. "All your stuff is long gone by now. Probably Marines from up at Cherry Point. Commander, I think you just have to look at it as gone and you are never going to see any of the stuff again."

The break-in left us both with an uneasy sense of having been violated. Our personal space had been invaded. Strangers had entered our world and done us wrong. We lost more than jewelry and a rifle—we had lost our sense of peace. Every strange night-sound emanating from the dark woods surrounding us became a hair-raising alert for the rest of our tour.

Kimberly did not react well to my first rescue call. I called Carol from the ship and told her we had to get underway to search for a man reported overdue. I didn't know how long it would be. When Carol told Kimberly, "Kim, daddy will not be home for a while, maybe a few days. He had to take the *Chilula* to try to find a man lost at sea." Kim's response was crying, gasping-never-ending crying. When we were at Alameda, I had come home from work at the end of the day just like any other dad. Carol tried everything to console her.

"Just think, Kimberly, how happy that man is going to be. He's probably been scared all night. He'll be so glad to see Daddy's big Coast Guard ship coming toward him to save him."

Through gulping, shoulder heaving sobs, Kimberly's angry response was, "Why didn't the man just take a flashlight!"

We enrolled Kimberly in nursery school which helped some, but she needed companionship at home, too. A dog. That should do it. A nice little Beagle that could grow with her— disaster!

She and the young pup, which we called Sailor, never hit it off. He scratched and nibbled at her, she poked and jabbed at him. When she wanted to go out to play, she begged for us to keep the dog inside, when she played inside, the dog had to go out. We often found one of them under her bed, and the other on top. This was not working. It was worse. One of them was going to have to go. We gave Sailor away to a nice family (any one that would take him) and we had peace again.

The second dog was a loving black Cocker Spaniel who became a member of the family for fifteen years. He came to us from a Marine family who was moving and could not take him with them. He had already been named, Andy, so we just kept it. Even poor Andy had trouble with Morehead City. One day, Carol, responding to his pitiful whining outside the back door, found him with a snapping turtle dangling from his left ear. Andy couldn't shake him off. The slightest attempt was too painful. The turtle, which had an eight inch shell, had clamped his iron jaws onto one thick cocker ear and was not about to let go. Carol scrambled around and grabbed the closest stick and wacked at the turtle until he finally released Andy's ear and crept on down the driveway. Andy's natural sense of curiosity had been seriously dampened.

There was a certain quaintness to Morehead City. It was a town with family restaurants named *Sanitary Fish Market*, and *Cap'n Bills* where cute Southern waitresses, with charming accents, kept your hush-puppy basket filled, and left you with a cheery, "N'ya'll come back and see us again, ya hear." It was a town with people grounded enough to shut down their business because the "blues are runnin.'" A town with a railroad track running in the middle of the main street. A town with three and a half hour Sunday church services. A town whose men celebrated Thanksgiving by sitting in duck blinds from the break of dawn, while the women prepared the traditional family dinner that the men were often late for, or even missed.

We did enjoy the beach, the easy living, and the pot luck dinners at the Catholic and Baptist churches. The local Catholic priest, a large beefy man who had sort of unofficially appointed himself the *Chilula*'s chaplain, our own Friar Tuck, made sure my family was included in such affairs. In turn, I often invited him to eat with the crew aboard ship. My experience with chaplains at Alameda had taught me how much good they could do. Father William Frost, pastor of St. Egbert's Catholic Church, was a positive influence on the ship, and the crew had grown accustomed to him, and I suspect, some may have even sought a little counseling. Friar Tuck was a good thing.

Mr. Smith lived in a sprawling house at the marina at the end of our road. A retired Wilson, NC businessman, he had a financial interest in Gull Harbor, but really fancied himself as a gentleman farmer who functioned as the superintendent/groundskeeper. We had a waving relationship. He would swing by on his tractor, under a broad straw hat, pulling dust-raising, clanking chains, and other strange equipment through the development, all day, every day. We would wave at him, and though he never glanced up, he took one hand off the wheel and stuck a fist high in the air in return salute.

Mr. Smith also farmed a large garden on the neighboring property. He sold vegetables to the local stores. In a neighborly gesture, he offered us three rows to work. We paid for seed and fertilizer, and he plowed, disked, and planted the seed with his tractor. We just had to keep it up and harvest our rows. When we accepted his offer, we did not know our "rows" were each fifty yards long. We had *a lot* of corn, tomatoes, snap beans, pole beans, and peas. Learning how to prepare, blanch, and put up the vegetables provided memorable family time as well as fresh frozen food that lasted us into our next assignment.

Mr. Smith had also informed us that North Carolina led the country with largest percentage of all the species of North American poisonous snakes. He seemed a little too proud of that. We didn't ask what numbers of them might be living with us in Gull Harbor. We just became a little more wary.

As time went on, we gradually became more acquainted with the local folks. They were always friendly, and openly expressed their appreciation of the Coast Guard. Carol and I soon discovered that if we couldn't talk about basketball, the bible, or tobacco, (maybe even in that order), any extended conversations would be limited. One lady expressed it best, "We just lo-o-ve having y'all here, but you *do* know that y'all never be one of us, right?"

I felt dangerously close to breeching that gap one evening, while I was reading the newspaper waiting for Carol to announce dinner. I leaned up from my recliner and yelled to Carol in the kitchen, "Hey, babe, did you see this article on the front page? They're going to cut the ribbon for the opening of the new A & P tomorrow. The high school band is going to play in the parking lot. Do you want to go?" Carol leaned back from the stove and peeked into the den.

"Reeeeally? Are you kidding me?"

"Oh, my God, Carol, I felt an honest tinge of excitement there!" I put the paper in my lap and just stared ahead for a half-minute. "I feel like I'm in an episode of 'Mayberry, RFD.'"

So, I was not surprised with Carol's response when I came home from the ship a few weeks after that with a copy of a message from the Commandant. He was going to form a team, led by a Commander, to research, design, and develop a service-wide Leadership and Management Training Program. Interested Commanders were invited to apply.

"Carol, this sounds really interesting to me. I'd love to have a chance to do this. It sounds like a really big deal. But, I'm only mid-tour in a sea-going command, so I don't know how real my chances are. Do you mind if I apply?" You *know* what she said.

Ninety men had applied. I made the short-list, and was called to CG Headquarters for an interview. Within weeks, I had orders to report to Yorktown, Virginia, where the school would be located. I turned my command over after fourteen months, rented my house to the *Chilula's* engineer, Charlie Kidd, and we headed for our next adventure.

As if snakes and snapping turtles had not been enough, Carol had been fighting major health issues ever since we arrived in Morehead. Her gallbladder attacks had reached the point where surgery was the only answer. Because of our pending transfer, the doctors at Cherry Point recommended she wait and have the surgery in Newport News, Virginia, at the Army hospital at Fort Eustis.

I regretted not having had the chance to work more to bring the ship and crew along further. Performance was weak, and their morale was low. Fortunately, we had been assigned two good morale-building missions: One to re-locate and confirm the finding of the USS *Monitor*, and the other was being assigned as the "enemy" ship trying to run a U.S. Navy blockade in a war game exercise. Both missions had a positive impact on the ship. Maybe the *Chilula* crew was turning the corner.

31

USS Monitor

I FIRST MET DR. HAROLD Edgerton at a cocktail reception at a private home in Beaufort, NC. It was the early summer of 1974 and "Doc" Edgerton was to embark on an expedition aboard my command, the U.S. Coast Guard Cutter *Chilula*. The famous scientist from MIT and I were to confirm the reported sighting of an ocean wreck as the USS *Monitor*. The Civil War "ironclad" had sunk in a turbulent storm off Cape Hatteras on New Year's Eve in 1862. I, of course, was providing transportation, and Doc Edgerton was providing his *side-scanning sonar* which would be used to search for the *Monitor*.

The expedition was sponsored by a consortium of Duke University, the National Geographic Society, and the National Science Foundation. A few representatives from those sponsors were at the reception to wish the Professor good luck. There was a small crowd of academicians and interested locals, along with the usual band of politicos with the felt the need to mark all such occasions with their presence. I was the only one in uniform, making it clear what my job was. While I admit that in private moments it was fun to toy with the idea that I was a joint partner in the *Great Monitor Expedition*—I was the seagoing bus driver.

Dr. Edgerton worked the room like a practiced celebrity, minus the Hollywood hubris. He was the most unassuming man I had ever met. His receding hairline rendered him bald to the top of his head, where an unruly patch of wispy gray hair danced freely in the slightest breeze. His worn sport jacket with suede elbow patches and a khaki shirt with no tie marked him as a professor. The button down flaps of both his breast

Dr. Edgerton and I on search for USS Monitor

pockets were held in the up position, against his chest, by multiple pens and pencils, scraps of folded paper, and miniature notebooks. This was no pretentious professor, this was an *engineer*.

His glasses were perched a far down on his nose, and thin lines fanned out from the corners of his eyes. He had a soft-spoken manner, and was easy to talk to. Everyone Doc met got a big smile and one of his favorite post cards that he pulled from his bulging pockets. "Do you want the strobe picture of a milk drop splashing into a coronet, or the one with a bullet crashing through an apple?" He loved to talk about his first love, photography.

I thought, *This was not the scientist who invented the strobe camera, furnished Jacques Cousteau with underwater photographic equipment, and had photographed nuclear tests for the U.S. in the fifties and sixties—this was everyman's grandfather.*

Dr. Edgerton had already loaded his sonar equipment aboard the ship before I got there the morning after the reception. He was cheery, and had already been meeting the crew, distributing his strobe photos. They were intrigued by the technology and the man. I greeted him and we went to the wardroom along with my ship's officers to discuss our mission. We both pondered two questions that were raised at the reception the night before. If we do verify the wreck as the USS Monitor, who is it going to belong to, and what will anybody be able to do with it?

A civilian, Robert F. Marx, claimed to have discovered the wreck several years ago, had dived on it, and placed a Coke bottle with his name in it into one of the gun barrels in order to claim the wreck as his. However, he was never able to provide proof of his story. The U.S. Navy claimed that since the *Monitor* had been a U.S. warship, it still belonged to the federal government. The State of North Carolina felt that since the wreck was found in waters off its coast, the state should own the remains. Dr. Edgerton and I decided that while the expedition would raise interesting questions, somebody else would have to answer them. Right now, our job was to get underway and find it.

We had good weather for the search. The seas were calm and the sun warmed the decks of the *Chilula*. Dr. Edgerton had set up his equipment on the open fantail. There was a constant cluster of curious crewmen checking out the sonar rig, and asking Doc questions. He patiently answered them all as if he were in his lab back at MIT faced with eager students. While he did not invent the side-scan sonar, he had experimented with its systems in his lab at MIT in the 1950s. He was instrumental in the development of the technology into a usable form for scanning the sea floor for wrecks.

The side-scan sonar was towed from the ship. It transmitted conical or fan-shaped pulses in a wide angle across large areas of the sea floor. It could create images showing debris and other obstructions on the sea bottom. Back on deck, the electronic pulses were depicted in a pattern of short dashes burnt onto a moving sensitive paper roll. The print-out looked like a hospital monitor or a seismograph.

293

As soon as we arrived at the last-reported position of the wreck, I ordered an expanding-square search. In less than one day, horizontal dashes began burning a football shaped pattern, with a round appendage on one side, onto the moving paper roll. Dr. Edgerton was elated. He felt certain that we had indeed found the *Monitor*. I smiled at him and pointed to the crew members that were standing around with big grins on their faces and punching each other in the arm. "Looks like your fans agree, Doc. Great job. Wow, we made short work of that one." After confirming the find with two more passes with the same results, we logged the position as 35⁰01'N, 75⁰24'W in 220 feet of water.

Given the historical significance of the find, scientists were reluctant to make an official announcement without a second-source confirmation. The Navy's first effort to photograph the underwater wreck yielded photos that were too blurry for confirmation. It was not until sometime later—I had actually been transferred to my next assignment—that Navy photos re-confirmed our finding. The hull was upside down on top of the apparently broken off turret which was now extending out one side, creating the "bump" in the football-shaped hull. The picture was a match for the side-scan sonar recording.

In the final determination, it was ruled that since the Navy had formally abandoned the wreck in 1953, and it lay outside the territorial waters of North Carolina, it could be exploited by divers and private salvage companies. To protect the site, the U.S. established a half mile radius around the wreck as the *Monitor National Marine Sanctuary* in 1975. It was designated a *National Historic Landmark* in June 1986.Today, the turret and a few other artifacts are displayed at the Mariners Museum in Newport News, Virginia.

The success of the *Monitor* mission brought the crew alive. As far as I was concerned, it could not have come at a better time. The ship had gone months with no action to put them in the limelight, no "Coast-Guard-To-

The-Rescue" excitement. They were losing their esprit-de-corps. They were like ready-to-go kids warming the bench for the coach who never put them into the game.

Living conditions aboard a ship built in 1944 were relatively primitive. Then, to make matters worse, there had been the stressful overload of Bravo-2 standby time. Liberty for the single guy was limited to a one-hour radius before they had to find a phone to check on the ship's status. They already complained there was *"nothing to do"* within an hour's drive of the *Chilula*. Some took chances, stretched the standby limits, and got in trouble for it. Minor glitches, hardly worth a sailor's gripe, ballooned into major issues.

The successful *Monitor* mission gave the crew a renewed sense of purpose and pride in accomplishment. Local newspaper and even a little television coverage had the crew walking tall again.

—32—

Enemy Victory

The mid-morning sun was half-way on its climb into a clear blue sky portending a blistering summer day. The sun was directly astern of the USCGC *Chilula* as we headed west at twelve knots toward the beach at Onslow Bay and the U.S. Navy blockade ships that awaited us. Their purpose was to prevent us from reaching the beach. It was our wild hope that by coming out of the sun, they might have trouble making visual contact. Maybe we could sneak through.

We were a designated blockade runner. The enemy.

The *Chilula* was participating in *Operation Solid Shield*, a major joint service exercise held off the coast of North Carolina. Onslow Bay sits in the shallow scoop of the coastline below Cape Hatteras. Morehead City and Cape Lookout mark the northern end of the bay with Wilmington and Cape Fear at the southern end. Inland of the long sandy strand of Onslow Beach lies the huge U.S. Marine Base, Camp Lejeune, its vast exercise areas, and two near-by Marine Air Stations, Cherry Point and New River. The port of Morehead City, provides deep draft piers for the large Navy supply ships and troop transports. Onslow Bay is the perfect place to practice both offensive and defensive tactics of an amphibious assault.

The *Chilula* was participating in Solid Shield as part of our Coast Guard military readiness mission. In practicality, however, it was difficult for the Coast Guard to "fit in" entirely. In the first place, there was the mental block of accepting a ship painted white as being part of the noble gray fleet, but more importantly, our weapons suit and communications gear were inadequate for full participation. The result was we were asked to play the part of the enemy. In this case, we simulated a merchant ship trying to run the blockade to deliver contraband goods to the bad guys.

The highly scripted war-games scenario started with a breakdown in negotiations between Blue Country (the good guys), and Red Country (the bad guys). Blue country had established a blockade line of ships to prevent unfriendly forces from reaching shore and their army was dug in to fend off the invasion forces. I had received my instructions by mail several weeks before the exercise in an Operations Order (OPORDER). They were simple. I had a handful of scripted scenarios and was free to use them as I saw fit. The purpose of each was to see if I could get by the blockade. Eventually, the OPORDER time-line moved to the amphibious assault. When it did, my job would be done.

It did not take long for us to have our first encounter with the blockade. A Navy Destroyer Escort (DE) appeared on the horizon and was headed directly for us. So much for coming out of the sun. He ordered us to stop to be boarded. There were no instructions as to how "realistic" I should make my penetrations attempts, but I felt a reasonable merchant ship would comply.

"All stop!" I ordered.

"Sir, the engines are all stopped."

"Very well, maintain your heading until you lose steerage way."

"Aye, aye, sir. Heading 270.

We coasted to a stop. The DE had lowered a small boat with their boarding party. They were close aboard ordering us to "prepare to be boarded," and wanted us to take their lines and lower a boarding ladder. I was surprised, if not a little shocked, as I stepped to the wing of the bridge to see five rag-tag men in their boat. All were bare chested, three of them armed. Nothing identified them as naval officers. I presumed their CO was looking after the comfort of his men on a very hot day. Nevertheless, it seemed an overly-lax approach even if it were an exercise. My next decision set the tone for the *Chilula's* two-day experience as a blockade runner, and I probably set the Coast Guard- Navy relationships back a bit.

"Who are you?" I leaned over the bridge wing directing my inquiry at the one man who was at least posing as their leader.

"We are an official U.S. Navy boarding party enforcing the blockade of Blue Country. You are required to submit to inspection of your cargo."

"How do I know that? I see no uniform insignia of the U.S. Navy. Unless I do, you do not have permission to board." I turned to the quartermaster. "All ahead one-third!"

"Sir, the engine room answers all ahead one-third."

"Very well. Make turns for 12 knots, steer 270."

"Aye, aye. 12 knots, 270."

Their wide-eyed, droop-jawed gapes told me that this had never happened to them before. We had simply refused them permission to board and steamed away, for all they knew to deliver forbidden cargo to Red sympathizers. I could hear their walkie-talkie squawking as their boat threw a wake racing back to their mother ship.

After the DE raised their boat, they continued to move inland with us, but closer abeam. The boarding party was again lowered and the DE made it obvious that we had better stop this time. I did. The boarding party, *in uniform*, was permitted aboard. They inspected and found nothing suspect, and told us we were free to continue. Had they looked under the canvas that covered a large box sitting in full sight on the open fantail, they would have seen the large printed sign that identified the four foot wooden cube as CONTRABAND CARGO. Enemy 1- U.S. Navy 0.

I took the *Chilula* east of the exercise area and headed south a few miles before attempting our second penetration. The crew had reacted positively to the first run. I had watched a few of them elbow poke each other while chuckling when we left those poor Navy guys stranded in their small boat. Emboldened by the first attempt, I thought the Navy might benefit from another blockade reality—nobody on the penetrating third country ship could speak English. It made sense to me. I made announcement over the PA to the entire crew congratulating them on our first run and instructing them that on this next one, we were a Slavic country ship and nobody understood nor spoke any English. They were not to respond to U.S. Navy commands from the boarding party. We headed inland and within a half-hour we were being approached by a blockade ship.

The DE took a position off our starboard bow, running ahead of us and crossing from the starboard to port bow, all the time signaling us to stop to be boarded. I slowed a bit, but kept my westerly heading. He gave the exercise signal, via flashing light, that he was firing shots across our bow. He was forcing the event to a new level. I slowed to five knots, and his boarding party attempted to come alongside. I could not contain my laughter. Their wild arms swinging in an attempt to get our deck force crew's attention. My crew hunched shoulders and turned their palms out, nodding their heads—nobody understood anybody else—perfect! Then the borders began throwing lines that were landing on our deck, then trailing off back into the ocean; after a few attempts, I decided to stop and let them aboard. Still through the whole evolution, we spoke nothing but gibberish. The boarding crew was beginning to look like they wished they had live weapons.

Their boat crew stayed with the boat and stood off twenty yards or so. Three boarding officer made their way onto the bridge to be greeted by a red-faced, wild hand waving ships' master (me) shouting in gibberish, more than a little upset.

"Vie der BOOM, BOOM. Das kill us?" I screamed. Waving my arms all over, I tried to be as upset as the old Italian's bocchi ball players I used to watch back in Bradford when they thought they were being cheated.

I was in the groove. They looked at me as though I were crazy. I did not break character.

I jabbed my finger repeatedly onto the papers I shoved under their nose, forcing them to read. "Zee! Zee dar!"

Their leader took them from my hand, perused them for a minute, then turned to the other officers and said, "The papers indicate the ship is from a neutral country."

"So, what do we do, head back to the ship?"

"Yes, take a quick look around the topside deck on the way, and let's get out of here."

I jumped in, "You look. Ve go." I turned to the young man on the bridge, "Vas dnck zoot–nutsdool." He caught my meaning when I held up one finger with a nod of my head. He rang the engine order telegraph to ahead one-third.

We were underway *with the Navy boarding party on board.* Now what would the DE do to the neutral country kidnappers? Sink our ship with their men on board, fire on a neutral country's ship? It was a no win situation. After a few miles, I slowed and let boarding team get back to their boat, which had been diligently bounced along in our bow wake. They wasted no time getting back to the DE. I reversed course to set up for another run.

I knew the crew was really into the game when one of my chief petty officers came to me. "Captain, I have a great idea for our next run."

"Let's hear it."

"I can block out one of our three masthead towing lights then make the top one red and they'll think we are fishing."

"Red over white–fishing at night."

"Yes, sir. Then if we stay close to the beach, we might catch the command ship with her pants down."

"Make it happen, Chief."

Well after sunset, the *Chilula* entered the exercise area from the south, cruising at seven knots, showing her "fishing lights." We were already *inside* the blockade line about a mile off shore. We could see the lights of two blockade ships to the east, and nobody made a move toward us. It was working. We were taken as a trawler.

A little further north, when I saw the silhouette of Blue Country's amphibious command ship, I drew within three thousand yards, then opened fire using the flashing-light signal designated by the OPORDER. What happened next, of course, was not unexpected. The command ship returned fire and two DE's were moving quickly into position to destroy me. However, I was confident that the *Chilula* would have been given credit for rendering significant damage to the command ship.

The third, and last, day of our scheduled participation in Solid Shield was another extremely hot day. The sea was flat calm, as it had been throughout. I took the ship a couple of miles outside the exercise area where I decided to reward the crew with a swim break. We had taken all the precautions, a small boat in the water, boat beams rigged out, lookouts posted all over the ship as a shark watch, several armed with M-1's. When we piped "Swim Call," on the PA system, scores of my crew dove into the calm Atlantic from the main deck, some of the more adventurous, from bridge wings. They were joking, kidding, splashing and dunking their shipmates, celebrating the joys of leaving the Navy in our wake. Then the bridge lookout sounded off.

"Aircraft! Starboard Beam, low on horizon!"

By the time I got my binoculars up to my eyes, I didn't need them. In a blink of an eye, the target grew from a small black blot on the horizon to a roaring, ear-splitting, screaming jet, heading directly at us. It was low— below the bridge level—when it flashed over our bow and pulled into a vertical roll, again disappearing into a dot in the blue sky. The pilot transmitted a voice message back to his carrier (I suspect intentionally on a frequency he knew we had) that had joined the exercise that was about to move into the invasion phase.

"Identified and engaged white enemy vessel at southeastern corner exercise area. Significant damage. Disabled ship dead-in-the-water. Many survivors observed swimming alongside." At least he had a sense of humor.

When I reflect on the awesome jet "attack," I remember how quickly it happened, the sense of helplessness, the micro-second images of death and destruction that could follow. I felt what it must be like, in those seconds of impending doom, for the enemy about to experience she sheer power and horrifying magnificence of the U.S. Navy, and thanked God that I'm on their side.

The war games experience, like finding the USS Monitor the year before, had a positive effect on the crew. Spirits were high, and I felt the road to recovery for the ship was on track.

For us, the *good* news from Solid Shield 75 was: The *Chilula* had penetrated the blockade nearly at will.

For the Navy, the *bad* news from Solid Shield 75 was that The *Chilula* had penetrated the blockade nearly at will.

The Leadership Challenge
Coast Guard Leadership and
Management Development Staff

Yorktown, VA

Director
October 1975-June 1978

National Defense University

Washington, DC

Instructor, Executive Development Staff
July 1978-June 1983

The demands for cultural changes in the mid-sixties and seventies were a challenge to civilian businesses and industries as well as the military. First-line supervisors and managers in large corporations, and military non-commissioned officers, who had ascended to leadership positions in another era, were at odds with the new generation of young workers. Even when the violent aspects of protests and radical movements declined, there were many who felt the personal freedoms espoused by the countercultural generations of the sixties should be part of the main-stream today.

Everyone was looking for the cure for the hippie-sixties hangover. Corporate leadership seminars for first line supervisors and managers sprouted up all over the country. Military schools were developing leadership segments to be added to existing curricula. Admiral Elmo Zumwalt (Chief of Naval Operations) was famously dragging the U.S. Navy into the new world through his infamous "Z-Grams," messages directed to the fleet that re-examined many of what young sailors considered "chicken-shit regs," regulations that restricted personal behavior, and life styles. Grooming issues loomed to the top of the list; fights over hair and beards were classic time wasters. Some of his efforts did not have the support of many high ranking officers. Their old Navy was disappearing.

The Commandant of the Coast Guard, Admiral Owen Siler, (Commandant from 1974-1978) chose to celebrate the nation's bicentennial year, 1976, by debuting a service-wide leadership training effort. It was a major legacy of his term as was the opening of cadet appointments to women.

−33−

COAST GUARD LEADERSHIP AND MANAGEMENT SCHOOL

SITTING ALONE ON THE KITCHEN floor of the empty house at 599 Crown Point Drive in Newport News, Virginia, I had plenty of time to think about the last couple of months. Carol and my sister, Pat, who had flown down from Bradford to help us move, were still in Morehead City waiting for the North American Van to load. The plan was for Carol, Pat, Kimberly, who was four years old, and the Cocker, Andy, to pile into our station wagon and head north as soon as the van left. I had made reservations at a Newport News motel near the Village Green development where we were going to live. They were coming to the house first because they just could not wait until the next day to see it. But, it was getting late.

This house, our seventh, was by far the finest we had owned. I was anxious for Carol to see it. It was a two story brick colonial with a front porch that ran the full width of the house. Four majestic white pillars stretched to the high porch ceiling, creating a picture-frame view of what was known as the Colonial five-over-four design: five second story windows, over four on the first floor. A center double-door entrance invited you into a spacious foyer that lifted to the second floor ceiling. The house, though it would have been more grand were it isolated at the end a long curved driveway—southern style, nevertheless commanded a corner lot at the entrance to a short cul-de-sac. A large shade tree protected the front from the hot Virginia sun, and a cluster of tall pines did the same for the small wooden deck that extended out the back.

I chuckled to myself recalling my conversation with the previous owner, whom I had bought the house from directly.

"Tell me about your neighbors." I asked. The final item on my check-off list.

"Well, let's see." He ticked off on his fingertips. "An Air Force major lives in the house just like yours across the street. The next one down is an Engineer at the Newport News Shipyard. He has a daughter about the same age as yours. Two doors down from you is a big Newport News Real Estate developer, Lamar Jolly." He has kids, too.

"What! Wait! Who! Lamar Jolly?" I couldn't believe it.

"Do you know him?"

"I must. How many people can there be in the world named Lamar Jolly? When I taught in Officer Candidate School in Yorktown fourteen years ago the chief yeoman in the training office was named Jolly."

Sure enough; retired CPO Lamar Jolly was now the hottest real estate mogul in the Newport News–Williamsburg area. We were neighbors for a couple of years then he moved on to his new development, the well-known King's Mill Resort near Busch Gardens in Williamsburg.

I lifted my cramped body from the kitchen floor. I stretch-walked my way to the living-room windows. There was no sign of the family yet. I stared into the darkened night, and rehashed the chain of events that led me to this career milestone.

The Commandant of the Coast Guard, Admiral Owen Siler, had chosen to celebrate the nation's bicentennial year, 1976, by debuting a service-wide leadership training effort. (Adm. Siler served as Commandant from 1974-1978.) He was determined to take all the time needed for research and developmental to ensure service wide acceptance of the program. He wanted it to be one of the legacies of his term as Commandant. He had another major legacy that year. The first women to be selected for the Coast Guard Academy reported that bicentennial summer as members of the class of 1980.

I was proud of my selection as the first Chief of the Leadership Development Staff. I looked forward to the challenge. I had already met with Captain Paul Schroeder, the Chief of the Training and Education Division, in the Office of Personnel. I was to report to him directly despite being physically located at The Reserve Training Center in Yorktown. The Captain assured me a free hand in the development effort, and I had already enjoyed the unprecedented opportunity to work with the assignment officers to hand pick my staff. We were given a year to research existing programs, both military and civilian, consider options, and design and develop the schools. It just doesn't get any better than that.

I also felt better about rotating from the *Chilula* early. Headquarters had found Commander Dan Sessions, a dedicated, experienced, and well known officer, who had agreed to postpone his retirement to take command at least for what would have been the remainder of my tour.

Car lights in the driveway broke me out of my reverie. Carol had finally arrived. It was three o'clock in the morning. Carol and Pat both laughed telling me about Kimberly's reaction when the toll booth operator bid them, "Good morning." Lifting her head in a stupor she said, "Mama, how does the man know that?" Exhausted, and a little giddy, everyone trooped a quick tour of the house then we headed to the motel to get what sleep we could. We had to meet the movers in the morning.

We settled into the house and the neighborhood quickly. Within hardly a month: Carol had her gallbladder surgery at Ft. Eustis; Kimberly was enrolled in school and embraced by the neighborhood kids; we found a church to attend. The little red wagon from down the street loaded with free kittens could no longer be ignored, so, the dog, Andy, adjusted to his new status—cats rule—and accepted the solid gray critter with four white feet, named Boots, into the family. Boots showed his appreciation by occasionally gifting us with a garter snake or a red-belly-racer that he unceremoniously deposited at the back door. We were a regular family again, and I went to work.

The development staff for the Coast Guard Leadership and Management School (CGLAMS or LAMS) had all reported for duty. We were assigned office and classroom space, and we were quickly immersed in the design and development a service-wide leadership program.

Lt. Gary Heil, USCGA class of 1972, was super smart, well liked, well known, and one of those extraordinarily coordinated athletes that could excel in any sport after one or two "show me how it's done" sessions. His reputation was well known in the junior office circles. A little on the cocky side perhaps, but with his handsome looks, good sense of humor, and an easy-going classroom style, he was a natural.

Chief Warrant Officer (CWO) Ron Hudson, had a studious mind, and easy going manner. He was intelligent, well liked with an impressive technical background. He took to the academic material extremely well. His formal, but not stilted, classroom style was considerably less flamboyant than either Gary's or mine. I think the contrast was good for the students. He also took great pride in helping our enlisted staff's venture into the previously unknown world of academia. He was good at it, and they often sought him out for help.

Four terrific Chief Petty Officers (E7-E9) rounded out our team. They were Robert Huff, Denny Thomas, George Conrad, and Don Eberle. They had outstanding records, were well known in their rating specialties, and had served on variety of ship and shore assignments. We worked with the enlisted assignment officer, to let them know what we needed. We did not need—nor did we want—enlisted men with college experience. We would teach our staff whatever academic background was necessary. What we needed was men with established *credibility*. Credibility as successful career Coastguardsmen. We could not give them that. Their performance record would. Students needed to respect them as competent, successful senior petty officers. They had to be role models.

The assignment process for everyone resulted in an assembled group of competent, super willing, enthusiastic winners. To a man, we were excited with the opportunity to be part of this milestone in leadership development for the Coast Guard. We all experienced personal growth in this assignment, particularly the enlisted men. One of the chiefs said to me about a year into the project, "Commander, you have no idea how much this whole thing has changed me."

"How so, Master Chief?"

"My wife and I were talking about it last night. Before this tour, I don't think I had read two books in my entire life." He smiled and looked around his desk. "Now, I'm surrounded with them. They have changed my life. I *never, never* would have said I'd end up teaching masters level course material to smart young officers with bachelor's degrees."

"What does your wife say about that, Master Chief?"

"Same thing...she never saw me doing that either." We both laughed. I loved these guys.

Our early research effort took us on the road attending courses and seminars, both civilian and military, some good, some not so good. Gary Heil and I, and to a lesser extent, Ron, traveled the country from coast to coast. After several months of research and studying, we had a pretty good handle on what the trends were in leadership training. Short term schools and seminars were turning up all over the country. We developed a good picture of what worked and what didn't.

Trying to teach leadership by talking about personnel traits of successful leaders, hoping to inspire students to mold their leadership style after them, had not worked for decades, if not centuries. Telling young men that they should be trustworthy, loyal, decisive, consistent, etc., worked no more than many pastors' messages on Sunday. I know I have had times when I felt sincerely moved by an inspirational message from the pulpit on Sunday, and vowed to change my ways—only to find that by Tuesday afternoon, I was behaving the way I always did.

Everyone was looking for concrete skills for the leader to develop, things he could *actually do*, not just talk about, when faced with a group or individual that was not contributing to the overall unit mission.

Enter the world of behavioral scientists. The teachings of Skinner, Herzberg, Maslow, and others, were affecting the design of leadership development programs. Leaders needed to understand group dynamics and individual psychology, they needed to assess situations, and they needed to respond with appropriate behavior. They needed to understand how their own personality could affect their flexibility in choosing an appropriate leadership style.

After attending many seminars over a period of months, we decided the best approach for us was to build our program around the Situational Leadership model of Paul Hearsey and Ken Blanchard. As we developed the curricula, I knew from my previous teaching experience that teaching method would be almost as important as the content. We built the course around the Adult learning theory of Malcolm Knowles. Adults were experiential learners rather than didactic. They needed less front-of-the class lectures and more experienced based opportunities to analyze what was happening and draw their own conclusions. That meant case studies.

I wrote a totally fictional case study, *The Disgruntled Deck Force*, with characters and situations applicable at the shipboard level involving a chief petty officer, young seamen, and a junior officer in his first assignment. For a story line, I had placed the incident on the USCGC *Absecon*, my first ship. The reaction in the pilot class, and all that followed was the same. A participant would approach one of our staff, and in confidential tones would share, "I know that you disguised the unit as the *Absecon*, but I know the real ship that really happened on." While that was total fiction, it told us we had successfully hit on such universal people problems that everyone could relate to, even "identify" the real place and players.

Our research also made it clear that for acceptance and success of a service-wide leadership program, we had to gain the understanding and support of the most senior officials. We developed a one week senior officer course, for captains and commanders. But, even that would be hard to sell. When I visited HQ, I asked for a round-robin trip to all the Coast Guard District Offices to present a one hour brief explaining the program.

Admiral Siler was very supportive, and he had greased the way for me with a message to all districts as to the importance of the briefing. I visited all twelve Coast Guard Districts, including Hawaii, and Alaska, enjoyed great cooperation in each. My briefings were attended by nearly all captains assigned to the district offices, from the Chief of Staff on down, and often included the Rear Admiral who was the District Commander. I was smart enough not to tell them *they* needed leadership training. My approach was to let them know how much more effective the people they sent could be if their "boss" had a common experience. Graduates would have a new more sophisticated vocabulary of leadership, and would bene-fit most if their superiors shared the common language.

The first Coast Guard Leadership and Management course to con-vene was the senior officer course. There was a message there in itself. It was a resounding success. I had rewritten the *Case of the Disgruntled Deck Force* into a higher level, but still fictional scenario. It had the same basic characters, except they were a Captain who was a District Operations Officer, and a Group Commander. The people problems were nearly the same, but at a much higher level.

Of course, in every class, at least one Captain let me know he "knew where that actually occurred."

From that point on, the success of CGLAMS was fixed. Quotas were filled, accolades poured in. I couldn't have been more proud of the staff.

We planned for expansion by adding a second school on the west coast at the Coast Guard Training Center, Petaluma. One of our officer students, LCDR Roger Chevellier applied to be the officer-in-charge. Roger got the job, and then spent a year with us before moving to California to establish the school there.

The other services had not been standing still during our development effort. The National Defense University in Washington DC had called for a two day conference for all military services elements that were involved in teaching leadership. That included all the academies, and senior service schools. The conference was to exchange ideas and discuss the general "state of the art."

I drove to DC for the conference—a totally unexpected life-changing event.

THE NATIONAL DEFENSE UNIVERSITY

I ENTERED THE GATES OF Fort McNair, in Washington, DC, and gazed to the southern end of the nearly quarter-mile of greensward to see a building that could only be the National War College (NWC). The large neoclassical brick building with granite trim was built by President Teddy Roosevelt in 1903 for that express purpose. The Roman-like high arched loggia with huge pillars provided a nest in the peak for a very war-like granite sculpture of a really pissed off eagle. It had to be a war building; it could never be anything else. Fort McNair sits on Buzzards Point, at the junction of the Potomac, and Anacostia River, giving the south side of the NWC a commanding strategic view down the Potomac River.

The NWC was one of two colleges that made up the National Defense University (NDU). The other was the Industrial College of the Armed Forces (ICAF). The two colleges had been formed into a university in the summer of 1976. The President of NDU, Army Lieutenant General Robert Gard, who had called this conference, had offices in the ICAF Building.

I joined the conference along with representatives from all the Service Academies, the senior service schools, the Army, Navy, and Air Force War colleges, as well as the independent staff level schools of each of the services. There were also representatives from various Pentagon offices and, of course, the staff of NDU.

After we had completed a vigorous two days of discussion, General Gard addressed the group on the last day. He thanked us for our effort and said he "looked forward to a final report." Then he ended the thank you session with a question.

"Before I take off, let me ask. Of all of you here today, how many have actually stood in the front of a classroom of successful senior officers, Colonels, and Captains, and tried to tell them anything about this leadership stuff?"

I raised my hand. Glancing around the room—I was the only one with my hand up.

General Gard pointed at me and said, "Commander, may I see you in my office after the closing session?"

"Of course, sir."

Later that afternoon, I reported to the president's office. General Gard beckoned for me to take a seat. He was a tall, good looking man with a thin athletic frame. The fifty-year-old General's amicable, easy going style veiled the status symbols of the three shiny silver stars that dominated his short sleeve khaki shirt. Conversation was easy. He offered a cold drink, we chatted for five minutes about my experience and the Coast Guard Leadership program, then he leaned against his desk front, paused for an interminable five seconds and said, "Do you think you are in a position to rotate out of your present assignment?"

I didn't know what to say. I had no idea where he might be going with this. Actually, I had been approached by our own Chief of Personnel about taking a new assignment nearly a year ago, but I asked for and was granted the a third year to button up expansion plans. That year was nearly over. My hesitation spurred him to follow up, "Commander, I'd like to add you to my staff. I'm putting together an Executive Development Staff of joint service officers to work out of my office and do just what you have already done, find ways to encourage our senior officer students to examine the concepts of leadership."

"Sir, I have no idea if that can happen." I smiled a little and added, "The Coast Guard doesn't even have a billet here, which might be a problem."

"I'll call Owen in the morning." He thanked me for coming in, looked forward to the conference report and he hoped he would see me soon. Our meeting was over. The "Owen" he was going to call, I realized after a two second delay, was the Coast Guard Commandant. I was not used to conversations at this level, and I sure as hell never thought of him as "Owen."

"Thank you, General. It's been my pleasure. Thanks for including us."

In three days, I had orders to report to the President of the National Defense University to fill a position on his Executive Development Staff. Other than as a student, there had never been a Coast Guard officer assigned to the NDU. Today there is a Coast Guard Faculty chair.

On the first of July, Carol joined Captain Charlie Blaha, the CO of Training Center Yorktown, in a small ceremony in the CGLAMS classroom. I had been promoted to the rank of Captain; they attached new shoulder boards bearing my fourth stripe, and the Captain pinned me with the Coast Guard Meritorious Service Medal, awarded for my work in establishing the Leadership School. It was a memorable day. Within a few weeks, we were settling into our new house, the eighth, in Vienna, Virginia.

Our house was a typical split-level perched on the peak of a hill in the suburbs. It was a growing area, long considered too far away for the Washington, DC commuter, but the newly built DC Metro transportation system was changing the landscape. The Vienna Metro station was scheduled to open soon.

The house at 2120 Statute Lane fronted onto Client Drive, and was in an older, established, named housing development with streets like

Lawyers Rd., Docket Ln., and Judge Ct. The houses were on good sized lots, with grown shrubs and trees and large lawns. It was not one of those clear-cuts with cloned houses plopped in rows that were springing up like weeds to feed the Metro even before it opened.

We settled quickly. Kimberly was enrolled in an historic grade school, and her mom volunteered in the library and helped with school projects. Kimberly started horseback riding lessons in Mrs. Dillon's English Riding school. She rode competitively, and watching her handle big "Will," was always a thrill.

I enjoyed the commute along the George Washington Parkway, a little long, but the sunrises over the Potomac River were often spectacular. Drivers talked, kibitzed, entertained, and passed on traffic information to each other on the old CD radios mounted on their dashboards. "Good morn'n good buddies, how can you not believe in God driving into this sunrise, c'mon back."

Everyone was happy except Andy, who was more than leery of the big German Short Hair, named Gunther, who patrolled behind our backyard fence. Andy also hated the paper boy whom he chased for blocks every chance he got.

The Executive Development staff was headed by U.S. Army Colonel Irv Katenbrink. In addition to myself, there was a Navy Captain in the Chaplain Corps, and two Lieutenant Colonels, One Army and one Air Force. We were a good team that worked well together to get our leadership material ready before the new classes arrived for the fall term. I briefed them on the key points of how we had used the situational leadership model. I rewrote the *Disgruntled Deck Force* case again, but needed help from Bob Landers, our Army member, to create relatable positions and believable language for the ICAF students. My character of the Coast Guard Seaman became an Army Lieutenant Colonel serving as a

Battalion Commander. It went over well. The "real battalion" had been identified as one in Korea, Germany, and one in Fort Ord, California.

I was a little more concerned about the case for the National War College. While there was no official difference between the senior school students, I felt an aura of relative superiority from the NWC students, at least when they were in a group. It was as if any issues below the world crisis level, were beneath them. What to do with my *Deckforce* seaman now?

Improbably, he became the Ambassador to *Blue Country*. His leadership conflict involved the Deputy Assistant Secretary of State and a potential national embarrassment hung in the balance. There had to be a change in leadership style.

I was walking back to my office after running the case at NWC when I became aware someone was following me. He continued behind me into the ICAF building and down the corridor to my office. He slipped in close behind me without a word, and closed the door behind him.

"Captain, I have to know how you got the information on that Embassy. I know where that happened and it was supposed to have been all taken care of." He was a little out of breath and his eyes showed genuine concern. He was a civilian student from the State Department.

"The case study is a fictional case. I wrote it myself, and I assure you, I had no inside information to go on. It is designed to bring forth what has proven to be amazingly common leadership problems at many levels."

I don't think he believed me. He never revealed where it was, (after all, he *knew* I already knew that). He quietly left my office, I suspect upset about the breech in secure communications... if there ever was any.

One of the great opportunities for students at (NDU) was the joint Friday afternoon lecture series. Students of both schools sat in the ICAF auditorium to hear such presenters as the Secretaries of State, Defense, and other Cabinet level officials. Foreign leaders, major news anchors,

CEO's of major industries like Piper Aircraft, and General Motors also made presentations. On occasions, presidents and vice presidents have chosen that audience to make significant announcements.

For my two years on the NDU staff, I enjoyed the same opportunity as the students for these lectures. I enjoyed many great presentations, but the one that impressed me the most was given by former Secretary of State, Henry Kissinger. He faced the audience on the stage, sitting in a large leather chair, an end table next to it holding a pitcher of water. Were it not for the large projection of a world map behind him, It was as though he were sharing his world vision with us from the comfort of his den. The map was for the audience, he never looked at it.

In his sonorous voice and deep accent, he walked us through the geographical and political pinch points in the world, the narrow sea straits and mountain passes that historically had caused many warring conflicts. Our eyes followed the places on the map as he ticked them off by heart. He traced the history of nations competing for natural resources, and seeking to control land and sea access routes as they drew lines, formed and broke alliances, and fought wars to get what their nations needed. It was an impressive history lesson.

Every year, each of the service chiefs was invited to address the joint students at a Friday lecture. When it was the Coast Guard Commandant's turn, General Gard called me to his office.

"Captain, you know that the Commandant of the Coast Guard will be here in two weeks. I would like you to introduce him at the Friday lecture and of course join us at the informal reception for him after the lecture."

"Thank you, sir, I'd be honored."

"Now listen, I hope you can move beyond the usual boring intro, 'From this year to that year he served as...etc.' I like to keep these introductions a little more upbeat and interesting. Can you do that?"

"Yes, sir, no problem."

"Good. Thank you. Join me in my office with five minutes to go, and we'll head to the auditorium together." I thanked the General again for the opportunity. I know I had a grin on my face as I walked back to my office thinking—*ooh I'll make it different.*

At the appointed hour the General, the Commandant, and I headed to the auditorium. The General motioned for the commandant and me to take chairs on the stage. He proceeded to the podium to introduce me as the only Coast guard Officer on the staff and the appropriate one to introduce his own service Chief. I stepped to the podium, receiving polite applause from the eight hundred students and instructional staff of the two colleges. The applause died down and I began.

"When I was a young high school lad, I lived in the small rust-belt community of Bradford, Pennsylvania. Bradford lay in the western foot-hills. My family was poor, and I wanted to go to college. Out of necessity as much as anything else, I thought about the service academies as a way to get my education." At about this point, I had visions of General Gard behind me wondering, "Where the hell is he going with this?" I could see questioning looks from a few student officers in the first couple of rows. I marched on.

"I read a lot about Annapolis and West Point, but I didn't know much about the Coast Guard. Somebody told my dad that one of the doctors in town had a son that went to the Coast Guard Academy, so I went to see him. When we met, I asked if he could tell me how his son liked the Coast Guard. He said, "Well, my boy, Jack, likes it a lot. He's a Lieutenant now, loves what he's doing and actually, he's doing pretty well.""

I smiled and said, "Today, the presence on our stage of Dr. Hayes' boy, Jack, is testimony to his father's wisdom. He is indeed...doing pretty well. Ladies and gentlemen, it's a pleasure to present the Commandant of the Coast Guard, Admiral John B. Hayes."

There was a ripple of laughter in the auditorium that grew as General Gard rose with a smile, gave me a strong handshake and said, "That was a terrific introduction. I can tell you we've never had one like that before." I smiled at Admiral Hayes who turned to address the joint student body.

The reception afterward was a small affair with just key staff of the two colleges. One of the ICAF student, I recognized, but didn't really know, snuck his head into the door, caught my eye and half whispered, "Hey, Dick, are you really from Bradford?"

"Yeah, I sure am."

"How about that, I'm from Salamanca." (Yes...that same destination of my overnight train trips home while I was at the Academy.) I wondered if he was ever on the same train on his way home from West Point.

At the end of two years, I said goodbye to the NDU Staff. General Gard awarded me the Defense Meritorious Service Medal. My new assignment was in CG Headquarters as Chief of the Training and Education Division. The assignment came with the bonus of no household move. We stayed in our Vienna, Virginia, home.

Coast Guard Headquarters II

Washington, DC

Chief Training and Education Division
Office of Personnel

June 1980-June 1983

—35—

CHIEF, TRAINING, AND EDUCATION

IT HAD BEEN TWELVE YEARS since my first HQ assignment. A lot had changed. Most notably, Coast Guard headquarters was now in SE Washington at Buzzards Point, within walking distance of NDU. The old Pennsylvania Avenue building had been razzed years before to make way for new construction. I was a Captain now, and although I loved the experience at NDU, I was ready to move back into the Coast Guard training business.

The former CG Training Branch was now the Training and Education Division. As the Division chief, I managed a $200 million dollar program involving seven separate training commands. I had direct control of $25 million dollars in training funds. Thankfully, I had a knowledgeable, experienced, and dedicated staff of over thirty officer, enlisted, and civilians who kept me on track.

In 1980, Ronald Reagan was elected to his first term as president. Early in the transition period, I received a phone call from Dr. Dennis Bark who had been a senior fellow at the Hoover Institution at Stanford University, and now worked in the Office of the Secretary of Transportation. He was an assistant to one of the politically appointed deputy's secretaries.

"Captain, I would like to set an appointment with you to discuss a Coast Guard Academy issue."

"Of course, sir. Can you tell me something about the issue?"

"Well, it's a question of whether the country needs two federal academies in maritime related missions. In the interest of the administration's goal of keeping government small, the secretary wants to examine alternatives. Interest is especially keen since there is now a Department of Transportation (DOT) with both the Coast Guard Academy and the Merchant Marine Academy. I thought it best to start with you."

I might have been shaken by this question, except it was not a new one. However, it usually concerned the Naval Academy vs. Coast Guard Academy. It wasn't hard to dig up the old arguments, update them, and relate them to the current question. With both academies operating in (DOT), the discomfort level increased some. The staff at CGA had done significant research on this question before and they were a great help this time.

Dr. Bark and I had met several times, in both my office and his, coffee shops, and one familiarization trip to the CG Academy. I don't know if he visited the MMA, but I presumed he had. I enjoyed working with him. We became quite friendly, in a Dick-and-Dennis having-coffee-kin-da-way, and when he reached a favorable conclusion and sold the Deputy Secretary of Transportation on it, I was not surprised.

I liked to think that by my fostering our congenial relationship, I may have played some small part in "saving the Academy." But, then, he told me that actually he had enlisted in the Coast Guard Reserve some time ago, went to boot camp at Alameda, and, even without active duty, had a soft spot for the Coast Guard. So, maybe I didn't convince him. But, I convinced myself that he must have gone to boot camp *after* the reforms that I had helped established. I never asked him. It was nicer to just leave it alone.

At one of our last meetings, Dennis gave me a gift. A three pound, nine-hundred page tome, *The United States in the 1980's*. It was published by the Hoover Institution

"Dick, spend some time with this, and you'll get a pretty good picture where this administration wants to take the country."

"Wow, thank you, Dennis." I took the book from him and automatically opened to the front flap. I scanned while Dennis talked.

"Hoover Institute is a major conservative think tank. There are others, but this is a favorite with President Reagan's group. It is a collection of essays from well-known and respected specialists. They recommend specific courses of action to address problems, both foreign and domestic, that they feel the country will face in the next decade."

"I can see they don't miss much," I said, skimming the contents: Welfare Reform, Energy Options, Your Health and the Government, Arms Control, Global Nuclear Conflict, The Middle East." I stopped, set the book down and thanked Dennis again.

"Dick, you'll find many of these contributors end up appointed at the under and assistant secretary level of the departments. The more visible secretaries, frequently appointed as political payback, bring these guys on board to put strategy into action. Many of them end up on the white house staff also. It won't happen all at once, but don't be surprised if you see many of these proposal march to the front in state of the union address over the years."

The United States in the 1980's taught me a lot about how government works. As I was writing these memoirs, I was drawn to an essay included in the book by Dr. Edward Teller. I think the universal truth of his piece is as applicable today as it was in the 80s.

Technology: the Imbalance of Power.

"Today all on earth are close neighbors: the First World, which is liberal; the Second World, which is dictatorial; and the Third World, where changes are rapid and often violent. The fate of all hinges on the development and use of technology. If we want to understand and influence the future, we should review and understand humankind's new tools."

The "new tools" are different today than thirty years ago, but think: cell phones, smart bombs, and social media...then think Middle East.

Administrative oversight of all the training commands called for a modest amount of travel, but I made more trips to the Academy than all others combined. On special occasion, because of the nature of planned activities, it was appropriate for the visiting HQ personnel to include their wives. I was pleased that Carol was included on one of the trips. We flew to New London on CG air when Admiral Hayes was the Commandant. Carol and I both enjoyed the interaction with the Admiral's wife "Boggy" as we discussed Bradford memories. I, of course, had grown up there and Boggy had made several visits with her husband in the early days of his career. The Admiral, a bit remote and standoffish in general, not just to us, but to other guests on the air plane as well, rarely joined in. Carol and I stayed overnight in Quarters B, overlooking the parade ground. We were guests of the Assistant Superintendent of the Academy, Captain Arnold "Danny" Danielson and his wife, Joan.

Of all the trips I made to the Academy, none were more *pleasurable* than the one with Carol, and none were more *memorable* than the one I when I nearly lost Ambassador Elliot Richardson.

—36—

The Doodling Ambassador

HE WAS A FASCINATING MAN. Ambassador Elliot Richardson served as
the U.S. Ambassador to the United Kingdom from 1975-1976. He still
held the title, although was better known to Americans for his earlier rolls
in the U.S. Government. President Nixon had appointed the Harvard Law
graduate as Secretary of Health, Education, and Welfare (HEW) in 1970.
He later served as Nixon's Secretary of Defense and Attorney General. In
1974, rather than follow Nixon's order to fire the special prosecutor in the
Watergate scandal, he resigned.

On this day, however, as a member of a Coast Guard advisory board,
he was receiving a briefing from senior military and civilian staff of the
Academy. The meeting was held in the Henreques Room of Hamilton
Hall, a beautiful gathering room of the library, surrounded by walnut and
glass-front bookcases and large mahogany tables.

There was a Spartan handsomeness about him. His hair was neatly
parted, and combed in a modest pompadour. He wore dark horn-rimmed
glasses. His straight lined thin lips receded modestly to set off his square
cleft chin. He looked like Gregory Peck playing Atticus Finch playing
Ambassador Richardson.

As I watched him, it bothered me that he appeared to be more interested in the magnificent Aldis Brown murals of historic Coast Guard battles
that encircled the room above the bookcases than the business at hand.
Seemingly bored by the drone of the Academy briefer, he kept glancing at
the murals. And, of all things, I could see that he was *doodling*! His ink pen
swirled, stopped, checked, scratched, reversed, and blocked every figure

and form known to man in a never ending tribute to nothing until his 8 x 10 notebook paper was filled with artistic gibberish. I was disappointed. What politico put this "distinguished visitor" on the committee? Nice trip, great meal, interesting tour of the Academy? He was useless!

Until the end of the Academy briefer's presentation.

Then, following mundane comments from the other members of the committee and the Academy staff, the Ambassador unwound his lanky frame from the chair he had surrendered to nearly an hour before, and stood.

"It seems to me, from what I have been hearing, that the main issues fall into categories...."

His slow Tennessee-like drawl silenced the room as he gave the most erudite, yet simple, summary that captured the essence of the entire meeting. He even laid out potential solutions. I couldn't belief it! The man was brilliant! I relearned a big lesson that day: never prejudge the capabilities of a person on appearances.

I later learned that other high profile figures were famed doodlers: Notably, Congressman Barber Conable of New York, and Nelson Rockefeller. Both have large collections of their doodles (some see them as being artistic enough call them pen and ink drawings). Both men have claimed that doodling kept them "more active, intellectually." They have also agreed that Elliot Richardson was probably "the most prolific doodler on Capitol Hill." His aides fought for his doodles after staff meeting; they were collectibles.

That was my second mistake of the day, albeit through innocent ignorance, I did nothing to recoup his doodle. It did not live on, but, rather, found its way into the janitor's trash...lost forever.

Rear Admiral William Stewart, the Chief of the Office of Personnel, and I had flown via Coast Guard aircraft from Washington, DC to the Academy for the single day of the whirlwind briefings for the committee.

I was the chief of Training and Education Division and therefore the Admiral's chief staff officer for Academy affairs. The Ambassador and several other DC politicos had flown with us.

After a hectic day, our Coast Guard pilots informed us that bad weather was going to delay our departure. Ambassador Richardson expressed mild concern. He was scheduled to speak at a Smithsonian Institution dinner that evening honoring former British Prime Minister Harold Macmillan.

A series of squalls were sliding up the east coast. Takeoff was delayed and progress was slow. Admiral Stewart had asked for several ETA checks as we made our way to Washington National. He seemed more nervous about the delay than the Ambassador. The Admiral was devising alternative plans. He had guests from the Academy returning with him so he was tied up. The Air Station didn't have a driver available. He turned to me.

"Dick, I know your car is parked at the Air Station. Could you hightail the Ambassador to the Smithsonian Castle? I think it's going to be close to get him to the dinner on time."

"Yes, sir, of course."

As soon as we touched down, the plane crew moved to get the door open, the ground crew already had the boarding steps at the ready. We taxied directly to the CG hanger, and the Ambassador and I hustled off the plane as soon as the wheel chocks were in place. Fortunately my car was close to the CG hanger. I ran ahead and opened the front door for the Ambassador, who climbed in just in time...it was starting to sprinkle.

As I maneuvered to get to the highway, I could see the Ambassador scanning my dashboard. "This is a very nice car," he drawled. He smoothed his hand along the tan imitation leather beneath the windshield, "Is it new?"

"No, sir. Not really. It's a two-year-old Toyota Corona."

"Well, it's very nice."

"Thank you, sir." I smiled to myself thinking about his reaction to my car when it dawned on me. I had placed my distinguished passenger in alien territory....the front seat of a compact family sedan. Hell, he probably hadn't even sat in the front seat of *any* car for years, much less a little foreign model. I smiled again to myself and thought, "I'll just let him dream on of the day he might own one too."

I never understood Washington traffic. Why were people snarled *inbound* on the 14th Street Bridge? They were supposed to be getting *out* of D.C. not trying to get back *in*. The light rain didn't help. At the slightest sprinkle, cars, like automatons, merged into tight jams. Drivers had fought hard for their own precious space, and they were protecting it. I was blocked out of the only exit I knew, two lanes over, not enough time. Now I was headed into unknown territory, downtown Washington at dusk. When I glanced at the Ambassador to explain our situation, I saw his head swivel to the right lamely pointing at the Smithsonian Castle as it passed down our right side, a quarter-mile away. "I think that's where we are supposed to be going," he said as the Castle faded out of sight. *No shit!*

"Sir, I've been forced out of the exit lane and we are headed into the heart of DC. I don't know the city well, could you help me with directions?"

"I'm sorry, he said, "but I don't know the city at all. Someone picks me up in the morning. I sit in the back seat with that little over-the-shoulder-pin-light and read the overnight mail that the driver brings with him. Now, that I think about it, I don't think I could even find my way to work."

Of course he couldn't. Why should a Secretary of Defense waste away his time finding his way to work, fighting traffic while he hunts for the best route? This man operated in a whole different world than I could even imagine.

"That's all right, sir, we'll make it in plenty of time. I'm sure I can feel my way around a block or two." *Did that sound convincing?*

My strategy was to go far enough north, head east a block or two, and then head south. We should run into the Mall and then I'd be home free. It was working...for a while. Without warning, my street split into four lanes. The right and left lanes offered exits to the Mall, the center two continued to a down ramp that disappeared. Blocked out of an exit again, I entered the short tunnel, and then I saw the sign, "Welcome to Virginia." I don't know how that happened. I tried not to react and hoped the Ambassador did not see the same sign. He didn't. I calmly felt my way into a return loop, crossed the 14th Street Bridge back into D.C. again, successfully this time, just like it was the plan. I don't think my passenger was even aware.

This could have been the end to a good story, except, I was not at the front entrance to the Smithsonian Castle when I did find it. I was on the back side, no obvious way to get in. I spotted a uniformed guard walking the perimeter, and I pulled to the curb.

"I'll be just a moment, Ambassador," I said. I jumped out of the car, called to the guard, explained the situation, and asked if he could help. He could. I returned to the car, opened the front door for the Ambassador and said. "Sir, this guard knows exactly where you are to be and will escort you there. It's been my pleasure to meet you sir, good luck with your speech."- *No sweat...fifteen minutes to spare.*

On the way home, I envisioned what the *Washington Post* headlines could have been: "Coast Guard Captain lost for hours in endless loop from DC to Virginia: Ambassador Richardson late for Macmillan honors."

With apologies to Shakespeare... *All's Well That Ends Well.*

USCG Training Center

Petaluma, CA

Commanding Officer
June 1983-August 1985

Richard Marcott

The Coast Guard Training Center, Petaluma, is located in the pastoral countryside of Northern California. It sits on eight hundred acres of land on the Sonoma-Marin county line. It was once owned by the U.S. Army who operated a secret code breaking site there in WWII. Camouflaged to avoid enemy aerial detection, the buildings were built to blend in with the common chicken farms in this region known as the "Chicken Capital of the World." The Coast Guard purchased the site in 1971, establishing the training command which now functions as the Coast Guard's major resident training facility on the West Coast.

It is one of the few CG bases providing dependent housing. Remotely located, it is a full service community with: student and dependent housing for officers and enlisted personnel, a retail exchange facility, medical and dental units, and recreational facilities including athletic fields, gymnasium, tennis courts, and a recreational lake. The base provides its own fire and police protection. Dependent students are bused from the base to Petaluma schools.

Initially the center operated three schools offering three courses for eight hundred students a year. It grew over the years to offer fifteen courses for over two thousand students a year. They offered training in basic occupational skills for Petty Officer ratings: Radioman, Yeoman, Subsistence Specialist, and Storekeepers. They also convene special courses in Leadership and Management for officers and petty officers, and have added an Emergency Medical Technicians school.

A major building program begun in 1985 added training for Telephone Technicians, Electronic Technicians, and Health Service Technicians. By 1989 Petaluma's eleven schools offered forty courses to four thousand students a year.

—37—

RETIREMENT

I JUST FINISHED MY LAST drive-around. I didn't do it often, but on the eve of my retirement it felt right. I was alone in the government car that had been assigned to me as CO. It was quiet, a few students playing softball, and one or two families having a picnic at the lake. I pulled onto the north perimeter road. It was late afternoon and the sun would soon be disappearing below the rolling hills to the west. I got out of the car.

I scuffed through the loose bark and leaves beneath the trashy eucalyptus trees which lined the road; their medicinal smell filled my nostrils like a Vick's inhaler. I stood quietly looking down the hill from the best overall view of the station. Twenty-eight years. I had hoped to make it thirty. When I left PTE in Washington, I knew that in four years I would have the mandatory limit of thirty years active duty. The last two Chiefs of Personnel had both advised me to seriously consider broadening my experience at a district office. I knew they were giving me their best advice if I wanted to be at all competitive for flag selection. But, I also knew the odds of being selected for Rear Admiral were slim, to say the least. Our world was filled with popular Captains with great records who didn't break the barrier. I also knew that I wanted to continue in the training business in retirement. I had eighteen years experience in training and education. I thought I would have a better shot, especially at age 52, at a suitable civilian job coming directly from running a large resident training center. The choice had been mine. When the assignment officer called me months ago to talk about transfer I was surprised...sort of.

I said, "Hey, wait a minute. I've only been here two years. We both know this is a three year assignment."

"Yeah, but then what are we going to do with you with only one year to go?"

"Logically, I would think you would just extend me for the one year, and I'll retire from here with thirty."

He laughed. "Are you kidding me? I have a long line of Captains now who are ready to move you out of there. You know you have had two years in the best damned job in the Coast Guard, and a lot of other guys want it, too."

When the captain's assignment slate was published, I had orders that were not going to help me transition to a civilian training job and I submitted my request for retirement.

The family had a few anxious moments in the following months. I would have to vacate government quarters when I retired, and I didn't have a job. Carol had asked every night for two months, "Where are we going to send the furniture, and where are we going to live if you don't get a job—soon." To complicate matters, options I was exploring were all over the country. Feeling the pinch, I came close to accepting a position with Ross Perot, but it was in Detroit, a deal breaker for both Carol and I. A month before retirement, I landed a job with the Bank of America in San Francisco, and we bought a house in Petaluma. I would commute from there, and that would keep Kimberly going to the same school system and with her friends.

I stared down the hill over the golden hay fields, to what a few months ago had been a large flat plowed spot below the administration building. I was proud to see steel cropping out of the ground that would soon be the new training building. I had worked with Petaluma when I was Chief of PTE in Headquarters for a major expansion of the base to include shifting electronics technician training to Petaluma. It felt good to see construction start on my watch. Congresswoman Barbara Boxer and I had turned over the ceremonial first shovel in December. Additional base housing had also been approved and construction would start soon. It would have been nice to see these projects completed before I left, but at least I was handing off a base with visible evidence of progress. Petaluma was coming up in the Coast Guard training world.

I walked back to the car to head back to quarters A, and thought, *My detailer had been right about one thing...this had been the best damned job in the Coast Guard.* I had known that since the day I reported aboard.

I thought back two years to the Change of Command ceremony when I reported as the new CO. The reception for my family had been a great way to meet the staff, and to introduce us to our civilian neighbors and the sizable retired community, both Coast Guard and Army, that still used the base for many things. The military base has always been an important part of the community. The receiving line at the reception was long. People were saying goodbye to the outgoing CO and welcoming the new CO and his family. The mayors of Petaluma, Santa Rosa, and other politicos had all been through the line. We met other community leaders who had longstanding ties with the base.

There was the immigrant Austrian furniture maker, who sold exotic furniture to Arab potentates and large corporations who flew his own plane from which he famously dropped thousands of roses onto our picnicking dependents celebrating Mothers' Day at our recreational lake. A retired Army Colonel pulled me toward him when shaking hands to say quietly in my ear, "Every CO of this base has been a Rotarian...I'll call you in a few days." The head of the Santa Rosa Navy League reminded me of their long positive relationship with the Coast Guard.

Kimberly, a very poised seventh grader, was receiving greeters along with Carol and I. At one point I heard the woman, who had just introduced herself to us as Mrs. Williams, saying to her, "Hello, Kimberly, I'm

Mrs. Williams from the ranch next door. Do I understand right that you ride?" I have no idea how rumors preceded a new CO's arrival— they just did, both true and false. Kimberly was getting her first taste of what life in a fish bowl could be for the new CO's daughter.

"Yes, ma'am...well, I did in Virginia."

"Wonderful," Mrs. Williams gushed. "Maybe you can help me. My husband's dental business in Marin County keeps him so busy these days that his horse doesn't get the exercise he should. I ride my own horse, but don't have time for his. Maybe you could exercise him sometime...we could ride together. You are welcome to ride him anytime, but, you'll need your own saddle, though."

This was the perfect answer as far as I was concerned. When we left Virginia, Kimberly had enjoyed riding, and I knew that at one time the Army had recreational stables. They were gone, but we still had eight hundred acres of open hayfields. If we were ever going to feel pressure to get a horse, it would be here. I lucked out with buying only a saddle. Kimberly rode with Mrs. Williams a number of times, but after being thrown and bitten a few times, she parted company with the Williams' horse.

Kimberly enjoyed free range of the base, and we were comfortable that it was a safe environment. We lived in the protection of a gated ranch, with our own, security police, and fire protection. We had small retail store, library, recreation fields, a movie house, and a lake with canoes and picnic tables. The permanent population of 850 Coastguardsmen and their dependents lived in clustered enlisted and officer housing areas. The 1500 students lived in barracks on the other end of the base near their training buildings. They kept pretty much to themselves.

Kimberly became a close friend of Justin Freeman, the son of one of the assigned Warrant Officers. There were seen together all over the base and they spent a lot of time at each other's house, going to movies, and just hanging out.

The open ranch setting was vastly different from the more suburban experiences of Walnut Creek, Newport News, or Vienna. The city of Petaluma, itself, had a split personality. East of Highway 101, the great divide, new modern suburban housing developments spilled business commuters onto 101. They wore uptight dark three piece suits and carried Burberry raincoats, and black umbrellas on their fifty mile trek over the Golden Gate Bridge into San Francisco.

West of 101 was more like old town Petaluma. Quaint main street stores that had avoided obnoxious growth. The land to the west was wide open ranches. They didn't commute here. They lived on the ranch. There were no "farms." Everything was a ranch. There were cattle, sheep, and pig ranches, even apple ranches, spread among magnificent fields of cut flowers, grown for the vast California market. Vineyards were not far away. Rolling hills of golden grass led all the way to Bodega Bay where they filmed Hitchcock's *The Birds*. The uniform of the day west of the great divide was more like baggy jeans or bib overalls, plaid shirts, and rubber barn boots.

A school bus trip to Petaluma was not like most Kimberly had experienced. There were classic stories of kids leaving the bus to coax an errant cow out of the middle of the road...funny; and of the bus pulling to the side of the road to let children witness the live birth of a calf...priceless.

The musical strains of the 504th Air Force Band from Travis Air Force Base filled the air as the bleachers filled with invited guests and visitors. My mother, sister Pat, and cousin Irene were in their reserved seats. I was so glad I had family here. Ironically it was the same people, except for dad, who had passed, that took me to the Academy in New London thirty two years before. An official car brought Carol and Kimberly to the front. Kim was escorted to her seat next to my mother, while Carol was taken to the reviewing stand. I arrived with RADM Henry Bell, Chief of the Office of

Personnel, and we inspected the ships company who were in formation facing the reviewing stand.

Carol and RADM Bell at retirement ceremony

The retirement ceremony followed a simple, time honored tradition. RADM Bell made his official remarks, and then presented me with the Coast Guard Meritorious Service Medal. Before it was my turn, the Admiral presented Carol with a certificate from the Commandant recognizing her leadership efforts in working with the Training Center Wives Clubs. She had taken the young enlisted wives under her wing and I know she enjoyed a special relationship with them. I made my retirement speech and read my retirement orders.

The new CO, Capt. Wilhelm Wolff read his orders and made brief remarks. He then made saluted me with the familiar, "Sir, I relieve you."

I, in turn, faced the Admiral, saluted him with, "Sir, I have been properly relieved."

That's was the magic moment. It was over. The Air Force Band played the crowd off the field, and everyone enjoyed a terrific retirement reception.

I was so proud of Carol. From the time she swallowed that awful cup of coffee in 1958, she has been my steadfast support, companion, and partner. This is her retirement as much as mine.

After tomorrow, our family would enter Petaluma, Phase II.

Family at Retirement

—*Epilogue*—

I went to work for the Bank of America the day after I retired from the Coast Guard. I was the Training Manager for the recently formed corporate Payment Services Division. We had bought a small house on an impossible hillside slope in Petaluma. A large swimming pool occupied the only flat piece of property in the back yard. Carol and I enjoyed California living, Kimberly was doing great in school, and we maintained contact with the friends we had made at the Training Center. Once again we were living the good life...except.

I did not enjoy the life-style-crunching commute. I was standing in line at 6:30 a.m. for a bus to San Francisco, and I didn't get home until 7:00 p.m. or later. The bank was in turmoil and facing personnel cuts. I had been hired in the middle of a large reorganization, so I was not the most welcome new manager for people who were being laid off all around me. In addition, my commute schedule eliminated significant community involvement which I had looked forward to.

Thirteen months later, the B of A was undergoing another major adjustment—I volunteered to be cut. Soon after I left the Bank, I accepted an offer from Santa Rosa Jr. College to conduct leadership seminars for their Industry Training Program. The program would start in a month. We took advantage of the break and Carol and I made a quick visit home to Bradford while Kimberly went to Japan on a three weeks exchange visit. Things were going to be OK. Until I got home.

A casual inquiry to see if the University of Pittsburgh at Bradford was doing anything similar to Santa Rosa led to an interview with five minutes' notice. The search committee was meeting to look for a Director of the UPB Outreach Program. Ten minutes into my conversation with the Dean, he asked me if I would mind meeting with them. Later that afternoon, I went back to discuss the position with the President of UPB, Dr. Richard McDowell. I could feel the chemistry. When I questioned the long range prognoses for the position, which was funded by a three year federal grant, he proffered, "Don't worry about that, they never shut down a project they once approved."

I came home and said to Carol, "I can feel it. Those people are going to screw up our life."

They did. Dick McDowell called me the day after we got back to Petaluma. "We want you to come home and be our Director of Outreach." In fact, Carol and I had become more concerned about her parents in Florida, and my mom in Pennsylvania. They were facing health issues, and it might be better if we were closer.

We told Kimberly when she stepped off the plane from Japan... "Hon, we're moving back to Bradford." It would be mild to say she had issues with that, but she knew it was a change she had to accept. She would be entering her sophomore year at Bradford Area High School in the fall, not knowing a soul. I felt for her, and knew that leaving her boyfriend wasn't easy to take either. She was too young to be experiencing another life-changing event over which she had no control.

When the moving van left our driveway, I gave the driver directions. "You've got two turns. You know, when you get on the San Francisco-Oakland Bay Bridge, well, just continue for 2624 miles and hang a left at Dubois, and drive for 80 more miles...you're in Bradford."

We were all adjusting well, but Kimberly made my day when she came home from school a month or so into the fall term and announced, "Dad, I just realized today that I'll be graduating from the same school as you did. That's neat." After living in California, Virginia, Maryland, and Virginia again, it was as though we both had just discovered that she had roots after all.

Kimberly had a covey of new friends, and was doing very well in school. Carol was active in church activities and The Women's Literary Club. I was in heaven back in the classroom, and active in the community. I was elected as a School Board Director, and I served as a Director of Beacon Light Behavioral Health Systems, and I sat on several community oriented commissions. We enjoyed reconnecting with my mom and my sister, Pat, who had never left Bradford. In short, we were enjoying the good life again.

Remember that three year government grant that funded the Director of Outreach? Surprise—it disappeared at the end of three years. Hit the reset switch.

We stayed in Bradford. I started my own consulting company and held Leadership and Management workshops and seminars for business and industries in the surrounding six counties.

Carol and I suffered through the parental withdrawal pains of losing our child to college four hundred miles away. To our great joy, the English major from Washington and Lee University in Lexington, Virginia, came back to Bradford after working for a weekly newspaper in Lexington, where she grew her chops as a terrific writer. She wrote for the Bradford Era, married, and later moved to the marketing and communications staff of UPB. She and Rick blessed us with two grandchildren, Preston and Maddy. Ah...The good life again.

I decided after three years of Leadership Seminars with my own company that I wanted to retire and really do something different. One Saturday morning, we were watching Norm Abrams on his TV show, *The New Yankee Workshop*. I said to Carol, "Woodworking has always been something I thought I'd like to do."

Her quick response was, "Well, Rich, you're sixty damned years old... if that's what you want...you better get started." A cellar full of equipment later and a reasonable learning curve led to passable household furniture: desks, end tables, book cases, baby cribs, and porch furniture.

I had always enjoyed acting in high school. Now that I had more time, I became heavily involved with the Bradford Little Theatre. I was treasurer, then president for two years, and I appeared in over twenty BLT productions and directed four.

When a group wanted to start a Barbershop Harmony chorus for Bradford, I was first in line. After experiencing the quartet at the Academy, I knew how much fun it could be. I became a charter member of the Mountain Laurel Harmonizers, the chorus where I sang lead, and I sang base in a quartet, The Northern Knights. What a great time I was having.

When an infection laid me low with a permanently paralyzed vocal cord, my singing days were over. I finally had time to start "writing those stories down for the grandchildren."

Now that I've finished *The View From The Rigging*, I'll have to decide on my next project.

A novel? (I have one hell of a story burning to get told.)

Get back to the woodworking shop? (We could use credenza in the study.)

Maybe I'll give harmonica playing another try. (I hate to accept defeat.)

I'll find something.

Change is inevitable in everyone's life, whether you brought it on yourself or it was foisted upon you. It happens not just to you, but to your family. We have experienced it in our military life as well as in our world after retirement. What matters in either case is how you figure out a way to accept a new challenge and continue to grow. Face it: life's a crap shoot... deal with it.

> *Continuity gives us roots; change gives us branches,*
> *letting us stretch and grow, and reach new heights.*
> Pauline R. Kezer

The End

Made in the USA
Middletown, DE
28 June 2017